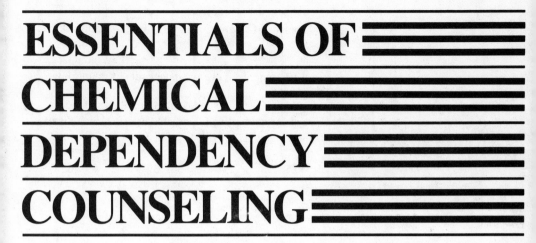

ESSENTIALS OF CHEMICAL DEPENDENCY COUNSELING

Gary W. Lawson
Dan C. Ellis
P. Clayton Rivers

AN ASPEN PUBLICATION®
Aspen Systems Corporation
Rockville, Maryland
Royal Tunbridge Wells
1984

Library of Congress Cataloging in Publication Data

Lawson, Gary.
Essentials of chemical dependency counseling.

Includes bibliographies and index.
1. Drug abuse counseling—United States. 2. Alcoholism
counseling—United States. I. Ellis, Dan C. II. Rivers, P. Clayton.
III. Title.
HV5825.L38   1984   362.2'9386   83-26573
ISBN 0-89443-583-3

Publisher: John Marozsan
Editorial Director: Margaret Quinlin
Executive Managing Editor: Margot Raphael
Editorial Services: Ruth Judy
Printing and Manufacturing: Debbie Collins

Library of Congress Catalog Card Number: 83-26573
ISBN: 0-89443-583-3

Printed in the United States of America

2   3   4   5

To our students and our patients

Table of Contents

   *Gary W. Lawson, P. Clayton Rivers, and James S.
   Peterson*

Introduction

There is an ever-increasing body of knowledge in the field of chemical dependency. More than ever before counselors in this field need to keep abreast of the new developments in their profession. The reduction in the age of the average patient or client, the involvement of family members in treatment, and new intervention and prevention programs are all helping to bring new and diverse client populations to the chemical dependency counselor. New treatment methods and strategies will be necessary for the counselor to be effective with this diverse group. Therapy designed for a 45-year-old white male alcoholic will not be effective with an 18-year-old, female American Indian cocaine user, nor will it work for chemically dependent persons' family members, who are equally in need of treatment. The chemical dependency counselor of today must be more knowledgeable and flexible than the chemical dependency counselor of previous years.

This text was not designed to provide *all* the knowledge that is needed to be proficient as a counselor. It was written, however, to introduce the basic skills, concepts, and issues of chemical dependency counseling as well as to provide the counselor with provocative questions and the motivation to continue learning about this most perplexing of human conditions.

Chapter 1 will help the new counselor to unravel some of the mysteries of the counseling relationship. Chapter 2 will briefly describe some of the often forgotten factors involved in chemical dependency. Chapter 3 will assist the counseling student in understanding diagnosis, and Chapter 4 will assist the counselor in developing a personal theory of counseling. Chapter 5 provides some basic counseling techniques. Chapter 6 is an overview of group counseling and Chapter 7 a unique look at the potential problems counselors could and often do have in a position as an agency counselor. We have ended the book with some questions that we as counselors and counselor trainers have been asked most often.

We encourage the reader to use this book as a starting point to begin a lifelong study of the therapeutic relationship and its use in the treatment of those people involved in chemical dependency. Be open to new answers as well as new questions.

Gary W. Lawson
Dan C. Ellis
P. Clayton Rivers

Chapter 1

The Counselor As Enigma

Dan C. Ellis

Before embarking upon how and when to do counseling there are several fundamental issues to consider. This chapter will focus upon some basic issues of identity and prerequisites and motivations that counselors should consider before sitting down with their first client.

COUNSELOR IDENTITY

The first question to ask yourself if you are or hope to be a counselor is "Why am I doing this?" What are the motivations that brought you to want to work as a chemical dependency counselor? People come to this field for many reasons and with varying expectations. It would not be possible to account for all the expectations and motivations a person could have; yet it is possible to outline some general considerations. We would say that there are some helpful, positive, and constructive motivations as well as some unhelpful, negative, and potentially destructive motivations.

The general public perceives counselors, psychologists, and psychiatrists in a variety of ways. However there seems to be a common cultural tendency to perceive these professionals as some kind of social enigma. We are a society of many classes, groups, sects, etc., and this is true in the professional world as well. Those people who treat our psyches, minds, emotions, phobias, addictions, etc., still somehow fall (subliminally at times, more obviously at others) into the role of shamans, priests, medicine men, and even gods. They do something to us, for us, and with us that we often believe to be mysterious, mystical, or just plain peculiar. They deal with a side of ourselves we do not fully understand and find uncomfortable to look at, think about, or explore.

Because of all the mystification associated with counseling, psychology, and psychiatry we tend to pigeonhole these professionals into this enigmatic, hard-to-define role or identity. As people consider entering these roles as a career the enigma certainly plays some part in their decision making. For some the enigmatic lure may simply consist of innocent fantasizing tempered by other, more realistic expectations. For others this extraordinary status may seem to be a way of escaping humanness, transcending personal problems, or even gaining power over others. These latter motivations we would say are unhelpful and can lead to potentially destructive client-counselor relationships.

COUNSELOR MOTIVATION

Chemical dependency is a serious health problem that demands that only the most skilled professionals provide treatment to its victims. These professionals need to enter the field with what we would describe as "clean" motivations. Clean, to us, would mean a realistic and mature understanding of the pressures and demands of the job as a counselor. In other words, counselors need to possess an ability to see the world and their own selves objectively. To do this counselor trainees need to do a complete personal inventory of why they wish to become counselors.

What are some of the personal reasons that motivate people to want to enter a helping profession, particularly chemical dependency counseling? It has been the authors' experience that the most commonly expressed motivation of the new counselor is *the need to help other addicts overcome their dependency*. This is true partly out of a sense of comradery, or a deeply felt obligation to assist another suffering addict because you have had the same experience. This kind of motivation can prove to be one of the most rewarding and satisfying for counselors who truly wish to serve their fellow addicts.

Obviously the kind of motivation mentioned above is fundamental to the tremendous success of Alcoholics Anonymous (AA). The principle of helping those who suffer from a common problem can be experienced as one of the most fulfilling opportunities in life. The benefits of doing this essentially unselfish act can also continually reaffirm the counselor's commitment to his or her own growth and sobriety. This type of motivation also serves to affirm and increase the counselor's self-worth and basic value as a human being. This experience helps counselors perceive themselves as moving from a nonproductive, failure identity to a contributing, socially responsible, sober member of society. Thus the motivation to help another suffering addict not only enhances one's inner being, it also allows the counselor to experience public recognition as a positive, successful contributor to the betterment of his fellow citizens. This need to move from a failure identity to a success identity is a basic tenet of William Glasser's work in reality therapy (1965). Furthermore, the work of people such as Abraham Maslow (1967), Clark Moustakas (1969), Sidney Jourard (1971), Carl Rogers (1961), and

Arthur Combs (1971) support this fundamental human need to seek a greater sense of worth and purpose.

Not all counselors in this field are recovering alcoholics and addicts, yet they may experience some of the same motivations mentioned above. For example, people who have lived with an addicted person (spouses and children) may feel a sense of responsibility to help others overcome and/or cope with the tragedy of chemical dependency. Also, by doing this counselors can further enhance their own sense of self-worth and progress toward a healthier identity.

The need or desire to help someone who is experiencing a problem similar to your own may not always manifest itself in a constructive way. Some chemically dependent people and their family members enter the counseling field as a way to "work out" lingering, unresolved personal problems. This counselor's motivation may on the surface seem similar to those mentioned above. The counselor still desires to move from a failure identity to a success identity, which is certainly important. Unfortunately, some counselors do not honestly consider their "real" motivations and end up deluding themselves into believing they only wish to be helpful to other addicts.

The counselor caught (unknowingly) in this dilemma will use his or her work with clients as a way to overcome serious personal problems. An example might be the counselor who sincerely believes that each time a client is stopped from drinking or using drugs, his or her own resolve to remain abstinent is solidified. As long as the counselor's clients get better, the counselor is fine, but a client who does not improve can become a personal threat to the counselor's stability. This kind of motivation can result in potentially unrealistic expectations and destructive client-counselor relationships. In this situation it is too easy for the counselor's needs to take precedence over the client's needs. For this reason it is essential that persons considering chemical dependency counseling as a career first seriously consider their reasons for doing so. It is important that counselors be well-adjusted people who are able to effectively separate themselves from their own concerns and focus totally on the needs of the client.

Another motivation for counselors in the chemical dependency field is *developing the knowledge and skills required to pursue a chosen professional career and strive for fulfillment through their own competency.* In this case the counselor, whether chemically dependent or not, chooses this field as a way of reaching a personal sense of accomplishment. These people tend to be more career oriented. Their self-worth and professional pride are enhanced by a job well done. This type of motivation focuses more upon the individual's learning and improving and is less affected by what the client does or does not do. The client's welfare is still important to the counselor and does influence the counselor's sense of self-worth but is not the primary motivating factor in choosing a career. This type of motivation would tend to identify the counselor as an ambitious, goal-oriented person who actively seeks out a challenge. This person can experience frustration upon realizing that the chemically dependent client is more challenging than originally expected. This can make goal attainment more difficult, but not impossible.

UNDESIRABLE MOTIVATING FACTORS

The preceding was a brief discussion of two common types of motivations that chemical dependency counselors tend to experience. There are other, less desirable motivations that we will mention briefly. Some counselors enter the field because they were favorably impressed by their counselor while in treatment for their own addiction. This kind of transference reaction does not seem to have much sustaining power as a primary motivator for a career in counseling. The mystique of counseling soon wears off and the starry-eyed new counselor may be unable to accept the reality of the career. Some of the work is drudgery and repetitive. It is always important to caution clients who have just completed treatment to wait before they make a decision on becoming counselors.

Others make a decision to enter chemical dependency counseling based upon inaccurate information and expectations. For some, counseling is viewed as a way to control other people, to have power over them, or as a way to be admired by the clients. Fortunately few people with these motivations ever make it into the field. Their heavy-handed tactics, insatiable egos, and manipulative games tend to give them away early. Their concern is obviously for their own prestige and power over the client, whose well-being has little to do with the therapeutic decisions made.

Another common, but unhelpful, motivator for some chemical dependency counselors is guilt. Whether the counselor is a recovering addict, a spouse, or a family member of an addict, guilt can become another type of addiction. It is our belief that people can become addicted to many substances or feelings, including guilt. Persons feeling bad about their past destructive behaviors will tend to seek ways of feeling better. When using drugs and alcohol is no longer an option some people may seek a career in counseling to help cope with their guilt feelings. The reasoning behind this kind of motivation is certainly well intentioned and altruistic. What better way could there be to "atone" for one's misdeeds than devoting oneself to helping others with similar problems? This is an important dimension of the AA program and has helped thousands to stay sober as well as gain a new sense of freedom from the past. However, the authors question the appropriateness of chemical dependency counselors entering the field to relieve their guilt feelings. Such counselors would most likely be more effective if they took the time to either (1) seek counseling first or (2) deal openly with those people or experiences in the past that still produce feelings of guilt.

In comparing guilt to an addiction we find that it can be an insatiable burden if not confronted directly. Doing "good deeds" for others as a career in order to eliminate past guilt can be a never-ending struggle. It seems that no matter how hard one works one is still left feeling guilty and lonely because one carries the burden inside and tells no one else about it. This is an unnecessary cross to bear and can be effectively overcome if openly discussed in counseling prior to embarking on a career as a counselor.

CONSIDERING YOUR OWN MOTIVATIONS

After reading this section readers may become worried over their own motivations. They may have identified some of the helpful, as well as unhelpful, motivations in themselves and may be questioning whether they have chosen the right career. It is true that most of us in the counseling field will at times stop and ask, "Why am I doing this, what were my original motivations, and have they changed?" We believe the process of asking and answering this question is one of the keys to being a successful and happy counselor. You may not always like the answers you come up with. Yet, reaching the answers and knowing why is better than not knowing. It has been our experience that most counselors can identify with many of the motivations mentioned earlier. It is our hope that the positive motivators are the ones that most counselors can identify with strongly. Our experience as trainers has shown that people who strongly identify with these motivations tend to be more successful as counselors. Those counselors who tend to enter counseling primarily, but not exclusively, for some of the more unhelpful motivations will have a difficult adjustment.

As a counselor or a counselor trainee it is essential that from time to time you consider your motivations. If you should uncover some not-so-desirable motivations, give consideration to what you can do about this. Rather than flying into a panic or slipping into a depression, try to devise a plan to help yourself overcome the problems you find. In other words, "practice what you preach." But if you find that your motivations and attitudes seem too deeply rooted to be overcome and that they interfere with your effectiveness as a counselor, it would be best to seek assistance from a mentor, friend, counselor, or teacher before pursuing this career further.

When attempting to assess your motivations, ask your peers and colleagues to give you feedback. What, in their opinion, seems to motivate you to be a counselor and does this enhance your counseling effectiveness? Then match this feedback against your own perceptions. Again, we must emphasize that periodically assessing your motivations is a healthy and necessary activity for all counselors. Do not expect to always come up with completely admirable motivations and do not expect that they won't change. This experience will help you stay "in touch" with what is going on inside you and how this relates to your work. This is a characteristic of competent, professional counselors who are concerned with taking care of themselves.

COUNSELING MISCONCEPTIONS

In the chemical dependency field there seems to be a definite linkage between clients and counselors. It is not uncommon to find people in the counselor's role who were only a few short months before in the client's role. This kind of rapid transition from the helped to the helper is certainly not the norm in other social service fields. Because of this phenomenon it is essential for counselors and aspiring counselors to take a close look at what they believe counseling to be.

In the more traditional fields of psychology, psychiatry, and social work, students spend several years in school formulating attitudes and belief systems about their future careers. This development generally takes place under the watchful eye of the experienced professor. As a result of this experience students have ample time to reorient their beliefs if they prove to be out of step with the rest of the field. This experience becomes a kind of gradual shaping period, with plenty of time later on for adjustments. This is not necessarily the case in the chemical dependency field. Learning opportunities are diverse and sometimes haphazard. Chemical dependency counselors frequently are faced with a confusing array of short-term learning events where they must "grab the skills and run." Here there are not always enough opportunities to integrate what has been learned, if learned at all. The work of David Powell has shown this to be a common occurrence (Powell, 1980). Due to the state of the training situation there is not always enough time to make sure trainees can actually internalize and then replicate what they have been taught. If trainees enter the field with misconceptions about counseling, it can be difficult to retrain them because of the short duration of most training efforts.

It has been the authors' experience that many new counselors believe that counseling is an effort to "get the client to see the right way to be." This is a questionable assumption to make. What is right? What does getting the client to see "the right way" mean? This kind of belief tends to indicate that the counselor views counseling as some kind of moralistic upgrading process. The counselor is supposed to get the client to see the errors in his or her ways and then rectify them. The counseling process is viewed as a coercive, manipulative, corrective effort to change clients' behavior. Counseling deteriorates into an effort to simply talk the client into behaving better.

One other commonplace misconception about counseling is that it must be intense if it is to work. This kind of belief is generally learned in treatment. Clients who go on to be counselors were taught while in treatment that good counseling occurred when people were crying, screaming, gnashing their teeth, and so on. This kind of counseling can lead to some disastrous results. Counselors can force clients into feeling states that they are not ready for and that can be terrifying to other clients who might be observing (such as in a group setting). Frequently counseling is slow moving, methodical, and even boring as the client moves toward change.

These are some of the less-than-desirable beliefs about counseling that trainees may have. Some of the more helpful and more appropriate beliefs regarding counseling are discussed below.

APPROPRIATE COUNSELING BELIEFS

One essential belief is that counseling is a conscious effort to facilitate the client's self-understanding and self-acceptance. This belief does not presume there is one right way to behave or feel. The intent is to help bring the client in touch with who he or she is. In order to accomplish this the counselor must set aside judgments and focus upon the client as an individual. Clients, however, may discover through this experience that it would be helpful to change some of their behavior.

Another essential belief is a clear sense of who is responsible for the client getting better. This must be a shared responsibility between client and counselor if helpful counseling is to take place. Of course in emergency situations where the client's life is at stake the counselor may have to take action without consulting the client. It has been our experience that counselors who believe they are solely responsible for their clients' getting well tend to have difficulties in maintaining a detached attitude and, in particular, with stress. It is difficult to be a healthy and happy chemical dependency counselor when you take your clients home with you each night (figuratively speaking, of course).

There are certainly many other beliefs important to consider when entering or practicing counseling. We simply wish to stress that it is important to give careful thought to one's beliefs about counseling and to see how they match with beliefs held by more experienced counselors. The remainder of this book will, in more detail, flesh out what has been discussed here.

THE MAKING OF A COUNSELOR

What does it take to become a counselor? Does it take a particular type of person, and, if so, how do you know if you are one? What are the characteristics of a successful counselor? Our answer to these questions would be that a successful counselor is a combination of different attitudes, knowledge, skills, and motivations that will vary from person to person. This section will explore some general guidelines for determining whether one possesses the necessary characteristics to do well in this field. Many of the characteristics discussed below were identified by psychologists and educators such as Carl Rogers, Sidney Wolf, Abraham Maslow,

Gerald Egan, and Arthur Combs. The authors believe these characteristics, based upon scientific research and experience, are essential in any counseling situation.

The Self As Instrument

Arthur Combs has proposed that the counselor is the primary instrument of therapy. This is a fundamental concept contributing to the effectiveness of any counseling effort. The individual who wishes to become a counselor must first be able to serve as an example of a healthy human being because either directly or indirectly the counselor functions as a model for his clients. This is not to imply that counselors are perfect, but that they are people who are able to effectively deal with life in essentially healthy ways that in fact contribute to their self-esteem. The counselor's self is the medium through which he relates to the client. This medium should be uncluttered by pressing personal problems and other distractions that can interfere with human interactions. Furthermore, it is critical for new counselors and even experienced helpers to fully appreciate that they are the most important thing they have to offer the client.

To be oneself with the client demands courage and a willingness to be vulnerable and open. Carl Rogers has called this characteristic "self-disclosure," the willingness to share immediate reactions and feelings. Again this is the process of modeling for the client what it is to be mature, honest, human, and able to straightforwardly confront life. The chemically dependent client is particularly handicapped at dealing with life's problems. The addiction by its very nature has frequently retarded the normal maturing process. The client desperately needs someone to demonstrate what it is to be human without the aid of alcohol and chemicals.

Self-Actualization

When Abraham Maslow coined the phrase self-actualization, he was referring to the experience of living one's life as effectively as possible. It means having full access to one's resources and using them to their full potential. The self as instrument is the vehicle through which the counselor communicates his level of self-actualization. A self-actualized person is not one who has achieved perfection but one who has managed to meet basic physiologic, safety, security, and ego needs. Once these needs have been met, one can concentrate on higher goals such as helping others and expanding one's awareness of oneself. The counselor's motivation to be of help to others must come out of a clear sense of realism and honest self-reflection. Maslow has referred to this type of motivation as Meta-motivation, that is, taking an honest account of what one has to offer one's fellow human beings. Counselors must honestly feel they have experienced some degree of success in resolving basic living needs before attempting to help others do the same.

Empathy

This is a particularly essential skill, yet it is also one that the novice counselor can learn through training and experience. It is helpful, however, if the novice counselor has some preexisting, native capacity to experience empathy. Empathy means the ability to accurately understand another person's experience and to communicate that understanding. This is simply a skill or characteristic, but one that frequently becomes confused and complicated by the uninformed counselor. When the authors are involved in selecting new trainees from the many candidates who apply, one of the special characteristics we look for is the ability to empathize with another human being. We do not believe it is essential for applicants to have had the same experiences as potential clients, but it is essential that they be able to express an understanding of another person's situation. More simply put: Can applicants see beyond their own concerns and accurately perceive those of others? The authors believe that if applicants understand the concepts presented above, they will probably do well in the chemical dependency counseling field. Self as instrument, self-actualization, and empathy, in our opinion, are the core characteristics of any successful counselor. If the counselor possesses these essentials in an observable degree, then the following characteristics should fall into place naturally.

Respect

Becoming naturally therapeutic is a concept that implies the development of one's inherent abilities to help others. Besides the characteristics and aspects listed above there are several others that add to the process of becoming naturally therapeutic. One of these is respect. This is particularly essential when working with chemically dependent clients who may demonstrate little respect for themselves or others. Every client has the right to his own identity, even if it means the continuation of alcohol or drug abuse. We as counselors may not like all that our clients do, but we must respect their right to do so, as long as it does not endanger someone else. This is difficult to do but necessary for the maintenance of counselor sanity. The bottom line on respect is that the counselor must truly believe that the client possesses the capacity to behave effectively and overcome addiction if allowed the opportunity and given a supportive environment.

Respect also implies a fundamental caring and concern for the client. Even when confronting the inaccuracies in a client's perception it is important to do so in a way that is not demeaning. The use of foul language, yelling, and rejection as means to shock a client into a new awareness does not imply respect for that person. Counselors who use these tactics frequently are demonstrating their lack of skill and nothing else.

Warmth

Another prerequisite of becoming naturally therapeutic is the ability to express warmth to the client. There is real therapeutic value in simply expressing genuine concern and caring for the client and his or her situation. Warmth can be expressed by listening, smiling, appropriate touching, laughter, and a sincere interest in the person. Part of being warm is being "real," being oneself. The counselor must be perceived as honest, not phony. Your actions must match your words. Insincere warmth can be destructive to the client-counselor relationship and can confirm for the client that he is really not OK.

Concreteness

Another essential skill is the ability to help the client be specific. Chemically dependent clients have particular difficulty in being honest with themselves and in looking at the what, when, where, and how of their lives. We do not all naturally possess these skills, and as counselors we must help clients to share the details of their lives, not just the broad issues and vague feelings. The counselor's job is to focus on details, to probe into clients' lives as if conducting an investigation. Always remember this: "There is generally more that is unspoken and there is valuable information in what is left unsaid."

Confrontation

Confrontation is an essential skill of the chemical dependency counselor because of clients' adeptness at concealing, avoiding, and distorting the truth in order to protect their addiction. Clients must come to understand the discrepancies between their words and behavior. It is essential to point out reality to clients who insist they feel nothing even as they turn red with anger. Sometimes this must be done in a kind, firm way, emphasizing the strengths of the client, and at other times the counselor must be assertive and even aggressive in order to get clients to see inconsistencies. This is a very important skill and will be discussed further in later chapters.

Self-Disclosure

The effective counselor must be willing to share his own experiences, to be "transparent," as Jourard (1971) says. But, as mentioned earlier, the counselor's own backyard must be in order before it is shown to the client. It is, at times, helpful to share with the client how you may have been confronted with problems similar to theirs. This helps you to seem more human and can be encouraging to the client. However, self-disclosure is best used sparingly as it may become a barrier to counseling. The more time spent talking about yourself leaves that much less time for the client to talk. Inexperienced counselors can easily get caught in the "self-disclosure trap," going on and on about themselves because they don't know what else to do. A little silence won't hurt and will teach clients that you expect them to talk when they feel ready.

Immediacy

Immediacy refers to the ability to live in the "now" and deal with life's experiences as they happen. The chemically dependent client has a long history of putting off till tomorrow what he can get drunk over today. Too many feelings and experiences have been repressed, suppressed, and forgotten by the chemically dependent client. The counselor must teach the client, by example, that "we are going to deal with your problems in the here and now, not tomorrow or next year." Frequently this can be accomplished by exploring the client's and the counselor's feelings for each other.

Potency

Another way of referring to potency would be to call it charisma or power. The honest, strong, and caring counselor can, it is hoped, elicit trust, security, and motivation from his clients. To take command of a situation and effectively move the client toward healthier living is what potency is all about. Potency implies the ability of one person to influence another. As stated earlier there always exists the potential for abusing skills. To assert your potency is to let the client know that you are secure in what you believe and that you expect the client to trust you. Using your potency is not intended to mean you should attempt to dominate or overpower a client.

This has been a brief discussion of the necessary characteristics of a successful counselor. Our experience as trainers and the research of others (Rogers, 1967; Carkhuff, 1969; Wolf, 1974) have shown that these characteristics are in fact related to effective counseling. Beginning counselors cannot expect to possess all of these qualities when they first begin counseling. They are simply goals to strive for. Later chapters will discuss when and how to apply these skills.

REFERENCES

Carkuff, R. *Helping and human relations: A primer for lay and professional helpers.* New York: Holt, Rinehart and Winston, 1969.

Combs, A.W., Avila, D.L., & Purkey, W.W. *Helping relationships: Basic concepts for the helping professions*. Boston: Allyn and Bacon, 1971.

Glasser, W. *Reality therapy: A new approach to psychiatry*. New York: Harper and Row, 1965.

Ivey, Allen E. *Counseling and psychotherapy: Skills, theories, and practice*. Englewood Cliffs, N.J.: Prentice Hall, 1980.

Jourard, S. *Self-disclosure: An experimental analysis of the transparent self*. New York: Wiley Interscience, 1971.

Maslow, A. *Toward a psychology of being*. New York: Van Nostrand, 1967.

Moustakas, C. *Personal growth: The struggle for identity and human values*. Cambridge, Mass.: H.A. Doyle, 1969.

Powell, D. *Clinical supervision: Skills for substance abuse counselors*. Human Sciences Press, 1980.

Rogers, C. *On becoming a person*. Boston: Houghton-Mifflin, 1961.

Rogers, C., Gendlin, G.T., Kiesler, D.J. & Truax, C.B. *The therapeutic relationship and its impact: A study of psychotherapy with schizophrenics*. Madison: University of Wisconsin Press, 1967.

Wolf, S. *Counseling skills evaluation*. Psychological Development Corporation, 1974.

SOME QUESTIONS TO CONSIDER

1. Why do I want to be a chemical dependency counselor?
2. What are some biases I bring to this field?
3. What are my positive attributes that will make me a good counselor?
4. What are some areas that I need to work on?

Chapter 2

Human Development, Sexuality, and the Family

Gary W. Lawson

It might seem odd to the reader that we would include human development, sexuality, and the family in the same chapter. In fact, some might ask, what do human development, sexuality, and the family have to do with chemical dependency counseling? We believe a great deal. All three are important to chemical dependency counselors and their clients, and very often they are not included as part of the chemical dependency counselor's basic training program. We will begin our discussion with a look at human development.

HUMAN DEVELOPMENT

Many alcoholism and drug treatment programs pay little, if any, attention to the past development of their clients. It is felt, by some, that "what's past is past, and there is nothing we can do to change it, so why bring it up?" If the past is brought up during treatment, it is usually only in the context of the recent past. AA deals with the past in the eighth and ninth steps by suggesting that its members make a list of all persons they have harmed and become willing to make amends to all of them; and make direct amends to such people wherever possible, except where to do so would injure them or others. Although these steps deal with the past and offer the AA member an opportunity to rid himself of possible guilt about previous actions, they focus mainly on past behavior with regard to drinking—and that is not taking human development into full consideration; the drunk-a-log is similarly deficient.

The drunk-a-log is often part of an AA meeting. Members tell how drinking led them down the path to dependency and how they have turned their lives around through AA. Then they explain how they have learned to stay sober just one day at a time. This is fine as an attempt to remind the speaker and those listening of history, lest it repeat itself. But too often this dialogue leads the listeners and the speaker to the conclusion that all of these problems began when alcohol or drugs entered the picture. Often they assume that before alcohol and drugs the speaker lived a normal, happy life, and if alcohol were removed, life would again be a bowl of cherries. The very high rate of suicides for those recovering from chemical dependency suggests that this is not true. And the number of chemically dependent persons whose family histories include psychological, physical, and sexual abuse suggests that before alcohol or drugs, things were not that rosy either. In short, although each of us starts out much the same, some time between the womb and the beginning of alcohol or drug use, we experience life events that have a direct effect on how we relate to our world. The more information the chemical dependency counselor has about these life events, the better the treatment plan can be—and the greater the chances the client will be successful in treatment.

Developmental Stages

Each major theory of counseling or psychotherapy embraces some form of developmental theory. Usually this theory involves a rationale of how a person develops. This rationale is, in turn, related to some type of developmental dysfunction that the particular theory of psychotherapy is designed to treat. The first to theorize in this manner was Freud. Freud's theory involved different stages of development, and posited that for those individuals who could not successfully complete these stages, the outcome was mental illness or exhibited deviant behavior.

Freud believed that every child goes through a sequence of developmental stages, each associated with a specific erogenous zone. He claimed that individuals passed through these stages on the path to a personality that is divided into three major parts: the id, the ego, and the superego. His stages of development were the oral stage, the anal stage, the phallic stage, the latency stage, and, finally, the genital stage. Freud felt that each of these stages fulfilled a task in the development of a healthy personality. Freud's theories have had a great impact on how we view the development of personality today. One of the popular theories of psychotherapy, transactional analysis, uses personality divisions called the child, parent, and adult that closely parallel the id, ego, and super ego of Freud.

It is not our intent here to present developmental theories. For a review of these, we would suggest the reader refer to a basic text on developmental psychology. Our aim is to suggest to the chemical dependency counselor that to provide the best treatment for chemical dependency one should have an idea about how the chemically dependent person develops. We propose several basic reasons why this is important.

Chemical Dependency Development

First, we believe that drinking alcohol or taking drugs is a behavior. We further believe that the way one acts or behaves under the influence of drugs or alcohol is also a behavior. We also believe that for each behavior there is an antecedent or a reason. Although an individual's behavior may seem to be self-destructive, there is a reason, a "payoff," for his behavior. At the least, the behavior is leading that person in a direction that, for him, appears to be logical or the only direction available. *Removing* the alcohol or drugs is just a beginning; something therapeutic must happen to an individual before he will *give up* drugs or alcohol. Something must also assist individuals in making the choice to change negative or self-destructive behaviors.

Thus, we believe that to focus only on alcohol- or drug-taking behavior is a mistake therapeutically. Even AA appears to have accepted this view. Of the 12 AA steps toward recovery from alcoholism, only one even mentions alcohol. The others deal with behaviors, emotions, attitudes, and changes regarding control of one's life. These are positive steps toward recovery that can be enhanced by using information regarding early personality development. Information that provides a key to the question "Why does this person behave the way he does?" will provide a direction for treatment. This includes what needs to change before the individual can behave in a more rational, self-fulfilling way. For many chemically dependent people, a change in behavior is brought about by a change in attitude. This change in attitude (sometimes known as therapeutic movement) is often brought about by one or more significant events in the person's life. When these events are manipulated or caused by the counselor, *that is therapy*. For example, if a person in a group experience becomes moved by the caring the other group members show toward him and changes his behavior as a result of this experience, that is therapy. It is only common sense to believe that the more the counselor knows about what motivates the chemically dependent person, the more accurately the counselor can set up these significant emotional events in order to bring about therapeutic change, that is, changes in attitude and behavior.

Unresolved Emotions As a Factor in Chemical Dependency

It is not difficult for the counselor to identify major emotions in chemically dependent persons. But often it is hard to get clients to let go of, or change, these emotions. Anger is one of these emotions. Anger may or may not appear to be directed toward a specific person or event. In some cases the alcoholic or drug addict may deny that this anger even exists. Yet, there is a repeated history of destructive, aggressive behavior toward others while intoxicated. A look into the chemically dependent person's developmental history might reveal a family background where anger and violence were not tolerated. So the only time it becomes OK to get angry or aggressive is while intoxicated. Further examination might find that a great deal of unexpressed anger toward a parent or a sibling exists and that the issues involved therein had never been resolved. If this were the case, the therapist could help resolve the issue by bringing in the family or providing some type of substitute treatment such as the "empty chair technique" (where the empty chair represents a person unable to attend therapy) for dealing with unresolved past issues. The therapist would also want to provide the client with alternative, positive ways of expressing anger. For some persons, just the knowledge of how they have been affected by past events is motivation enough to assist them in changing their behavior.

Persons who come from alcoholic families often have the type of difficulties described above. As we know, about 50 percent of all alcoholics come from alcoholic families. What we do not know for sure is why only some of the children of alcoholics become alcoholic themselves and why others drink only moderately or choose not to drink at all. Of the ones who do become alcoholic, it is clear their lives as children in alcoholic families had a great deal to do with their existing alcoholism. We know that modeling played a part in the development of their problem drinking. We also know that they may be at higher risk biologically or genetically. But most of all, we know that they were affected psychologically.

The Psychological Factor

It has been our clinical experience that the psychological factor is most important in chemical dependency development. Children from alcoholic homes who themselves have drinking problems generally do not like themselves, and they do not feel in control over what they see as their hostile environment. Furthermore, most, if not all, of their basically negative attitudes can be traced directly to their experiences as a child in an alcoholic family. What is unfortunate is that many of their ideas and attitudes are erroneous and based on the sometimes distorted view of the world they had as children. For example, because of their parents' behavior they believed, and still believe, that their parents did not love them. Therefore, they see themselves as unlovable. After all, "If one's own parents don't love one, who will?" Seemingly logical reasoning, but a child has no understanding of the complexities of alcoholism and the behavior connected with it. To the child, the behavior is clear and the message is clear. Because my parents treat me as they do, I must be unloved and unwanted. At the very least, the message is confusing. "Daddy loves me but Daddy has a disease?" For a child and even many adults, a disease does not excuse past or future behavior. Missing a birthday or missing Christmas is a disappointment to a child, disease or no disease. And if the child resents the drinking parent for his neglectful behavior, telling the child not to, because the parent has a disease, only makes the child feel guilty about natural feelings. For the child, the only real option is to have the parent demonstrate his love through consistent, loving behavior.

For adults who grew up in an alcoholic family, an understanding of their parents' behavior—and the connection to why they are now behaving the way they do— could change some of their own destructive behavior. Most alcoholics do not make a connection between their own behavior and that of their parents. And they have given little, if any, thought as to why their parents behaved the way they did and to the impact their grandparents had on their parents. It is a common belief that we all have a set of choices and are free to make whatever choice we want. The reality is that long before we make many choices, we are programmed to make one choice over another and our choices are not always in our own best interest. However, if we know how we have been programmed, we can override our programming and make choices that are truly in our best interest. Hence, adults who grew up as children of alcoholics should reexamine the issue of their self-worth. Given additional information and evidence—i.e., people who care about them, past successes, parents who, perhaps, are now sober and can express love to them— they can decide they need to reassess their feelings of worthlessness and examine how they could make new decisions regarding their future behavior. For them, this might mean remaining sober and allowing themselves to enjoy life.

In most instances, it is possible to trace the antecedent of a behavior and to develop patterns of past behavior. It is also possible to predict, with some degree of accuracy, what future behavior will be based on past behavior. It is almost impossible to do this without a knowledge of each person's developmental history. Because of the many similarities between persons who are chemically dependent, it is easy for a chemical dependency counselor to come to believe that each client is basically like the others. There are far more differences between chemically dependent persons than there are similarities. The knowledge of these differences often separates a counselor who is mostly effective from one who is mostly ineffective.

Other Developmental Levels

Although early developmental theories include only the period from birth to early adulthood, it has become clear that we continue to develop in many areas for most of our lives. Erikson's theory of psychosocial development runs from birth through old age, with eight stages altogether. Each of these stages is meaningful to the understanding of individuals as they progress through life. We can best illustrate our point by reviewing a developmental stage and reflecting on how this information might be helpful to the chemical dependency counselor. Let us look at adolescence as a developmental stage, considering the important physical, emotional, and social characteristics of an adolescent. For the sake of simplicity, we will look only at the male adolescent.

Physically, the adolescent male is in a state of rapid maturation. Some boys mature at an early age and some later. Those who mature later are often not as self-confident and assured as those who mature earlier. However, late maturers often become more sensitive and insightful than their early maturing counterparts. There is likely to be a great deal of concern about appearance at this age, especially with regard to the opposite sex. The male sex drive is at a peak at the ages of 16 to

17. A strong sex drive and severely limited opportunities to satisfy it are sources of much concern to many young males.

Socially, the adolescent male becomes increasingly under the influence of his peer group. Often there are conflicts between peer group and family values. This is another source of conflict for the adolescent. Emotionally, the adolescent may be moody and unpredictable, partly because of biological changes associated with sexual maturation and partly because of confusion about identity. Adolescents also tend to be intolerant and opinionated, partly because of a lack of confidence, partly because of a lack of experience as formal thinkers. In a search for a sense of identity and in their efforts to become independent, many adolescents experience moments of confusion, anxiety, and anger. They may express their frustration by turning to alcohol or drugs or by otherwise rejecting established values. Adolescents also live for the here and now; they think very little about the future or consequences of present behavior. They look for immediate gratification rather than working toward some future goal. As a group, they look much the same, but on further examination they are each very different.

Adolescents have a completely different set of problems than adults. The goals for treatment may be the same, but the direction to take to reach the goals is dictated by the problems encountered on the way. For example, building self-image might be an appropriate goal. For the adult, this might be done through improved relationships with family members and improved performance on the job. For the adolescent, it might only be done through a peer group.

For a 45-year-old adult, the reality that alcohol intake is damaging his liver and that he might someday die as a result of this could be a motivating factor to give up drinking. This same news presented to the adolescent might have no effect whatsoever on his alcohol intake. Again, the more you know about the developmental factors of the individual you are working with, the more effective you can be in treatment planning and, thus, treatment.

HUMAN SEXUALITY

Just like human development, human sexuality is often neglected in training programs for chemical dependency counselors. Consequently, many chemical dependency counselors feel ill-equipped to deal with their clients' sexual problems, and often these problems are neglected in the treatment plan. However, sexual problems rarely resolve themselves, and, if nothing else, it is the responsibility of the counselor to make an appropriate referral to a therapist trained to deal with problems of a sexual nature. This section of the chapter will view sexuality as it affects the chemically dependent person and will suggest some prospects for treatment and referral.

Human sexuality is heavily intertwined in the development of each individual. The role that sex plays in establishing a positive self-image cannot be overstated. In turn, this variable also becomes critical to the treatment and rehabilitation of the chemically dependent person. Very often, the chemically dependent person has used drugs or alcohol to ease the anxiety or conflicts surrounding the issue of sexuality. These conflicts can easily complicate the rehabilitation effort if they are not considered, and dealt with, as a primary part of treatment.

Sex as a Source of Guilt

For the chemically dependent person, sex has often been instrumental in the establishment of a negative, rather than positive, self-image. Guilt about sexual behavior is sometimes a primary motivator for drug- or alcohol-taking behavior. This guilt need not be connected to sexual behavior that occurred while the person was drinking; it might even be sexual behavior that took place during a predrinking- or drug-taking period. For example, victims of childhood incest have many issues surrounding their sexuality that cause them guilt, great pain, conflict, and self-doubt. If incest is ignored as a factor by the chemical dependency counselor, the treatment for these individuals will be incomplete or altogether unsuccessful.

In other instances, sexual behavior that occurred during drinking may be a great source of guilt. The values regarding sex that a person has when sober are often violated when under the influence of alcohol. Promiscuous sex, homosexuality, and incest are all potential guilt producers. It is the responsibility of the chemical dependency counselor to determine the client's primary sexual issues and to establish how these factors are involved with the drinking or drug-taking behavior. The counselor can then intervene therapeutically to help the client resolve these matters. If this is done successfully, sexual problems will no longer be a source of negative feelings for the client.

Obtaining the Sexual History

As is suggested in Chapter 3, assessment, or diagnosis, is the cornerstone of a successful treatment program, and a successful diagnosis is only complete with an accurate sexual history. In order to gain access to information that is of a very personal nature, it is critical to ensure that rapport has been established between the counselor and the client. This rapport should be a natural part of a therapeutic counseling relationship. However, this may take time to establish, and the counselor should not rush to deal with sensitive subjects. Other, less threatening aspects of the client's history can be reviewed until the client is more comfortable with the counselor. With a subject such as sex, where values and feelings differ, it is only natural that some clients will be reluctant to bring the subject up regardless of the quality of the client-counselor relationship. This does not mean that the counselor should not bring the matter up. If the client is reluctant to talk about sexual subjects, the counselor should discuss the importance of such issues with the client and model openness toward sex. This might be done with a certain amount of self-disclosure by the counselor about his own experiences.

With regard to the sexual history of the individual, the counselor needs to pay particular attention to issues surrounding patterns of dominance and control, dependency, intimacy, and childhood experiences, including parental attitudes toward sex. Dominance issues should be examined with regard to the client's present and past interpersonal relationships. Questions concerning who has control, the level of control (Is there overcontrol? When? How?), and what this does to the self-esteem of the parties involved should be considered.

Dependency issues should be examined with regard to who is dependent upon whom, when, and under what circumstances. Levels of intimacy should be determined, and the influence of childhood experiences on sexuality should be considered with regard to parents and siblings. How did they relate to one another? Were they given opportunities for self-expression? What were, and are, the patterns of self-restraint they developed? For chemically dependent persons, it is important to assess self-image and the role sex has played in the development of that self-image. It is also of interest to note how they see their spouses. What kind of image do they have of their spouses? What is their image of their relationships? After a client's relationship has been evaluated from the point of view of both parties, a more profound sexual history can be developed.

The sexual history should include an attempt to ascertain any specific dysfunction and a history of that dysfunction. It should also include the client's feelings with regard to the dysfunction. To complete the picture of the client's sexual background and how this background might be influencing current destructive behavior, a sexual history of the childhood, adolescent, and teen-age years should be taken. Feelings regarding family, cultural, religious, and social influences should be explored. Premarital sexual experiences and feelings, first sexual experiences, first knowledge of sex, masturbation, and homosexuality, and a courtship and marital history are also important.

Some additional areas to explore in a sexual history would be the details (onset, duration, circumstances) of a specific problem and how the client views the problem. The client's physical and emotional condition plus forewarnings of the dysfunction and associated symptoms should also be considered.

Sexual problems have a variety of causes, both physiological and psychological. And, as noted earlier, these sexual problems are manifested in other psychological problems. It is not always clear which problem precedes the other; either way, the important issue is the current effect and how it can be dealt with therapeutically.

PHYSIOLOGICAL AND PSYCHOLOGICAL SEXUAL DYSFUNCTION

Some possible psychological causes of sexual dysfunction include anxiety, religious orthodoxy, hypertension, lack of arousal in one's partner, inability to communicate sexual desires, lack of knowledge, relationship problems and, of course, alcoholism and drug abuse. Some possible physiological causes of sexual dysfunction include diabetes, arthritis, central nervous system damage, vaginal infection, endometriosis, irritation from vaginal foam or jellies, menopausal atrophy, mumps, cancer, dietary insufficiencies, and drug and alcohol abuse.

Some specific female dysfunctions that women are likely to report are:

- not yet having had an orgasm
- pain during intercourse (dyspareunia)
- an involuntary vaginal spasm preventing penile penetration (vaginismus)
- absence of sexual feelings during intercourse
- little or no sexual desire

Some specific male dysfunctions that men are likely to report are:

- premature ejaculation (ejaculatio praecox)
- erection with delayed or no ejaculation (ejaculatio retardata)
- inability to produce an erection (This may be called impotence and can occur as a primary or secondary dysfunction)
- absence or diminution of sexual feelings during intercourse
- little or no sexual desire

It is not essential for a client to report one of these problems for sex to be a major issue in chemical dependency. In fact, more often than not the client will not report a specific problem. Sexual problems in the chemically dependent person are more likely to revolve around issues of guilt and self-image regarding prior sexual behavior and beliefs than specific dysfunctions. However, the counselor should be aware that specific dysfunctions do sometimes occur and that they are treatable when they do.

Should You Refer the Client to a Sex Therapist?

Whether the chemical dependency counselor wants to do sex therapy himself or refer clients with sexual dysfunctions to a competent sex therapist is an individual choice. This choice should be made with several things in mind. First, what is the counselor's personal comfort level when it comes to dealing with sexual problems? Do the counselor's own values and personal experiences make it difficult to work on issues involving sex? If so, we would recommend that the counselor refer clients with sexual problems. The counselor who is not comfortable with his own sexuality can hardly expect to be a good sex therapist. Counselors should also consider their training; sex therapy is not something one does without proper training and instruction. There are many good books on the subject (There is a list at the end of this chapter) and there are excellent workshops offered across the country on sex therapy. These workshops are most useful to the beginning sex therapist.

One other consideration is the availability of sex therapists in your community. If they are widely available and of good quality, the counselor may choose not to seek additional training in this area. However, if the counselor lives in a community where there are no competent sex therapists, the extra effort expended on training in sex therapy will be well worth the effort. Clients will benefit from the counselor's additional skills, and the counselor's understanding of the role sexuality plays in chemical dependency will be increased. Even with additional training, there may be times when it is more beneficial to send the client to an intensive sexuality treatment program such as the one operated in St. Louis by Masters and Johnson.

Another skill that the chemical dependency counselor will find useful in dealing with the client's sexual problems is marriage counseling. Sex is only part of a marital relationship, and often sex between marital partners is hampered by other issues in the relationship. For a relationship to thrive, it must have mutual understanding, trust, and acceptance. These qualities have sometimes eroded in a relationship where one member of the couple is chemically dependent. The counselor who can assist in establishing a positive marital relationship will not only resolve many sexual issues but will be working toward the resolution of the chemical dependency problem as well.

This book is not designed to train chemical dependency counselors as sex therapists or marriage counselors. Its purpose is to alert the counselor to potential problems that chemically dependent clients may exhibit and to direct the counselor in ways to establish resources to confront these problems as they become apparent. Marital and sexual problems are two of the complicating issues that a chemical dependency counselor must confront. They must be included as necessary parts of most treatment to provide a complete treatment plan for each client.

To summarize the counselors' goals with regard to sexual problems: the counselor should uncover the client's sexual problems, freely examine the issues, and clarify problem areas. The counselor should also provide insights and interpretations as to how these problems are affecting the client's chemical dependency; provide emotional support and reduce anxiety and hostility; and educate and give permission, when necessary, in an effort to reduce guilt and increase positive feelings of self-worth in the client.

Thus far we have discussed human development and sexuality. We have seen how important these issues are in developing a total picture of the chemically dependent client and how these issues can be used to develop a total treatment plan.

Now we will discuss perhaps the most important factor in gaining insight into the chemically dependent person—the family.

THE FAMILY

In the first section of this chapter, we discussed the importance of development and how this relates to problems that clients experience later in life. No period of development is more critical to the development of the adult personality than childhood. Almost without exception, the personality theorists link major adult personality characteristics to certain categories of childhood experience. (There are exceptions to this contention, however.) It seems reasonable to conclude that if childhood experiences are so important in molding various personality attributes, the way one interacts with drugs and alcohol would be greatly influenced as well. There is nothing that has a greater impact on these early experiences than the family. This section will examine the family and its role in the treatment and prevention of chemical dependency problems.

In our examination of the family, we will be looking at two types of families that influence the chemically dependent person. First, and perhaps more critical to the development of the individual, is the family of origin. This family includes the individual's parents, relatives, or significant others who played a major role in his rearing. The major importance of this system is that the individual's attitudes and values about himself and the world, as well as the use of alcohol and drugs, are mostly formed here, and thus play an important role in his present behavior.

The second family we shall examine is the nuclear family. The nuclear family consists of those individuals with whom the person is living at the present time. This system is important because it may serve to create, maintain, or worsen problems that the chemically dependent person is having at the time. The nuclear family is also important because it is a potential mechanism for positive change in the life of the chemically dependent person.

Identifying Factors in the Development of Chemical Dependency

There are three major areas where theories of the etiology of chemical dependency have arisen. There are those theories that are biologically or genetically based; those theories that are psychological in nature (these include theories that chemically dependent persons have a distinct personality flaw that leads to chemical dependency); and, finally, those theories that are sociocultural in nature (these propose that the largest determiner of drinking and drug use practices is the culture that the chemically dependent person lives in).

Theories in each of these major areas are based to some degree on research findings and other empirical data. There has been evidence linking drug dependency or alcoholism with genetic factors, psychological factors, and sociocultural factors. But none of the research has demonstrated that any one of these factors is the major contributor to the etiology of chemical dependency. So most theorists believe that it is a combination of these factors that causes one person to become chemically dependent and another person not to. One thing that is clear, and becoming more clear as research in the area continues, is that the family has a major impact, perhaps *the* major impact on the individual in each of these areas. The family influences all of the physiological, and a great deal of the psychological and sociological development, of the individual. It is the developmental foundation established early by the family that is reflected in how a person relates to his environment, including his relationship with drugs and alcohol.

We cannot conclude from this that the family is the cause of chemical dependency. But it seems clear that the family cannot be ignored, in regard to either etiology, treatment, or prevention of chemical dependency. To establish a clearer picture of the role the family plays in physiological, psychological, and sociological factors, let us look at each factor from the perspective of the development of a risk level for chemical dependency. Remember that each of us has a potential risk for problems with chemical dependency; however, some of us are at greater risk than others.

Genetic Predispositions

It has long been established that alcoholism runs in families. The evidence is not as conclusive for other forms of drug abuse or addiction, but more and more research has indicated a link between generations of those who experience chemical dependency problems. A number of studies have shown higher rates of alcoholism among relatives of alcoholics than in the population in general. While their findings suggest that genetic factors are involved, they provide no details on how a predisposition to alcoholism is transmitted. We can assume that just as eye color or metabolism rates are passed on genetically, so is the capacity for drug or alcohol abuse. The chemical dependency counselor can determine the physiological risk level for a client by asking if parents or grandparents have had chemical dependency problems. If the answer is yes, it can be assumed that the person is physiologically at a high risk to develop chemical dependency problems.

The chemical dependency counselor can use the information about parental problems with chemicals to let clients know they are at high risk and to establish the importance of reducing the risk levels in other areas, psychological and social. Although physiological susceptibility can be established, environmental factors will still play a major role in the development of chemical dependency. The client can simply be told: "We don't know for sure what causes chemical dependency, but we do know that each of us reacts differently to drugs or alcohol based on our size, chemical makeup, and other genetically predisposed factors. Because your parents or grandparents had a problem, you are physically at risk to have such problems, as your children will be, too. If you have a problem now or if you think you will at some time choose to use drugs or alcohol, you must pay particular attention to any signs of impending problems, you must work to keep your risk levels low in the other two areas." Figure 2-1 is useful in conceptualizing the primary goals in the treatment or prevention of chemical dependency, that is, identifying and lowering one's risk levels.

Figure 2–1 Risk Levels for Various Etiological Factors

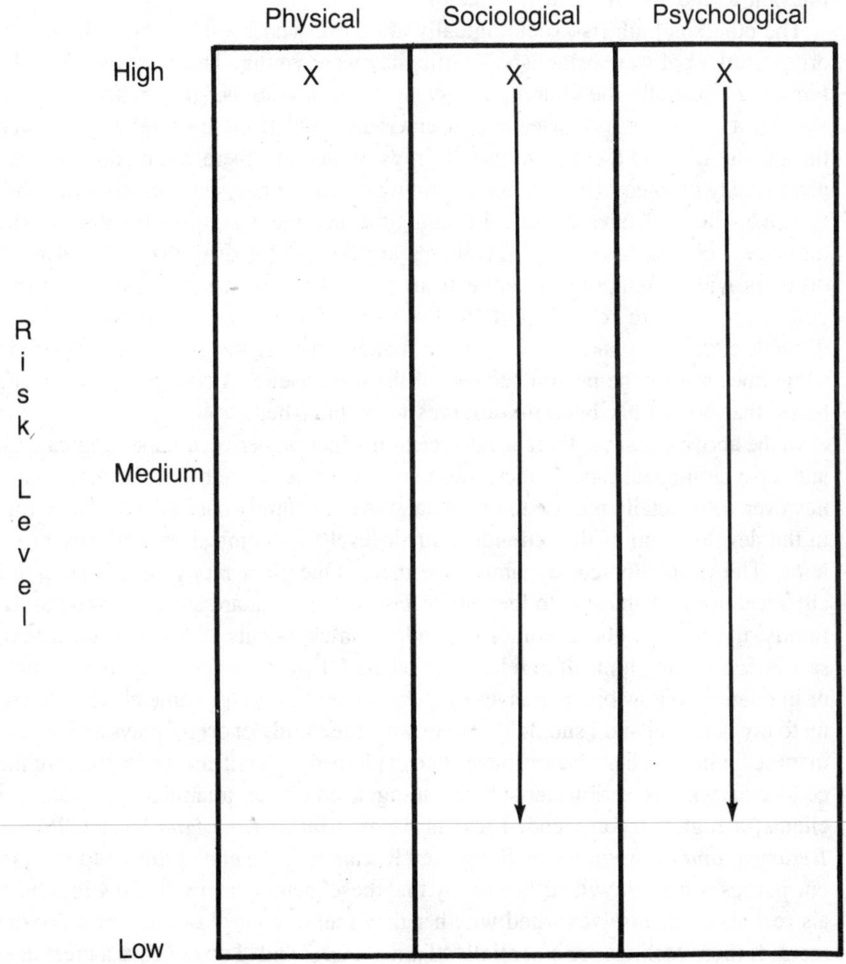

Sociological and Psychological Factors

The person who is sociologically at high risk is one whose primary support system, most often the family, either condones excessive chemical use (as a parent who is alcoholic might do) or does not tolerate the use of one or more chemicals (for example, a religious group with strong sanctions against the use of chemicals, commonly alcohol). In the first instance, the person is at risk because the abuse of chemicals is an option as a coping mechanism. Or it is an expected behavior: groups such as American Indians, Irish Catholics, and others have been identified as having high rates of alcoholism and other chemical dependency problems. The degree to which these social and cultural groups have influenced the individual is relevant to the sociological risk factor.

The others at high risk sociologically are those whose values about the use of drugs or alcohol were established while they were young. The message from the family, and usually the church, was clear: "Those who use are wicked." At the very least, "they (users) have not chosen God's way." If these values are followed throughout life and there is no use of drugs or alcohol, there can be no chemical dependency problem. But if, after becoming older, a person chooses to use alcohol or drugs, he will have a very difficult time not feeling guilty because of the messages received as a child. Problems are compounded by the fact that most drugs provide a temporary respite from guilt. The process becomes: use, feel guilty, use more to relieve guilt, feel even more guilty, use even more. It is a difficult cycle to break. To complicate matters even more, the family of origin sometimes rejects the person because of the drug use, thus confirming the user's belief that he is truly bad and deserves to be punished.

In the above instance, there is not a clear distinction between a sociological risk and a psychological risk; in fact, these are often interrelated. It is not necessary, however, to be totally precise to understand that the family has had a dramatic role in the development of the individual's risk level for chemical dependency problems. The psychological dynamics are there. One clear motivational factor for chemical use and abuse is to feel better. For reasons that are closely linked to the family, the person who becomes dependent on chemicals very often has a poor self-image, seeing himself in relation to others ("I am not as good as my parents") or in relation to how one perceives one *should* be ("I haven't come close to living up to my potential and I should"). Either way, the family of origin plays a vital role in these feelings. These factors have been explained in detail elsewhere, and for the counselor who is serious about providing a complete treatment program for clients, a highly recommended text is *Alcoholism and the Family: A Guide to Treatment and Prevention* (see Suggested Readings at the end of this chapter). For our purposes here, it will suffice to say that these factors determine how individuals feel about themselves—and whether they feel in control of the world around them. If these feelings are essentially "I am not OK" and "I do not have a great deal of control over things that happen around me or to me," these persons are psychologically at high risk to develop some form of chemical dependency problem, if they use chemicals.

The one variable that remains constant is, of course, use. It is impossible to become chemically dependent if one does not use chemicals. This is not to say that it is impossible to have chemical dependency problems after one gives up the use of chemicals. On the contrary, very often the problems only begin when the person stops using. This is where the nuclear family becomes important: we believe that the family is a system, and if one or more members of that system are chemically dependent then the system is sick, not just the person who is chemically dependent. The system must be treated, and is best treated as a unit. That does not translate to placing the chemically dependent person in treatment, while educating the family about the "disease" of chemical dependency and teaching them to live with, yet psychologically apart from, the chemically dependent person. The family system, when functioning as a unit, is the place where family members should meet many of their needs (the need to be loved, the need for security, and the need to be wanted and needed, among others). If the family does not meet these needs, the system needs repair or redirection. When the family is intact, we highly recommend that family therapy be used to restructure the family system so that all members are meeting appropriate needs through the family.

Meeting Interpersonal Needs Through Alcoholics Anonymous

If the family is not available, the second best approach is to provide a surrogate family to meet these needs: AA serves this purpose for many. A problem may arise if AA meets these needs at the expense of the real family (if it is intact). We have known many an alcoholic who took refuge at an AA meeting rather than working out unresolved family matters at home. When used properly, AA is often very successful at reducing both the psychological and sociological risk levels enough to allow individuals to seek family therapy to resolve family problems.

Sociologically, AA provides a new social group with a new set of values with regard to drinking. Often this means a change from a group where drinking to excess is not only acceptable but encouraged to a group where drinking in any fashion is not acceptable. This group, if it becomes a major influence on the individual, lowers the person's sociological risk level; if the individual maintains contact with AA and AA members, he will continue to have a reduced sociological risk level.

Psychologically, people reduce their risk level if they respect and identify with the other members of AA whom they meet. They reduce their own feelings of hopelessness by seeing people who have had problems similar to theirs become better because they were able to stop drinking. There is some psychological relief in the knowledge that others in the world share similar problems; there is a feeling of acceptance that helps people feel better about themselves. Perhaps what is most important, there is a feeling that by sharing experiences with other members, there is a chance that one could be helping other members stay sober. This is carried even further when the member is asked to do 12-step work, which includes making house calls and home visits to individuals who are suffering from alcoholism and volunteering to share with them the answers that have been successful in maintaining sobriety. The 12-step call is a great esteem builder, and it serves to further reduce the psychological risk level by making the caller feel needed and useful.

Again, risk reduction is best done through the family for several reasons, and even if AA is used in the beginning, the counselor should help clients work toward meeting their goals through the family. The first reason is that the family is the logical place for these needs to be met. Second, the family needs help just as much, or perhaps more, than the chemically dependent person. By conducting family therapy, the counselor helps each family member meet his personal needs through the family system. This pays off not only for the chemically dependent person but for the children in the family as well, by teaching them to meet their interpersonal needs through the family and thus reducing their risk of future problems.

The chemical dependency counselor who has a knowledge of human development, skills in identifying and treating sexual problems, and the ability to treat the family as a system will find the field of chemical dependency treatment rewarding and a continual challenge. Counselors who do not possess this knowledge or these skills will be constantly perplexed by the chemically dependent client. They will have to rely on the old standby, "This client wasn't ready for treatment," when one person after another is unsuccessful in treatment. They will be unable or unwilling to see that it was not the client who was not ready for treatment; it was the counselor who lacked the skills to identify appropriate treatment plans. Meanwhile, the counselor with an understanding based on knowledge in these and other areas will be able and willing to take the appropriate responsibility for what happens in treatment and to make adjustments as necessary to provide a successful treatment plan.

SUGGESTED READINGS

Alcohol and Sexuality, by Lois Fleit, Arlington, Va.: H/P Publishing Co., 1979.

Alcoholism and the Family: A Guide to Treatment and Prevention, by G. Lawson, J. Peterson, and A. Lawson. Rockville, Md.: Aspen Systems, 1983.

An Introduction to Theories of Personality, by B. Hergenhahn. Englewood Cliffs, N.J.: Prentice-Hall, 1980.

Becoming Partners: Marriage and Its Alternatives, by C. Rogers. Calif.: Delta, 1972.

Human Sexual Response, by Masters and Johnson. Boston: Little, Brown, 1966.

Marriage Happiness, by D. Knox. Champaign, Ill.: Research Press, 1971.

SOME QUESTIONS TO CONSIDER

1. What happened developmentally to me to put me where I am today?
2. How comfortable am I with my own sexuality?
3. What was my family of origin like and how has it affected me?
4. What do I want and what am I willing to give to my current family?

Chapter 3

Characterizing Clients and Assessing Their Needs

Gary W. Lawson

> *The eyes believe themselves;*
> *The ears believe other people.*
> Old Chinese Proverb

There is no "typical" chemically dependent person; they are as different as fingerprints. There is no specific personality type, family history, socioeconomic situation, or stressful experience that has been found to categorically predict the development of chemical dependency. Chemically dependent persons include doctors, ministers, lawyers, truck drivers, teachers, and members of virtually every profession known. Chemical dependency transcends race, religion, social class, intelligence, and ethnic affiliation. Chemical dependency is a complex behavioral disorder, and attitudes and concepts about chemical dependency are changing for those who work in the field. As more objective information concerning chemical dependency accumulates, the total picture will become more clear. The issues of use, misuse, and abuse are now being examined from many perspectives: legal, clinical, professional, personal, social, and cultural, among others. Chemical dependency is now seen as a series of complex interactions between people, their environment, and the chemical they choose to use. Chemical dependency problems should be seen on a continuum. For example, alcohol problems are not limited just to alcoholics: they also include problem drinkers, prealcoholics, and families of alcoholics. Not only are there different types of people who have chemical dependency problems, there are many types of chemical dependency problems. The type of person, his environment, the chemical involved, and the use pattern should all be considered in the diagnosis and treatment plan for the chemically dependent person. Simple definitions and simple methods of diagnosis sacrifice important scientific and clinical distinctions. Quality treatment is preceded by quality diagnosis. Counselors *must* know their clients and be able to assess their needs with accuracy.

DIAGNOSIS

The therapeutic relationship that a counselor establishes with a client is usually called counseling or therapy. This process is discussed in detail in Chapter 5. The importance of this relationship should be self-evident. The relationship may be therapeutic to a greater or lesser degree depending on its quality; however, in most instances therapy does not end with the counseling relationship. Therapy can include many things, for example, relaxation training, assertiveness training, group counseling, recreation therapy, or a bibliotherapy (reading) program. The counseling session, besides providing some direct therapeutic value, is the appropriate place for the counselor to assess the client's other therapeutic needs. During the initial counseling sessions the counselor should evaluate the client and his therapeutic needs. The quality of this assessment, or diagnosis, will be based on the quality and depth of the counseling relationship, and the outcome of treatment, or therapy, will have a direct relationship to the accuracy of the diagnosis and how it has been reflected in the treatment plan. Therefore, diagnosis becomes an integral part of the outcome, or prognosis. Counselors who know how to diagnose and how to translate this diagnosis into an individualized treatment plan are maximizing the benefits from their efforts.

CHEMICAL DEPENDENCY BEHAVIOR CLASSIFICATION

There are two major ways to classify deviant behavior such as chemical dependency: the first is as immoral or sinful, the second is as nonmoral and beyond the control of the individual. In turn, this deviant behavior is either addressed through the social institutions of the judicial system or the social institutions of the health care system: often this means jail versus a hospital treatment program. Alcoholism and the abuse of medically prescribed drugs are now viewed less as immoral, sinful behavior (legal diagnosis) and more as personal sickness (medical diagnosis). The use or abuse of illegal drugs, however, has not made this transition. "Alcoholism is a disease" is a slogan that has a great deal of public acceptance. "Heroin addiction is a disease" or "Drug addiction is a disease" has less chance for such acceptance because of the legal status of the substance involved. Addiction may be addiction; however, the social context of use has special meaning when legal and political aspects of diagnosis are considered.

Diagnosis As a Social Process

Diagnosis may be viewed as a social process: at issue is how a specific society or subsegment of society creates and uses social rules to define chemical use versus abuse. These rules may be narrow or broad, depending on the drug and the particular society. The abuse of alcohol, for example, is seen rather consistently in American culture as a pattern of repetitive, heavy drinking with obvious personal deterioration; consequently, almost anyone can make an accurate "social" diagnosis of alcoholism. However, this process of collective identification of alcoholics or of seeing all alcoholics as only those who have shown obvious deterioration, such as "skid row" alcoholics, has probably done more to deter progressive treatment and rehabilitation of the individual alcoholic than any other single variable, for two reasons. First, as part of the alcoholic's denial system problem drinkers or prealcoholics must see the "alcoholic" from a skid row perspective. In the process they can deny the existence of their own alcohol problems for as many years as it takes to reach "skid row" (Forrest, 1978). Second, persons may resist being labeled as alcoholic because they view alcoholics as down-and-outs. They may refuse treatment under that label, although they might accept treatment without the label.

Diagnosis As a Clinical Process

The counselor is primarily involved with diagnosis from a clinical or treatment perspective. The first aspect of this diagnosis is to establish that chemical dependency problems are present. This "screening diagnosis" is conducted to establish whether or not the client is appropriate for the counselor and his treatment agency. Some agencies have intake specialists to make these evaluations. But many other agencies place this responsibility on the person who will be the client's individual counselor. A key question here is "Are mood-altering chemicals involved?" or "Does this person ingest drugs?" (McAuliffe & McAuliffe, 1975). After this has been established the counselor can proceed to the second phase of diagnosis.

Diagnostic Classifications

The precise detail of this in-depth diagnosis is closely related to precision treatment. Where treatment is general and imprecise, there is little need for detailed diagnosis. This has, in the past, been the case in the field of alcoholism and drug abuse. Until recently most treatment approaches for alcoholism and drug abuse have been global and imprecise. Each person would go through the same treatment program, regardless of diagnosis. However, as significantly different treatment methods and treatment goals are established, the need for more detailed and precise diagnostic methods increases (Pattison & Kaufman, 1982).

There are two major types of diagnosis: binary diagnosis and multivariate diagnosis. The binary type of diagnosis is an either/or method: one is either chemically dependent or one is not. This approach may be based on either a unitary or multivariate framework. When the assumption is that there is a discrete entity termed "chemical dependency" or "drug addiction" or "alcoholism," the diagnostic goal is simply to find an effective way to distinguish those who are dependent on chemicals from those who are not. However, even though many still believe such entities exist, the research data of the past 20 years clearly demonstrate that the unitary concept is incorrect. The adverse effects of chemical use depend on many factors, and the binary diagnosis of chemically dependent persons leaves much to be desired.

Conjunctive and Disjunctive Classifications

Concepts or categories can either be conjunctive or disjunctive. A conjunctive classification is one in which *all* the defining attributes must be present for any individual to be classified in that category. For example, one must be over 18 and registered to be classified as a voter. This does not occur in the classification of alcoholism: alcoholism is disjunctively categorized. That is, a person classified as alcoholic can have a number of different defining attributes: blackouts, legal problems, family problems, physical problems, or many other problems related to alcohol use. The alcoholic may have experienced any one or any combination of these problems (Wallace, 1977).

As might be expected, the alcoholic in treatment denies alcoholism and focuses on the areas where no problems exist. The focus for the counselor is on the problems. The following exchange is typical:

COUNSELOR: "You appear to have an alcohol problem, because you were picked up twice for drinking and driving."

CLIENT: "Yes, but I still have a good job and my family life is fine; besides, many of my friends have been picked up for drinking and driving."

These encounters often end with the counselor concluding that the client is in denial and that nothing can be done until the client drinks some more and "hits bottom." The client is left feeling that "the counselor does not understand the situation and has only one goal, and that is, to diagnose me as an alcoholic." These sessions often end without resolution, with both counselor and client feeling frustrated. Too often, the binary method of either/or diagnosis identifies only those in the late stages of alcoholism. Early stage alcoholics and problem drinkers typically are not treated but are sent on their way until they hit bottom. Those who do enter treatment are likely to drop out or exhibit resistance. This approach is no longer acceptable, given the different types of treatment interventions available for all types of alcohol problems (Lawson et al., 1983).

Multivariate Syndromes

Most scientific authorities in the field of chemical dependency now agree that the factors involved in chemical dependency, drug addiction, and alcoholism are most accurately viewed as multivariate syndromes (that is, multiple patterns of dysfunctional chemical use that occur in many different types of personalities, with multiple combinations of adverse consequences and multiple outcomes, that may require different treatment interventions). Pattison and Kaufman (1982) list six implications of multivariate syndromes that apply to alcoholism. (They are presented here in adapted form to show their relevance to chemical dependency.)

1. There are multiple patterns of use, misuse, and abuse that may be denoted as a pattern of chemical dependency.
2. There are multiple interactional etiological variables that combine to produce a pattern of chemical dependency.
3. All persons are vulnerable to the development of some type of chemical dependency problem.
4. Treatment interventions must be multimodal to correspond to the particular pattern of alcoholism or chemical dependency in a specific person.
5. Treatment outcomes will vary in accord with specific chemical use patterns, persons, and social contexts.
6. Preventive interventions must be multiple and diverse to address diverse etiological factors.

The future of the chemical dependency field will, no doubt, include the description of consistently interrelated sets of symptoms with implications for etiology, prognosis, treatment and prevention. The chemical dependency counselor will contribute to this by providing a multivariate diagnosis that is free of imprecise and ambiguous definitions that binarily impose a diagnosis of chemical dependency. The chemical dependency counselor will be expected to identify and treat all manner of people on all points of the chemical dependency continuum.

DEFINING THE PROBLEM

How is "the problem" defined? There are many terms that are used in the field of chemical dependency. Some have clear meanings, others are confusing and less well defined. It is difficult for counselors to talk to one another (or to clients or other professionals) if they are using similar words, but these words have different meanings to each person. To begin with, what is chemical dependency? (Does it refer only to physical dependency, or does it also include psychological dependency? What is considered a chemical? Alcohol? Nicotine? Caffeine?) For the purpose of this book, and as a general guide for the counselor, this definition is offered: chemical dependency is a condition where there are perceivable signs or indications that the ingestion of a psychoactive or mood-altering chemical is causing the individual continuous life problems, yet this individual continues to use psychoactive chemicals. Although this is a rather broad definition, it does not fully encompass the range of clients that a chemical dependency counselor is likely to see.

The important aspects of this definition of chemical dependency are "life problems" and "continued use." What are these life problems and what treatment approach is best suited to assist the client in dealing with them? What role does chemical use play in these problems and what is the payoff for continued use? Note that the rationale behind this definition is not to seek an either/or diagnosis but to determine at what level these problems exist. For the individual who is beginning to experience problems related to chemical use, the counselor may only want to point out the relationship between the problems and the chemical use. The counselor may imply that the use must change, or the problems will likely remain or get worse. It can no longer be assumed, however, that the only choice available to the client is to give up chemical use or progressively develop more and more problems. Chemical dependency problems are similar to other chronic medical disorders in that the condition may improve, remain stable, or become worse. As is also the case with most behavioral disorders, the client's economic, intellectual, and personal resources are often a major determinant of outcomes, with or without therapeutic intervention (Mendelson & Mello, 1979). The prognosis for problem drinkers, for example, is far more encouraging than once believed. Rapid, spontaneous remission or gradual disappearance of alcohol-related problems may occur in a relatively high number of people. Cahalan (1970) reported that approximately 20 percent of those surveyed who reported alcohol-related problems no longer had these problems three years following the onset of the problem even though they had not sought help.

Others have reported on those who "cure" themselves of addictions, on alcoholics who reduce their alcohol intake to nonproblem levels, and on former heroin addicts who returned from Vietnam to a drug-free life without treatment (Peele, 1982). It is true that many factors are now clear regarding chemical dependency; however, other pertinent issues remain unclear. One reason for this is the use of circular definitions. The counselor should avoid these semantic traps. For example, if, by definition, an alcoholic is a person who cannot drink alcohol without experiencing problems, it is impossible for an alcoholic to return to nonproblem drinking, and the only acceptable treatment goal for an alcoholic is total abstinence. If an alcoholic should, by chance, return to nonproblem drinking, then by definition he is not really an alcoholic. This definition eliminates the possibility of scientific inquiry.

Denial

Denial is another concept that can be used to distort issues. If alcoholism is a "disease of denial," as many contend, then the only logical diagnosis that can be made of the problem drinker is alcoholism. If a "problem drinker" or "prealco-holic" diagnosed as alcoholic rightfully denies his alcoholism, the denial is seen as the first stage of alcoholism (denial). If the problem drinker doesn't deny alcohol-ism the only alternative is to accept it. These "yes-you-are–no-I'm-not" games only cloud the issues with regard to a specific diagnosis. They also detract from the counselor-client relationship. Definitions should be for the benefit of the counselor and client, and they should not detract from the therapeutic process. They should be flexible, yet understandable to both the counselor and the client.

Defining Terms

Some of the words counselors should examine in their own minds are use, misuse, abuse, addiction, habituation, and dependence. The following brief definitions are offered to assist counselors in developing their own meanings for these words relative to their own personal, social, and physical criteria:

- *Use.* The intake of a chemical substance into the body with the goal of somehow altering one's state of consciousness. (Use may or may not cause problems.)
- *Misuse.* Using a chemical with some physical, psychological, social, or legal adverse consequence (often carries unnecessary moral implications).
- *Abuse.* Chronic, recurrent misuse of chemicals. (This term should, perhaps, be left for such situations as child abuse, animal abuse, and self-abuse. The term "chemical abuse" tends to anthropomorphize chemicals by making them the object of the abuse.)
- *Addiction.* A cellular change that occurs with the increased use of most depressant drugs. The primary clinical features are the development of tolerance and the development of withdrawal symptoms upon removal of the drug.
- *Habituation.* The repetition of behavior. (This behavior is often anxiety reducing for the individual.)
- *Dependence.* Physical dependency is much the same as addiction. Psycho-logical dependence is a state that occurs when there is a strong urge to alter one's state of consciousness through the use of a chemical. These two types of dependence may occur independently or in combination with each other.

These are not the only terms that the chemical dependency counselor needs to clarify; there are many others. The point is that the counselor cannot be too clear or too specific about a client's problems and how these problems relate to a treatment plan.

DEFINITIONS AND DIAGNOSIS

Even though alcoholism and drug abuse have many commonalities, and it can no longer be assumed that alcoholics abuse alcohol to the exclusion of other drugs, alcoholism and drug abuse are still regarded as distinct and separate disorders. Therefore, separate diagnostic and evaluation methods will be presented for each.

Diagnosing Alcoholism

Many approaches have been presented in the literature for evaluating and diagnosing alcoholism. There are biological methods, but these are indirect because they reflect consequences of alcohol use, and many persons may have alcoholism syndromes without biological damage.

There are psychological methods of diagnosis that include indirect psychometric measures, such as the McAndrews Scale of the Minnesota Multiphasic Personality Inventory (MMPI). There are also direct psychometric methods, such as the Michigan Alcoholism Screening Test (MAST). The National Council on Alcoholism's list of major and minor criteria for the diagnosis of alcoholism is presented here as an example.

- *Diagnostic Level 1:* Classical, definite, obligatory. A person who fits this criterion must be diagnosed as alcoholic.
- *Diagnostic Level 2:* Probable, frequent, indicative. A person who satisfies this criterion is under strong suspicion of alcoholism; other corroborative evidence should be obtained.
- *Diagnostic Level 3:* Potential, possible, incidental. These manifestations are common in people with alcoholism but do not by themselves give a strong indication of its existence. Other, significant evidence is needed before the diagnosis is made.

Tables 3-1 and 3-2 delineate these diagnostic levels in more detail.

Criteria such as these are helpful, but not foolproof, in diagnosing alcoholism. One of the problems is false positives; while some of these measures have a 99 percent accuracy rate for identifying those in an alcoholic population, they diagnose almost 50 percent of those who are not alcoholics *as* alcoholics. Often, too, the results from measures such as these do not translate well into treatment plans. Each of these measures has shown some degree of success in diagnosing a certain type of alcoholic, but often this is to the exclusion of many other types. Several authors have made an attempt to differentiate between these "types" of alcoholics. One such differentiation was reported by Greenblatt and Shader (1975). They suggested that alcoholism be divided into three distinct conceptual entities:

Table 3-1 Major Criteria for the Diagnosis of Alcoholism

Criterion	Diagnostic Level	Criterion	Diagnostic Level
TRACK I. PHYSIOLOGICAL AND CLINICAL		Alcoholic hepatitis	1
		Laennec's cirrhosis	2
A. Physiological Dependency		Pancreatitis in the absence of cholelithiasis	2
1. Physiological dependence as manifested by evidence of a *withdrawal syndrome* when the intake of alcohol is interrupted or decreased without substitution of other sedation. It must be remembered that overuse of other sedative drugs can produce a similar withdrawal state, which should be differentiated from withdrawal from alcohol.		Chronic gastritis	3
		Hematological disorders: Anemia: hypochromic, normocytic, macrocytic, hemolytic with stomatocytosis, low folic acid	3
a. Gross tremor (differentiated from other causes of tremor)	1	Clotting disorders: prothrombin elevation, thrombocytopenia	3
b. Hallucinosis (differentiated from schizophrenic hallucinations or other psychoses)	1	Wernicke-Korsakoff syndrome	2
c. Withdrawal seizures (differentiated from epilepsy and other seizure disorders)	1	Alcoholic cerebellar degeneration	1
d. Delirium tremens. Usually starts between the first and third day after withdrawal and minimally includes tremors, disorientation, and hallucinations.	1	Cerebral degeneration in absence of Alzheimer's disease or arteriosclerosis	2
2. Evidence of *tolerance* to the effects of alcohol. (There may be a decrease in previously high levels of tolerance late in the course.) Although the degree of tolerance to alcohol in no way matches the degree of tolerance to other drugs, the behavioral effects of a given amount of alcohol vary greatly between alcoholic and nonalcoholic subjects.		Central pontine myelinolysis ⎫ diagnosis only Marchiafava-Bignami's ⎬ possible disease ⎭ postmortem Peripheral neuropathy (see also beriberi)	2 / 2 / 2
		Toxic amblyopia	3
		Alcoholic myopathy	2
a. A blood alcohol level of more than 150 mg. without gross evidence of intoxication.	1	Alcoholic cardiomyopathy	2
b. The consumption of one-fifth of a gallon of whiskey or an equivalent amount of wine or beer daily, for more than one day, by a 180-lb individual.	1	Beriberi	3
		Pellagra	3
3. Alcoholic "blackout" periods. (Differential diagnosis from purely psychological fugue states and psychomotor seizures.)	2	**TRACK II. BEHAVIORAL, PSYCHOLOGICAL, AND ATTITUDINAL**	
B. Clinical: Major Alcohol-Associated Illnesses. Alcoholism can be assumed to exist if major alcohol-associated illnesses develop in a person who drinks regularly. In such individuals, evidence of physiological and psychological dependence should be searched for. Fatty degeneration in absence of other known cause	2	All chronic conditions of psychological dependence occur in dynamic equilibrium with intrapsychic and interpersonal consequences. In alcoholism, similarly, there are varied effects on character and family. Like other chronic relapsing diseases, alcoholism produces vocational, social, and physical impairments. Therefore, the implications of these disruptions must be evaluated and related to the individual and his pattern of alcoholism. The following behavior patterns show psychological dependence on alcohol in alcoholism:	
		1. Drinking despite strong medical contraindication known to patient	1
		2. Drinking despite strong, identified, social contraindication (job loss for intoxication, marriage disruption because of drinking, arrest for intoxication, driving while intoxicated)	1
		3. Patient's subjective complaint of loss of control of alcohol consumption.	2

Table 3-2 Minor Criteria for the Diagnosis of Alcoholism

Criterion	Diagnostic Level	Criterion	Diagnostic Level
TRACK I. PHYSIOLOGICAL AND CLINICAL		Urinary urobilinogen elevation	2
		Serum A/G ration reversal	2
A. Direct Effects (ascertained by examination)		Blood and blood clotting	
		Anemia: hypochromic, normocytic, macrocytic, hemolytic with stomatocytosis, low folic acid	3
1. Early			
Odor of alcohol on breath at time of medical appointment	2	Clotting disorders: prothrombin elevation, thrombocytopenia	3
2. Middle		ECG abnormalities	
Alcoholic Facies	2	Cardiac arrhythmias, tachycardia: T waves dimpled, cloven, or spinous; atrial fibrillation; ventricular premature contractions; abnormal P waves	2
Vascular engorgement of face	2		
Toxic amblyopia	3		
Increased incidence of infections	3		
Cardiac arrhythmias	3	EEG abnormalities	
Peripheral neuropathy (see also Major Criteria, Track I, B)	2	Decreased or increased REM sleep, depending on phase	3
3. Late (see Major Criteria, Track I, B)		Loss of delta sleep	3
B. Indirect Effects		Other reported findings	3
		Decreased immune response	
1. Early		Decreased response to Synachthen test	3
Tachycardia	3		
Flushed face	3	Chromosomal damage from alcoholism	3
Nocturnal diaphoresis	3		
2. Middle			
Ecchymoses on lower extremities, arms, or chest	3	**TRACK II. BEHAVIORAL, PSYCHOLOGICAL, AND ATTITUDINAL**	
Cigarette or other burns on hands or chest	3		
Hyperreflexia, or if drinking heavily, hyporeflexia may be a residuum of alcoholic polyneuritis)	3	A. Behavioral	
		1. Direct effects	
		Early	
3. Late		Gulping drinks	3
Decreased tolerance	3	Surreptitious drinking	2
C. Laboratory Tests		Morning drinking (assess nature of peer group behavior)	2
1. Major—Direct		Middle	
Blood alcohol level at any time of more than 300 mg/100 ml	1	Repeated conscious attempts at abstinence	2
Level of more than 100 mg/100 ml in routine examination	1	Late	
2. Major—Indirect		Blatant indiscriminate use of alcohol	1
Serum osmolality (reflects blood alcohol levels) every 224 increase over 200 mOsm/liter reflects 50 mg/100 ml alcohol	2	Skid row or equivalent social level	2
		2. Indirect effects	
3. Minor—Indirect		Early	
Results of alcohol ingestion		Medical excuses from work for variety of reasons	2
Hypoglycemia	3	Shifting from one alcoholic beverage to another	2
Hypochloremic alkalosis	3		
Low magnesium level	2	Preference for drinking companions, bars, and taverns	2
Lactic acid elevation	3		
Transient uric acid elevation	3	Loss of interest in activities not directly associated with drinking	2
Potassium depletion	3		
Indications of liver abnormality:		Late	
SGPT elevation	2	Chooses employment that facilitates drinking	3
SGOT elevation	3		
BSP elevation	2	Frequent automobile accidents	3
Bilirubin elevation	2		

Table 3–2 continued

Criterion	Diagnostic Level	Criterion	Diagnostic Level
History of family members undergoing psychiatric treatment: school and behavioral problems in children	3	2. Indirect effects Early Unexplained changes in family, social and business relationships, complaints about wife, job, and friends	3
Frequent change of residence for poorly defined reasons	3	Spouse makes complaints about drinking behavior, reported by patient or spouse	2
Anxiety-relieving mechanisms, such as telephone calls inappropriate in time, distance, person, or motive (telephonitis)	2	Major family disruptions, separation, divorce, threats of divorce	3
Outbursts of rage and suicidal gestures while drinking	2	Job loss (due to increasing interpersonal difficulties), frequent job changes, financial difficulties	3
B. Psychological and Attitudinal		Late	
1. Direct effects Early When talking freely, makes frequent reference to drinking alcohol, people being "bombed," "stoned," etc., or admits drinking more than peer group	2	Overt expression of more regressive defense mechanisms: denial, protection, etc.	3
Middle		Resentment, jealousy, paranoid attitudes	3
Drinking to relieve anger, insomnia, fatigue, depression, social discomfort	2	Symptoms of depression, isolation, crying, suicidal preoccupation	3
Late		Feelings that he is "losing his mind"	3
Psychological symptoms consistent with permanent organic brain syndrome (see also Major Criteria, Track I, B)	2		

1. A pathologic psychosocial behavior pattern, characterized by deteriorating function in occupation, family, and citizenship, resulting from excessive alcohol ingestion.
2. A drug addiction of the classic type. Cessation of alcohol ingestion is followed by withdrawal.
3. A medical disease with certain characteristic sequelae, such as cirrhosis, nutritional disorders, and neurological damage.

They suggest that for those alcoholics who have all three characteristics, a diagnosis of alcoholism is easy. However, the alcoholic may have only one of these disorders or perhaps a combination of two. (For example, the heavy-drinking executive may have characteristics 2 but not 1 or 3; the skid row alcoholic may have 1 and 2 but not 3, and so on.) These classifications are most useful for physicians.

Kuanert (1979) has divided alcoholism into three somewhat different categories. He classifies alcoholism as either reactive, secondary, or primary. Reactive alcoholics are those who become preoccupied with alcohol only after being overwhelmed by some external stress. Secondary alcoholics are suffering from a major psychiatric illness such as schizophrenia, and they medicate for this illness with alcohol. Primary alcoholics are those who find, from their first drinking experience, that their relationship with alcohol is extremely positive and highly desirable. They choose to involve themselves with alcohol and to capture the feelings evoked from this special relationship time and time again, and they disregard any negative consequences of their drinking. What is fundamentally useful about Kuanert's approach is that he supplies a different and varied treatment plan for the underlying psychiatric illness, then the alcoholism.

Chemical Dependency Diagnosis

Wright (1982) has presented a useful profile of the chemically dependent person. Each of the areas in the profile (below) could be addressed in a diagnostic interview and could also be included in a treatment plan:

1. Risk Factors
   a. Alcoholic relatives
   b. Disorder in family of origin
   c. Unusual early life history
2. Physical Symptoms
   a. Diseases related to substance usage
   b. Physical signs of usage
   c. Tolerance
   d. Withdrawal
   e. Stress-related or obscure illnesses
3. Mental Symptoms
   a. Decreased cognitive ability
   b. Memory failure
   c. Psychological dependency
   d. Obsession
   e. Defensiveness
   f. Delusioned denial
4. Emotional Symptoms
   a. Compulsive use
   b. Unstable moods
   c. Powerlessness
5. Social Symptoms
   a. Job
   b. Relationships
   c. Legal
   d. Financial
   e. Psychiatric

6. Spiritual Symptoms
   a. Rigid negative attitudes
   b. Low self-image
   c. Negative God concept
   d. Unusual religious observances
   e. Failure of humility
   f. Failure of love

Wright's list does not delineate all the potential problem areas of the chemically dependent person, but it does provide an excellent starting place. To provide more detail, each area would need to be expanded; for example, under relationships might be spouse and under that sexual, recreational, and so on.

The most extensive set of criteria for chemical dependency diagnosis that has been published to date is the diagnostic manual of McAuliffe and McAuliffe (1975). It is much too detailed to present here; however, the major areas covered are:

- Symptoms of mental obsession,
- Symptoms of emotional compulsion,
- Symptoms of low self-image,
- Symptoms of rigid, negative attitudes,
- Symptoms of rigid defense system,
- Symptoms of delusion,
- Symptoms of powerlessness, and
- Physical symptoms.

Although this manual is quite thorough, it might not translate as well into a specific treatment plan as other, less complicated approaches to diagnosis. However, the beginning counselor as well as the more advanced counselor could find this manual very useful with some adaptation to their own situation.

Other Diagnostic Manuals

Two other diagnostic manuals should be mentioned here, if only because of their wide acceptance by the mental health field and by insurance companies who need a specific diagnosis to evaluate claim payments. These are the Diagnostic and Statistical Manuals II and III of the American Psychiatric Association (DSM II and DSM III). These manuals base diagnosis on a description of the clinical features of the dysfunction.

DSM II divides alcoholism into three categories: episodic excessive drinking, habitual excessive drinking, and alcohol addiction. Drug dependence is classified according to the type of drug involved: e.g., opium dependence is one category, cocaine dependence another, and so on.

DSM III places more emphasis on the similarities between alcoholism and other forms of drug use. It contains a new category, "substance use disorders," which is subdivided into substance abuse and substance dependence. It would be wise for the chemical dependency counselor to become familiar with the two manuals. A local psychologist or mental health counselor would probably be happy to provide some training on DSM I and DSM II for the chemical dependency counselor.

Each of the diagnostic criteria presented here is accurate from the perspective of the person who established it. Chemically dependent persons can be evaluated, split up, divided, and diagnosed in hundreds of ways: all of these ways could conceivably be correct. Most likely, chemical dependency counselors will be expected to follow rules their agency has established with regard to diagnosis. However, the beginning counselor will soon be the experienced counselor and, in that regard, can have an effect on the agency's policies, including how diagnosis is used and what criteria are followed. There is one simple rule to follow when making these decisions: *make sure the diagnosis is helpful to the client*.

CASE EXAMPLES

To best illustrate the type of in-depth diagnosis that we encourage we will present two case examples. The first example has been taken directly from the case file of a very traditional alcoholism treatment program: note that almost anyone would fit into this treatment plan and that the treatment recommended does not necessarily relate to the patient as presented in the history. It is not at all unusual to see this traditional kind of diagnosis and treatment plan. Specific data have been changed to protect the individual and the agency.

Case No. 1

DATE OF ADMISSION:	3/14/80
DATE OF DISCHARGE:	4/10/80
DATA BASE:	Patient is a 25-year-old male from Scottsbluff, Nebraska; height, 75 inches; weight, 200 pounds.
	Patient came in voluntarily on 3/14/80.
CHIEF COMPLAINT:	Patient was pushed by authorities, after second DWI, to seek treatment at the present time. Went through detoxification.

HISTORY OF ILLNESS: Patient drinks only scotch, a pint per day. Drinks three or four days a week at a bar and at home. Some hangovers. Blackouts denied. No delirium tremens. Had one period of sobriety for three months.

PHYSICAL EXAMINATION: Liver was not enlarged.

LABORATORY REPORT: SGOT, 19. GGT, 18; Hemoglobin, 18; MCV, 84; Ua, negative; VDRL, negative.

CHEST X-RAY: 3/14/80, normal.

PSYCHOLOGICAL: Assessment on 3/16/80. I.Q. was 110. Test readministered on 4/1/80, and I.Q. was 121. A total of two hours with psychology department.

OBSERVATIONS: On entry, patient was cooperative, detoxification was not needed, no withdrawal symptoms.

MEDICATIONS: 500 mg. Antabuse, three times a week; Unicap T, two daily; Tennes lotion to back (patient's own medication), as needed.

MEDICATION ON DISCHARGE: 250 mg. Antabuse daily; B-complex daily; Tennes lotion to back (patient's own medication).

WARD: Patient was alert and compliant and cooperated reasonably well. Well aware of problems. Self-esteem improved. Patient was definitely serious about program. Family contacts—active girlfriend who picked him up after discharge.

SOCIAL WORKER: Mr. Smith entered treatment as the result of a DWI. He was verbally skilled throughout his stay. Felt he has gained maximum benefit. His recovery plans include AA, Antabuse, and continued individual

	counseling. Did have three consents that were signed.
COUNSELOR:	Mr. Smith completed program, including AA steps one through five. During the third week, he continued to play with the idea that a cured alcoholic could return to social drinking. His intellectualization and avoidance of responsibility for his recovery are a strong defense against accepting alcoholism. He made statements that his girlfriend and mother would keep him sober. No visible change in behavior or attitude was observed; unless he follows a supervised recovery plan, his prognosis is poor.
MEDICAL:	Patient was present when the medical goal was set to confront legal problems ensuing from alcohol ingestion. Patient needs very closely supervised follow-up or he will not do well. Was very compliant, a junior at the university, and used intellectualization as a defense. Would plan to return to school. Only mildly involved in program.
FINAL DIAGNOSIS:	Alcohol Addiction

PROBLEMS AND/OR SOLUTIONS:

Alcohol abuse—Patient was educated on alcoholism and completed the routine program. Patient was compliant throughout.

Legal problems ensuing from abnormal alcohol use and/or illegal drug use— Patient was educated on alcoholism and completed routine program. Patient was compliant throughout.

Anxiety—Reduced slightly through participation in individual and group therapy.

Lacks understanding in the dynamics of addiction—He was urged to follow recovery plan but was never able to work on a feeling level.

Intellectualization—Patient was always wondering whether he would be able to drink socially further. This attitude remained unchanged. Patient needs a supervised environment to stay sober.

TREATMENT MODALITIES:

Lectures, 21 hours; Group, 22½ hours; Movies, 8½ hours; Religious Therapy, 1½ hours; AA orientation, 6 hours; Reading and Tapes, 25½ hours; Social Skills, 5 hours; Counselor, 2½ hours; Social Worker, 1½ hours; Team, Completed Fifth Step; Testing, 1 hour; and Medical Exam, 1½ hours.

AFTERCARE PLAN:

Date of Discharge	4/10/80
Placement	Scottsbluff, Nebraska
Family	Contact own
Finances	Student at university
Legal	Second DWI in county
Follow-up	AA in city of residence

STAFF RECOMMENDATIONS:

AA meetings twice weekly; Antabuse daily for two years with supervision; outpatient counseling; seek sponsorship in AA and become active in AA or patient will not make it.

SUMMARY:

Participation good. Problems identified and treatment plan completed. Patient received moderate detoxification benefit from treatment.

Awareness of problems related to drinking were poor on entry—good on discharge. Plans for dealing with problems related to drinking were poor on entry—good on discharge. Changes in self (attitude, behavior, feelings) related to drinking were moderate.

PROGNOSIS:

Poor, unless follow-up is closely supervised.

Case No. 1 Discussion

Note that the presentation omits a great deal of information relating to this individual (for example, his feeling of self-worth, his sexuality, his family, his development, etc.). The treatment plan was not specific and did nothing or very little to meet the patient's specific needs.

The diagnosis was alcohol addiction, yet there was nothing to indicate that the patient was physically addicted. (Detoxification was noted as unnecessary although he did go through a detoxification procedure; it is not uncommon for programs to require all new patients to go through detoxification as a medical precaution.) Psychological addiction, if it existed, was not mentioned. Drinking did not occur daily but three to four times weekly. Very little was mentioned regarding his family. Anxiety was mentioned but with no specifics. (It is not unusual for a person to be anxious because of being in a treatment program.)

Treatment consisted mainly of lectures, group therapy (which some people respond to and others don't), movies, and AA orientation. Aftercare was simply "AA in city of residence."

Although the patient seemed poorly motivated, nothing was done to improve his motivation. Little wonder, then, that his prognosis is listed as poor; however, the poor prognosis is made to look as if it is the patient's fault. Statements such as "patient was always wondering whether he would be able to drink socially" or "lacks understanding in the dynamics of addiction" and "never able to work on a feeling level" were used to focus on the patient's deficiencies, but these issues were apparently never dealt with in treatment.

It is also interesting to note the counselor's conclusion, that "no visible change in behavior or attitude was observed." What did happen in treatment to change anything in the life of this patient? One would suspect very little by reading his records. A more appropriate statement to sum up what happened in treatment would be the following: a thorough diagnosis was never completed, and the patient was run through the standard treatment program.

To illustrate a more thorough approach that relates diagnosis to treatment, we will present this case again, with a narrative of what diagnosis and treatment could have been like.

Case No. 2

Upon admission a complete personal history was taken to determine basic demographic data; educational, vocational, health, treatment, social, and judicial histories; relationships with family and friends; recreational/community involvement; personality and emotional development; sexual functioning; and motivation for treatment.

A behavioral assessment of alcohol abuse was completed that included, in detail, what goes on before, during, and after the client consumes alcohol. This also includes the people he is with, when and where he drinks, the amount and type of available alcohol, concurrent activities, and any emotional state that could have influenced his drinking. The specific reinforcers for drinking were also identified.

Personal Data

Joe is an unmarried 25-year-old white male, third-year university student majoring in business. Joe presented March 14, 1980, for treatment of alcohol abuse, motivated by authorities due to a second DWI. At time of presenting, Joe had been drinking over a pint of scotch daily, three to four times per week. This pattern had existed for over a year.

Personal History

Joe is the oldest of three children. He has two brothers, five and seven years younger than he. He was born in Luke City, Nebraska. His attitude toward his parents and siblings, on the surface, appears positive. However, he reports that as a child he found it difficult to approach his father and that he never seemed able to please him. Most of his communications in the family were through his mother. He did report some resentment toward his brothers because he had to help his father, a farmer, with the chores, and his brothers did not because they were too young. This often involved getting up at 4:30 in the morning while his brothers slept in.

The youngest brother is a senior in high school, and the middle brother is a junior in college preparing to go to medical school.

His father, now 69, continues to farm but at a reduced level. His mother is a retired school teacher. Neither parent drinks, for religious reasons.

Joe does have a girlfriend whom he plans to marry some time after college. Their relationship seems tenuous due to his drinking behavior. He is often verbally abusive to her when he drinks heavily.

Joe is in the third year of college as a business major. However, his grades have been falling because of his drinking and sleeping through class. He is unsure about his business major and reports that he majored in business because he thought his father wanted him to. He has never seen a guidance counselor about his career plans, nor has he spoken to his parents or teachers. He has worked as a sales clerk in a clothing store for the past two years to help pay his way through school. He hates the job but needs the money.

Joe spent two years in the Army, stationed in Europe as a tank gunner during most of that time. He receives some military benefits to assist him through school. He loved Europe and hated the Army.

Joe's only encounters with the police are the two DWIs, which were approximately two years apart.

Joe has some interest in music, sports, reading, and movies. He seems to have led a fairly normal, middle class, small town existence.

Joe seems reluctant to adopt a treatment goal of total abstinence. However, he does seem anxious to attend to the other aspects of his life (i.e., vocation, sexual relationships, personal satisfaction in social relationships, and family relationships).

Joe attended AA after his first DWI, but he "didn't like it or the people in it." "A bunch of burned-out drunks" was the way he described it. The religious aspects reminded him of his Baptist upbringing, which he has rejected.

Behavioral Assessment

Joe's problems are:

1. Alcohol abuse
2. Vocational dissatisfaction
3. Relationship problems with—
   a. girlfriend
   b. family
4. Skill defect in expression of positive and confrontational statements to peers and family. Anxiety in presence of strangers and crowds.

Etiological Description

Alcohol Use. Joe's immediate concern is his inappropriate use of alcohol, the DWIs, and the problems drinking causes between him and his girlfriend. He first drank alcohol while in basic training in the Army; this was seven years ago. He found that alcohol made him feel at ease around other people. He drank nearly every day during his two years in the Army. Although he reported some hangovers, he had no blackouts or other alcohol-related problems. He has smoked marijuana but did not find it enjoyable; he reports no other drug use.

His beverage of choice is scotch, which accounts for 90 percent of his alcohol intake. Seventy-five percent of his drinking is done at bars, with friends; he reports that he often drinks with no related problems. He has had no suicide attempts, no psychiatric treatment, nor any formal treatment for his alcohol abuse.

Vocational Potential. Joe is also very concerned about his vocational future. He is afraid that a degree in business will limit him in his career choices. He is not sure what he wants to do. He does not particularly like school, and he did not like the Army. He doesn't feel that he is capable of much more in school than he is already doing. He does not see himself as bright; "close to average intelligence" is how he described himself. His teachers in high school always told him that he was not working up to his potential, but he thought he was.

Interpersonal Relationships. Joe does not seem to have much insight into the nature of relationships. Often he does not see the cause and effect relationship between his behavior and the way other people treat him. He also has given little thought to the relationship between how he feels about himself now and his personal needs, and his early family life. He feels that others just "don't understand him." In this way, he seems to externalize his problems, placing the responsibility for his happiness on those around him. He appears to have many unverbalized expectations of others, and he is hurt when these others do not live up to these expectations. This hurt is also hard to verbalize and is often expressed inappropriately as anger, during a drunken episode. He later regrets this behavior and feels guilty about it. This, in turn, makes him feel unworthy of any positive regard from others.

Joe indicated that while his home life as a child was mostly satisfactory, little, if any, real communication existed. He believes that strong emotions of any type were discouraged. His mother and father never fought; there was never a raised voice in the household. The only time his father showed any emotion was when his mother (Joe's grandmother) died. Even then there was very little; just one short crying episode then things were back to "normal."

Joe has indicated that he has felt ill at ease with other people most of his life. As a child he was physically smaller than most of his classmates and, as such, was not invited to participate in competitive sports; in adolescence he felt that his size frustrated his attempts at dating.

More recently, Joe has expressed skill deficit and anxiety in speaking with strangers and expressing himself in crowds. Joe is also unassertive in various social situations.

Treatment Techniques

Joe meets all the criteria of those people who have been successful on a controlled drinking program:

1. He has, at times, practiced social drinking.
2. He is under 40 years old.
3. He was never physically addicted to alcohol.
4. He has few life problems related to alcohol (in comparison to most alcoholics).
5. He has a relatively short problem drinking history (less than 10 years).
6. He does not see himself as alcoholic.
7. He does not subscribe to the disease concept of alcoholism.
8. He prefers the controlled drinking option to abstinence.
9. He has no family history of alcoholism.
10. He has environmental support (girlfriend, peers) for controlled drinking.

He will be offered such a program on an outpatient basis, after he completes the 30-day inpatient program: he must remain abstinent during the 30 days. If he is unsuccessful at controlled drinking, he has agreed to accept total abstinence as an alternative goal.

The following program will be adopted to deal with Joe's abuse of alcohol:

- Investigate situations, feelings, or thoughts that occur before, during, and after excessive drinking.
- Arrange effective alternative responses to excessive drinking.
- Learn how controlled drinking differs from alcoholic drinking.
- Practice drink refusal.

- Establish contract with the outpatient counselor, girlfriend, and family to reward period of controlled drinking and to levy penalties (e.g., loss of attention and monetary fines) for excessive drinking.
- Set up reading program on controlled drinking including *How to Control Your Drinking,* Miller and Muro, 1976.
- Complete Continuous Data Questionnaire at outset of program with counselor, and once every three months thereafter. (See Exhibit 3-1.)
- Joe will see a vocational counselor for testing and evaluation. He will set career and educational goals that he feels good about based upon the test results and vocational counseling.
- Joe will be seen in family therapy with his parents and brothers; he will be seen with his girlfriend, as well.
- Joe's current skill deficit in interpersonal relationships will be modified through assertiveness training.

In this example, the treatment plan is directly related to the diagnostic information. All of a person's problems cannot be dealt with in such a short time period, so someone—preferably a treatment team—must decide which problems should be selected for treatment to achieve the best overall results. This decision will depend, in part, on the resources of the treatment agency. Some treatments might include educational and vocational counseling; marital counseling; family counseling; sexual dysfunction, obesity, exercise, nutrition, or recreational counseling; and education as to nonalcoholic ways of getting "high."

GOAL SETTING

Alcohol- and nonalcohol-related treatment goals must be established as part of the treatment plan. The following steps for goal setting are suggested by Poley, Lea, and Vibe (1979):

1. Define each goal in terms of identifiable behaviors.
2. Define the goal in such a way that it is measurable in terms of frequency, quantity, or length of time.
3. Define the situations in which the desired behavior is to occur: the time, the place, with whom, how, and the client's emotional state.
   Some examples of behavioral goals are:
   a. to drink a maximum of two 12-ounce bottles of beer per 24-hour period, at a rate of no more than one bottle of beer per hour;
   b. to spend one hour per evening with the television off, speaking with one's spouse without arguing;

Exhibit 3–1 Continuous Data Questionnaire

To be completed by therapist in interview with the client. To be given: (1) during assessment, (2) at the start of treatment, and following that, (3), at regular three month intervals, and lastly, (4) at treatment completion (or termination). Following treatment completion, the CDQ will be given as a follow-up at three, six, and twelve month periods in post completion (or termination) of therapy. Report periods are defined as follows:

The first time the questionnaire is given is during the Assessment period. In all interviews, the questions are asked with respect to the previous three months of the client's life (or the period since the last CDQ, if that is less than three months). Thus the words "report period" in this questionnaire refer to the previous three months of the client's life. Please give responses to all questions, even is the answer is zero.

Name of Client _____

1. Stage of Treatment:

    1. Assessment
    2. Treatment initiation
    3. Treatment
    4. Treatment completion

    5. Follow-up (not in treatment, not yet discharged)
    6. Completed program (discharged)
    7. Terminated, explain
    8. Readmitted

2. Date administered _____
   Administered by _____

I. ALCOHOL USE

Regardless of treatment goal (abstinence or controlled drinking), answer the following as completely and as accurately as you can:

1. Over the past three months you have consumed alcohol on the average as follows:

    a. how much per week?
    b. how many days per week?
    c. how many days abstinent per week?
    d. amount per day?
    e. preference of beverage a) _____ b) _____ c) _____
    f. who with?
    g. where?
    h. note all other drugs taken whether licit or illicit include prescription and over the counter medications

2. Most of my friends are _____. My spouse (including common-law) is _____
   (place correct number in blank space).

    1) abstainers
    2) occasional users
    3) moderate or average users
    4) frequent or heavy users
    5) alcoholics
    6) not applicable

3. During the past report period what is the longest period of time over which you did not drink?

    Days _____ Weeks _____ Months _____ Always drank _____

Source: Reprinted from *Alcoholism: A Treatment Manual* by Wayne Poley, Gary Lea, and Gail Vibe with permission of Gardner Press, ©1979.

Exhibit 3–1 continued

4. How difficult is it for you to control the amount of alcohol that you consume?

1) extremely easy
2) moderately easy
3) neither difficult or easy
4) moderately difficult
5) extremely difficult

5. During the past report period your alcohol urges have been:

1) nil or almost none
2) quite weak
3) average
4) moderately strong
5) very strong

6. When do you drink?

A.
1) weekends only
2) during week
3) both
4) N/A

B.
1) morning mostly
2) afternoon mostly
3) evening mostly
4) at any time
5) N/A

7. General comment on drug-alcohol use (thoughts, feelings, attitudes, performance)

II. WORK-EDUCATION

1. Are you employed _____ Not employed _____

2. Has your place of employment changed since last report period? Yes _____ No _____. If yes, how many times? _____ If not employed proceed to #9.

   Name of employer (if changed since last report)_____

   Name and address of firm or company_____

   _____

   Telephone_____

3. Average monthly income from this job (indicate to nearest dollar)

   $ _____ None _____

4. Length of time in present job.

   Years _____ Months _____ Weeks _____

5. How many days have you missed from work during this report period?

   a. Alcohol-related _____
   b. Illness_____
   c. Leave of absence _____

6. How many times were you late for work in the last month? _____

7. How satisfied are you with your job?

1) Very satisfied
2) Moderately satisfied
3) Neither satisfied nor unsatisfied
4) Moderately unsatisfied
5) Very unsatisfied
6) N/A

Exhibit 3–1 continued

8. How would you rate yourself on your performance at work?

    1) Excellent
    2) Quite good
    3) Average
    4) Moderately poor
    5) Very poor
    6) N/A

9. Length of time unemployed. Yrs. _____ Months _____ Weeks _____

10. Usual occupational status.

    1) Full-time (more than six hours per day)
    2) Part-time (less than six hours per day)
    3) Temporarily unemployed
    4) Permanently unemployed
    5) Welfare

11. Usual occupational category.

    1) Professional, executive, or managerial
    2) White collar (secretary, clerk, etc.)
    3) Skilled labourer, tradesman (chef, electrician)
    4) Unskilled labourer
    5) Semi-professional (nurse, skilled technician)
    6) Houseperson
    7) Unemployed
    8) Student
    9) Other

    Also, please indicate the specific job title. _____

12. Additional Income other than job if employed (during report period) 1) welfare, 2) unemployment, 3) donations, 4) loans, 5) illegal sources, 6) personal wealth, 7) spouse/commonlaw partner, 8) family, 9) other, specify.

    Source _____   Amount _____
    Source _____   Amount _____
    Source _____   Amount _____

13. How much money do you presently owe?

    mortgage _____
    car debts _____
    credit cards _____
    family _____
    friends _____
    others _____   _____

14. How much money have you repaid on loans, etc. (during this report period)?

    mortgage _____
    car debts _____
    credit cards _____
    family _____
    friends _____
    others _____

Exhibit 3–1 continued

15. Have you been meeting required payments? Yes _____ No _____

16. Do you plan to continue your education or training?

    1) am currently doing so
    2) yes, most definitely
    3) yes, want to
    4) maybe, thinking about it
    5) undecided
    6) no plans
    7) never

    If #1 or #2, specify _____

17. General comments on work-education-income areas (thoughts, feelings, attitudes, etc.)

III. FAMILY INVOLVEMENT

1. Who do you live with? (use up to three categories)

	Now	Usually
1) Spouse/common-law partner	_____	_____
2) Parents	_____	_____
3) Grandparents	_____	_____
4) Brother or sister		
5) Other relatives		
6) Friends		
7) By yourself		
8) institution or at a residence		
9) members of the same commune		

2. Main type of place that you live in:

    1) no regular place (street, abandoned bldg., etc.)
    2) hostel, rooming or boarding house
    3) hotel
    4) apartment or other family dwelling
    5) jail, prison, or other correctional institution
    6) therapeutic community or other rehabilitation facility
    7) hospital
    8) school, college, or university residence
    9) employers housing, including armed forces
    10) own house
    11) other, specify _____

3. How well do you get along with your family? _____ (other than spouse)
   friends? _____
   spouse (incl. common-law)? _____

    1) very well
    2) moderately well
    3) neither well nor poorly
    4) moderately poor
    5) very poor
    6) N/A

Exhibit 3–1 continued

4. How often do you do things with your family? _____ (other than spouse)
   friends? _____
   spouse (incl. common-law)? _____
   alone? _____
   1) very often (every day)
   2) quite often (several times/week)
   3) sometimes (several times/month
   4) rarely (several times/year)
   5) never
   6) N/A

5. How important are your friends to you? _____
   family? _____ (other than spouse)
   spouse (incl. common-law)? _____
   1) very important
   2) moderately important
   3) neither important nor unimportant
   4) moderately unimportant
   5) very unimportant
   6) N/A

6. How important do you feel that you are to your spouse? _____ (incl. common-
   friends? _____   law)
   (other than spouse) family? _____
   1) very important
   2) moderately important
   3) neither important nor unimportant
   4) moderately unimportant
   5) very unimportant
   6) N/A

7. How well do you handle arguments with your spouse? _____ (incl. common-law)
   family? _____ (other than spouse)
   friends? _____
   1) very constructively
   2) moderately well
   3) neither well nor poorly
   4) moderately poorly
   5) very poorly
   6) ignore the problem
   7) don't argue (probe)
   8) N/A

8. Do you usually keep appointments, dates and obligations to your
   friends? _____
   family? _____ (other than spouse)
   spouse? _____ (incl. common-law)
   1) yes, always
   2) usually
   3) sometimes
   4) rarely
   5) almost never
   6) N/A

9. General comments on family involvement (thoughts, feelings, attitudes, performance, etc.)

Exhibit 3–1 continued

IV. SOCIAL-RECREATIONAL-COMMUNITY INVOLVEMENT

1. What were your social/recreational activities during the past report period? (Include informal activities like drinking with friends) (Indicate if any of these were new.)

Activities	New (Yes, No)
_____	_____
_____	_____
_____	_____
_____	_____
_____	_____

2. About how many times a week do you participate in these social/recreational activities?

1) four or more
2) two to three times
3) once a week
4) less than once
5) rarely or never

3. During the past report period, how many new friends have you met by participating in these events?

1) none
2) one friend
3) two friends
4) three friends
5) four friends
6) five or more friends

4. General comments on social-recreational-community involvement (thoughts, feelings, attitudes, performance).

V. JUDICIAL INVOLVEMENT

1. During this report period, has there been any change (less or more involvement) in your status with the criminal justice system?

Yes _____ No _____

** If "yes," complete judicial section, if "no" skip to Personality & Emotional Development.

2. Reasons for arrests during report period. Record number of arrests in each category (use zero where appropriate).

	Number
1) Crimes against person, e.g. assault, rape, homicide	_____
2) Crimes for profit, e.g. robbery, burglary, forgery, theft	_____
3) Prostitution, pimping, or soliciting	_____
4) Gambling	_____
5) Motor vehicle driving offences (excluding minor offences)	_____
6) Other, specify	_____

Exhibit 3-1 continued

3. If arrested during report period please indicate charge, conviction and sentence.

charge _____
conviction _____
sentence _____

charge _____
conviction _____
sentence _____

charge _____
conviction _____
sentence _____

charge _____
conviction _____
sentence _____

4. Do you have any outstanding bench warrants?

Yes _____   No _____

If yes, specify _____

5. Is there a presentence report outstanding?

Yes _____   No _____

6. Has there been a change towards less involvement with the criminal justice system (i.e., off parole, off probation, cleared bench warrant?) Yes _____ No _____

If yes, specify _____

7. General comments (thoughts, attitudes, feelings, performance, etc.).

VI. PERSONALITY AND EMOTIONAL DEVELOPMENT

1. Please rate the following characteristics as you feel they may apply to you.

1) very low
2) moderately low
3) neither high nor low
4) moderately high
5) very high

1) responsibility to self _____.
2) Responsibility to others _____.
3) Self-esteem (self-worth) _____.
4) Initiative (motivation) _____.
5) Anxiety _____.
6) Sociability _____.
7) Assertiveness _____.
8) General feeling of well-being _____.
9) Hostility-aggression-punishment towards others _____.
10) Depression _____.

Exhibit 3–1 continued

    2. Please indicate on each of these scales, how you felt during the report period. (circle correct number)

1) tense	1	2	3	4	5	relaxed
2) tolerant	1	2	3	4	5	critical
3) depressed	1	2	3	4	5	happy
4) hard (tough)	1	2	3	4	5	soft (tender)
5) calm	1	2	3	4	5	nervous
6) sickly	1	2	3	4	5	healthy
7) forgiving	1	2	3	4	5	unforgiving
8) sociable	1	2	3	4	5	unsociable
9) unfriendly	1	2	3	4	5	friendly

    3. Comments or reflections on personality and moods.

VII. HEALTH

    1. Your overall physical health has been: _____.Your overall mental health has been: _____.

        1) excellent
        2) very good
        3) average
        4) poor
        5) very poor

    2. During the past report period, have you had any major diseases or illnesses? Yes _____ No _____

        If yes, specify _____

    3. Have you been eating regular meals?

        1) all of the time
        2) most of the time
        3) occasionally
        4) rarely or never

    4. Have you been eating reasonably balanced or nutritious meals? (Probe what they have eaten over the last few days.) Answer to be rated by therapist.

        1) all of the time
        2) most of the time
        3) occasionally
        4) rarely or never

    5. On the average, how many hours of sleep do you get each night?

        1) more than 10 hours   4) 5-6 hours
        2) 9-10 hours   5) less than 5 hours
        3) 7-8 hours

    6. Is that enough? Yes _____ No _____

    7. Do you use drugs/alcohol to help get to sleep? Yes _____ No _____

    8. How much time do you spend doing physical exercise? (sports, work, bicycling, etc.)

        1) more than fifteen hours per week
        2) ten to fifteen hours per week
        3) five to ten hours per week

Exhibit 3–1 continued

4) one to five hours per week
5) less than one hour a week

9. Have you had any difficulties with menstruation?

Yes _____ No _____ N/A _____

If yes, specify. _____

10. During the past report period how many times did you see a medical doctor? _____
Psychiatrist? _____

11. How much time have you spent (during this report period) in the hospital for physical reasons? _____ Mental reasons? _____

1) no time
2) less than one day (not overnite)
3) one day to less than one week
4) one week to two weeks
5) two weeks to less than a month
6) one month to three months
7) three to six months
8) more than six months

12. Have you attempted to harm yourself during the report period?

No _____ Yes _____

(During Assessment, check for anytime in client history.) If yes, how many times have you attempted to harm yourself (including attempted suicide) and by what method. Please indicate approximate date(s).

SEXUAL HEALTH

1. Your sexual drive or urges are:

1) strong
2) average
3) weak
4) very weak
5) no urges

2. Can you reach orgasm through intercourse, masturbation, or other means?

1) all of the time
2) most of the time
3) occasionally
4) seldom
5) never

3. How satisfied are you with your sex life?

1) very satisfied
2) moderately satisfied
3) neither satisfied nor unsatisfied
4) moderately unsatisfied
5) very unsatisfied

4. General comments, thoughts, attitudes, etc. on general or sexual health.

Exhibit 3–1 continued

VIII. MOTIVATION

  1. What do you see as the most desirable goals of treatment here for you? And, giving your honest opinion, how well do you feel that you have achieved (i.e. your present success) or will achieve these goals (i.e. your expected success)?

    1) very successful
    2) moderately successful
    3) no indication (haven't attempted, no indication of success yet, etc.)
    4) moderately unsuccessful
    5) very unsuccessful
    6) N/A (no goals)

Goals	Present Success	Expected Success
1. _____	_____	_____
2. _____	_____	_____
3. _____	_____	_____
4. _____	_____	_____

  2. How important is it for you to stop abusing alcohol or abstain?

    1) very important
    2) moderately important
    3) undecided
    4) moderately unimportant
    5) very unimportant

  3. What do you feel would be your most desirable use of alcohol?

    1) never use
    2) use rarely
    3) use socially
    4) occasional heavy use (i.e. binge drinking)

  4. Rate your responses to the following items:

    1) strongly agree
    2) agree
    3) undecided
    4) disagree
    5) strongly disagree

    A. My alcohol problem is something I can get over soon. _____
    B. No one I know is really interested in my problem. _____
    C. Nowadays a person has to live pretty much for today and let tomorrow take care of itself. _____
    D. I have a good relationship with all my family. _____
    E. It's hardly fair to bring children into the world with the way things look for the future. _____

To be completed by interviewer

  5. Interviewer's rating of person's overall motivation.

    1) very motivated
    2) moderately motivated

Exhibit 3–1 continued

      3) neither motivated nor unmotivated
      4) moderately unmotivated
      5) very unmotivated

   6. Interviewer's expectancy of client success at decreasing/eliminating alcohol abuse.

      1) very successful
      2) moderately successful
      3) neither successful nor unsuccessful
      4) moderately unsuccessful
      5) very unsuccessful

   7. General comments, attitudes, feelings, thoughts, performance, etc. on motivation.

IX. THERAPIST'S SECTION

To be completed on second and subsequent administration of the Follow Up Questionnaire

   1. Problems experienced during the Report Period which involved any of the following (circle yes or no)

1) Family	Yes	No
2) Friends	Yes	No
3) Drugs	Yes	No
4) Alcohol	Yes	No
5) Legal Authorities	Yes	No
6) School	Yes	No
7) Work	Yes	No
8) Finances	Yes	No
9) Health (include pregnancy)	Yes	No

     If yes, explain briefly _____

     _____

     _____

     _____

     _____

   2. Treatment facilities to which client was referred during Report Period, in order of occurrence

      1) Inpatient (hospital)
      2) Therapeutic community or other residence for group living (Initiation)
      3) Partial hospitalization (day or night hospital)
      4) Out patient
      5) Other; specify_____
      6) None

      1) _____
      2) _____
      3) _____

   3. Number of days client received therapeutic or support contacts at clinic_____

   4. Where did therapeutic or support contacts occur? (list category letters in order or frequency with *most frequent* first

Exhibit 3–1 continued

1) Hospital
2) Therapeutic community or other residence for group living
3) Day or night hospital
4) Outpatient clinic
5) Pharmacy
6) Vocational counselling or taining center
7) Social rehabilitation center
8) Religious organization
9) Patient's home
10) Community meeting place
11) Social or community agency
12) Other, specify_____

	Category	Agency Name
1)		
2)		
3)		
4)		
5)		

5. Drugs prescribed or administered to the client during the Report Period. Specify drugs used within each category. Check whether drugs used for withdrawal, maintenance or support.

	Withdrawal	Support	Maintenance
1) Antabuse			
2) Antidepressants			
3) Barbiturates or sedatives			
4) Tranquilizers			
5) Others, including those for medical conditions, Specify: _____			

6. Types of therapy or support received (circle Yes or No)

1) Vocational counselling	Yes	No	
2) Vocational training	Yes	No	
3) Educational training	Yes	No	
4) Individual counselling	Yes	No	
5) Group counselling	Yes	No	
6) Family counselling	Yes	No	
7) Recreational therapy	Yes	No	
8) Therapeutic community or other living group	Yes	No	
9) Religious activities	Yes	No	
10) Other: Specify_____	Yes	No	

7. Contacts with therapeutic or support personnel during Report Period.

1) Medical practitioner, western trained	Yes	No	
2) Medical practitioner, indigenous	Yes	No	
3) Specialist in psychiatry	Yes	No	
4) Psychologist	Yes	No	

Exhibit 3–1 continued

5) Social worker or sociologist	Yes	No
6) Vocational counsellor or trainer	Yes	No
7) Ex-addict counsellor	Yes	No
8) Nurse	Yes	No
9) Clergy or religious leader	Yes	No
10) Agency counsellor	Yes	No
11) Other counsellor: specify _____	Yes	No

General Assessment by Therapist

8. Social Functioning (within treatment setting)

1) Well-adjusted socially	Yes	No
2) Co-operative with staff	Yes	No
3) Conforms to treatment regulations	Yes	No
4) Disrupts therapeutic milieu	Yes	No
5) Requires excessive therapeutic attention	Yes	No
6) Physically violent or threatening	Yes	No
7) Other problems: specify_____	Yes	No

9. Diagnosis of medical problems requiring treatment.

10. Source(s) of information for completing report.

1) Personal interview with client	Yes	No
2) Staff members involved in treatment	Yes	No
3) Medical records	Yes	No
4) Client's family	Yes	No
5) Friends of client	Yes	No
6) Other; specify_____	Yes	No

11. Where was tthe questionnaire completed:

1) At home
2) At clinic in interview
3) At clinic by client alone

12. If questionnaire done by client alone was it later reviewed in a client/therapist session?

Yes _____ No _____

c. to make the acquaintance of three new people every week (say Hello, find out their names, phone numbers, and two of their interests); and

d. to complete five applications for employment by 2:00 P.M. each weekday.

4. Determine *with the client* the relative importance of the treatment goals. Some clients may have five to seven treatment goals: in order to determine the order in which the goals are to be addressed, it is helpful to write each of the treatment goals on an index card and have the client do a card sort, identifying the priority of goals as he sees it. This is often an excellent, yet

simple, way of determining those goals that the client feels most motivated to work on. Counselor reservations about the ordering of the treatment goals should be aired and revisions of the priorities sought out with the client when indicated.

5. Determine baseline data, using questionnaire (Exhibit 3-1).
6. Once the final treatment goals are defined, and baseline data collected, intermediate goals may be determined. For instance, if the goal of a client who currently weighs 185 pounds is to weigh 145 in six months, an intermediate goal would be to weigh 175 in one month.

Once goals have been set, treatment may begin as outlined. Continue to gather data on the client's progress. Some behavior patterns, interventions, and goals are offered as examples in Table 3-3.

Table 3–3 Behavior Patterns, Interventions, and Goals

Behavior Pattern	Intervention	Goals
Low self-esteem, anxiety, high verbal hostility	Relationship therapy, client-centered model	Increase self-esteem, reduce verbal hostility and anxiety
Defective personal construct system, ignorance of interpersonal means	Cognitive restructuring using therapies that are directive, such as Ellis, Glasser, group therapy	Insight
Focal anxiety (i.e., fear of crowds)	Desensitization	Change response to same cues
Undesirable behaviors, lacking appropriate behaviors	Aversive conditioning, operant shaping, counter conditioning	Eliminate or replace behavior
Lack of information	Information giving	Give information, have client act on it
Client complaint indicates that social situation is causing difficulty	Organization intervention, environmental manipulation, family therapy	Remove cause of complaint, modify environment
Interpersonal rigidity, poor functioning in social situations	Sensitivity training, communication training, group therapy	Increase interpersonal repertoire, desensitization to group functioning
Grossly bizarre behavior	Medical referral	Medication or hospitalization to protect client from society, ready client for further treatment

CLIENT MOTIVATION

It is useful to divide clients into one of these two categories: motivated to change or not motivated. It is true that there are degrees of motivation, but, basically, clients either come to the counselor's office willingly or they do not. There are two types of motivation: intrinsic (motivation from within the individual) and extrinsic (motivation from outside sources such as the courts, family members, etc.). Clients who seek treatment because they will be fired if they don't are usually extrinsically motivated; clients who are just sick and tired of their life styles are intrinsically motivated.

The counselor can have a great deal of influence on both kinds of motivation. First, it is important to establish what motivation is already there. Then, build on that, and expand to the other area of motivation. Counselors who tell clients "You're the only one who can motivate yourself to stay straight" don't know much about motivation or their clients. Counselors *can* motivate their clients, and clients *can't* do it all by themselves. (If they could, they wouldn't need treatment.) The counselor can motivate in many ways: by example, by providing hope where there is none, by providing information and education where myths and misconceptions exist. The counselor can also aid in motivation by doing family therapy, working with the client's employer, or helping to find the client an employer.

MOTIVATIONAL TECHNIQUES

Some motivational techniques mentioned by Poley et al. (1979) include treatment deposit contracts (in which patients put up money that they will lose if they do not complete treatment or other goals); Antabuse treatment; bibliotherapy (reading assignments); essay assignments (e.g., write an essay on why, and what, you would like to change); involvement of significant others (e.g., family, employer); and audio-visual feedback that includes video replays of drunken and sober behavior. The counselor must not rely totally on the chemically dependent person to be self-motivated. Without outside assistance, some people will never succeed.

SUMMARY

Chemically dependent persons come in all ages, shapes, and sizes, and they have various physical, psychological, and sociological problems. They use various chemicals, and this chemical use interferes with their life functioning in various ways. It is the counselor's job to assess these many conditions and symptoms and put them into a usable diagnosis that will translate into an effective treatment plan.

In the past this was rarely done. Simplistic definitions led to general, nonspecific treatment programs. The alcoholic was diagnosed as either alcoholic or not alcoholic. Alcoholics were sent to AA or entered treatment; nonalcoholics went back to drinking. Drug addicts were sent to drug programs. There was only one goal for all of these programs—total abstinence. It was assumed that if abstinence was maintained, the problems would melt away. This did not happen. Many could not maintain abstinence, and for many who did the problems were just beginning.

Can a person diagnosed as chemically dependent ever return to drug or alcohol use? The answer to this question and others are being researched every day, and answers are being found. In some cases they may not be the answers everyone would like to have. But counselors who want to accurately assess their clients must have all the information that is available—and they must be able to adjust to the complex problems of each client with an individualized treatment plan. A thorough diagnosis is the key to that treatment plan.

REFERENCES

Cahalan, D. *Problem drinkers*. San Francisco, Calif.: Jossey-Bass, 1970, p. 202.

Forrest, G. *The diagnosis and treatment of alcoholism*. (2nd ed). Springfield, Ill.: Charles C Thomas, 1978.

Greenblatt, D.J., & Shader, R.I. Treatment of alcohol withdrawal syndrome. In Shader, R. (Ed.), *Manual of Psychiatric Therapeutics*. Boston, Mass.: Little, Brown & Co., 1975.

Kuanert, A.P. Perspectives from a private practice: The differential diagnosis of alcoholism. *Family and Community Health*—Alcoholism and Health, Part II, Vol. 2, No. 2, August 1979. Rockville, Md.: Aspen Systems Corp., pp. 1–11.

Lawson, G., Peterson, J., & Lawson, A. *Alcoholism and the family: A guide to treatment and prevention*. Rockville, Md.: Aspen Systems Corp., 1983.

McAuliffe, R.M., & McAuliffe, M.B. *Essentials for the diagnosis of chemical dependency*. Minneapolis, Minn.: The American Chemical Dependency Society, 1975.

Mendelson, J., & Mello, N.K. (Eds.). *The diagnosis and treatment of alcoholism*. New York: McGraw-Hill, 1979.

Miller, W.R. Controlled drinking. *Journal of Studies on Alcohol*, 1983, *44*(1).

Pattison, M.E., & Kaufman, E. (Eds.). *Encyclopedic handbook of alcoholism*. New York: Gardner Press, 1982.

Peele, S. The human side of addiction: People who cure themselves of addictions. *The U.S. Journal*, August 1982, p. 7.

Poley, W., Lea, G., & Vibe, G. *Alcoholism: A treatment manual*. New York: Gardner Press, 1979.

Wallace, J. Alcoholism from the inside out: A phenomonological analysis. In Estes, N., and Heineman, E. (Eds.), *Alcoholism, development, consequences, and interventions*. St. Louis, Mo.: C.V. Mosby Co., 1977.

Wright, C. New patterns in alcohol and drug addiction: The physician as a pusher. Presented at 33rd Alcohol and Drug Problems Association of North America (ADPA) Annual Meeting, August 29–September 1, 1982, Washington, D.C.

SOME QUESTIONS TO CONSIDER

1. How can I use diagnosis to develop an individualized treatment plan?
2. Am I willing to treat someone who refuses to stop drinking?
3. How can I improve the diagnosis and treatment planning in my agency?
4. Do I consider alcoholics different than drug abusers? How?
5. What does that mean in terms of treatment?

Chapter 4

The Counselor's Frame of Reference

Dan C. Ellis

Previous chapters have characterized the counselor and the client according to attitudes, beliefs, needs, motivations, and personality. This chapter discusses what to do and think about before the client arrives, that is, the counselor's frame of reference and how it is developed.

WHAT TO DO BEFORE THE CLIENT ARRIVES

There are several important factors to consider when preparing to greet your client for the first time. One way to help yourself in this preparation is to try and put yourself in the client's shoes. What is he thinking and feeling? What might he be anticipating? How might you feel if you were entering a chemical dependency counseling center for the first time? Consider what was said in Chapter 2 when thinking about the person you are about to meet.

Consider what clients have to contend with once they walk through the door of your agency. Are clients greeted by a warm and friendly receptionist who attempts to make them feel comfortable? Or, are the clients ignored when they enter and made to feel that they should have come at another time?

Remember, your agency is offering a professional service to clients, and you and your staff need to behave in the most cordial and respectful manner. However, your behavior needs to be acceptable within the context of its environment, that is, the community you work in. Who are your clients? Are they middle class suburbanites who would be most comfortable in an environment resembling a doctor's or businessman's office? Or, are they mostly ethnic minorities who are put off and intimidated by a typical "white man's social welfare" type of setting? Part of being a professional is being able to fit in with and understand the community or environment that you work in.

Setting the mood of the agency before a client arrives is essential to establishing a productive and non-threatening counseling environment and is the first step in initiating the counseling process. The second step is preparing the counselor's personal readiness to focus his attention upon the client. One of the authors recalls the story of a counselor frantically rushing to work to be on time for his first appointment. The counselor wheeled into the agency's parking lot, bolted out of his car, and ran into his office moments before the client arrived. Once the counseling session had begun the counselor realized that he might have left his keys locked in the car with the motor running. He was so distracted by the thought of this situation, he could not concentrate on anything the client said. Finally the counselor had to confess his dilemma to the client and asked to be excused to check his car. Sure enough, the keys were locked inside with the motor running. Sheepishly the counselor returned to his office and asked the client if he would be willing to reschedule the appointment for another time. Fortunately the client understood and arranged to come back later that week. Obviously this is a rather bizarre example of mental unpreparedness, yet it underscores the importance of being undistracted when initiating the counseling process.

If your primary work responsibility is to see clients, it is best not to fill spare moments with other activities. Staff meetings, committee meetings, inservice training, etc., are best scheduled on days when you see only a few clients. When you leave a staff meeting where policies and procedures that may affect you personally were discussed, it is frequently difficult to set those issues aside and concentrate on your client. Effective counseling requires a clear and calm mind and every effort should be made to keep your schedule as uncluttered as possible.

THE INTAKE PROCEDURE

When considering what your client must contend with when first entering the agency, the entire intake procedure must be examined. The intake procedure may be your responsibility, or it may be the responsibility of a staff person specifically assigned to this task. If you are fortunate enough to have someone who does intakes for you, you have already overcome one of the problems of counseling preparation. As necessary as the intake form is, it can become a barrier to the counseling process. You are there to be of help to the client, and it is sometimes difficult for a client to understand how an intake form could possibly be helpful.

If you do your own intakes (collecting background information, etc.), it is wise to inform the client that this is a necessary process required by agency administration. It is also important to make clear to the client that this must be done before the two of you can actually begin counseling. *You do not want the client to mistake the intake for a counseling session.* Furthermore, it is important to answer any questions the client may have about the intake form while conducting the interview. Intake forms frequently ask questions that do not on the surface seem to have any relevancy to the client's original purpose in seeking counseling. Generally, clients put up no resistance to the intake process and expect it as a matter of course when seeking any kind of professional service. However, occasionally a client may be particularly intimidated by the experience and test the counselor's patience with a rash of questions that seemingly attempt to impede the entire process. It is best to handle this situation with tact and answer each and every question. It is only fair to allow clients to gain as much information as they can in order to ensure more comfort with the idea of seeing a "counselor." It is best to do this even if you believe the client is just testing you and intentionally trying to frustrate you.

Finally, in preparing to greet the client you usually have at hand some initial client information. This information may be sketchy notes taken while talking on the phone with a referral source, or it may be a detailed history. Counselors who prefer a detailed history feel that this information reduces the possibility of being "conned" by the client, provides a more accurate picture of the client's needs, and puts the counselor in charge of the session.

The other side of the issue is that a detailed history may predetermine the counselor's attitude toward the client. There is some amount of research to support the occurrence of this phenomenon, commonly called the Rosenthal effect (Rosenthal & Jacobson, 1968). Even the most unbiased social history can influence the counselor in a way that could lead to an unproductive counseling relationship. Even with no prior information, it is possible for the counselor to have certain inaccurate expectations. Not every individual who comes to a drug or alcoholism treatment program has a problem with drugs or alcohol. The individual may be in the wrong place or may have been sent there by a well-meaning but misinformed friend.

In considering the counseling process and the client-counselor relationship, the authors conclude that little or no prior information is preferable. It is the quality of the client-counselor relationship, not knowledge of the client's history, that is of the utmost importance. This relationship will take time to develop. It is best, then, to set aside the intake information prior to the first interview and do your best to establish contact with the client in a way that will set the stage for a fulfilling relationship. After the client leaves the first session, review the intake information; you will find it is much more useful at this point because it is set within the context of knowing the client in person.

HOW TO GREET THE CLIENT AND INITIATE COUNSELING

Now that you and the client are in your office, what happens next? Having a clear sense of how to initiate the counseling process is very helpful at this time. As you introduce yourself and ask the client what it is he wants to talk about, it is important to have in mind your purposes and concerns.

The process is affected not only by what you say but also by how you look, how your office looks, and the overall atmosphere. Here are some considerations to keep in mind when first sitting down with a client:

- Reflect a genuine interest in the client. Be sure that there will be no interruptions during the session (e.g., phone calls, others walking into your office, etc.). Does your office reflect someone who is ready to do counseling, or is it disorganized and chaotic, as if you had other pressing business to attend to?
- Inform the client of how much time you have together and that this time has been cleared just for him.
- If the client appears particularly nervous, try to reassure him. For instance, you could say, "Many people are nervous when they first come here, but that goes away quickly."
- Opening statements are best if phrased in an open-ended manner as an invitation to get to know each other and to uncover the reasons that brought the client to your office. Such statements might be "How is it that I can help you?" "Would you please tell me in your own words why you came here today?"
- Accusatory statements tend to put the client on the defensive and set up an uncomfortable environment for the client to work within. Such statements as "How much do you drink?" "Did your use of drugs bring you here today?" "Do you think you are an alcoholic?" can be counterproductive.

Remember, the counselor is setting up an environment for himself, as well as the client, to work within. Consider the needs of the person who is new to your "turf" and how you can help this person feel more comfortable. You are the master of the process and must set the example.

THE COUNSELING SESSION

As you begin to consider what it is you do as a counselor, it is essential to have established a frame of reference that comes partially from experience and partially from some formal structure. Your frame of reference may be loosely organized around basic beliefs you have about counseling or it may be tightly structured, leading to a highly organized and sequential counseling process. Sorting through your own philosophical framework is where your preparation for the first counseling session begins. The authors are inclined toward a broad, flexible, and intuitive approach. From this model the counselor views each new client as a unique individual and does not commit himself to a specific procedure until he knows the client better. Yet this method may not be comfortable for every counselor. When employing a highly structured model, the counselor becomes the leader for the client as they both weave their way through the process. This model might typify the inpatient, or residential counselor's, approach. In this structured environment it makes sense to use a structured model of counseling. The counselor has specific goals to accomplish within a given amount of time, and each client will need to follow a fairly regimented style of treatment.

Yet even within the highly structured model of inpatient treatment there exists a need to respond to the individual needs of the client. The concept we advocate identifies the counselor as a follower, being led by the client at least for the first few sessions. From this frame of reference the counselor responds to the client with a wide array of skills and experiences.

Even within the loosely structured approach there is a clear and intentional process to be followed. Each counseling session, as well as the totality of the counselor-client relationship, is performed within clearly marked boundaries. The process, or model, we suggest has three phases, as follows:

1. Problem statement
2. Work phase
3. Decision for action (Ivey, 1980)

Within each phase there are many issues and procedures to be considered and discussed. The remainder of this chapter covers these three phases and some specific skills and techniques as they relate to the phases.

Problem Statement

For the novice counselor this can be the most difficult and frustrating phase. The new counselor may have the unrealistic expectation that the client will state the problem statement in a clearly organized fashion. If the client, particularly the chemically dependent one, could so simply state the problem, he wouldn't need the counselor. Identifying the problem or problems to be worked on can be a time-consuming process requiring a diligent and continuous effort. The nature of the client's problems will emerge further as counseling probes deeper.

As the counselor and the client consider the problem and its severity, the counselor needs to frame these efforts within the context of the individual and his environment. Are the problems influenced by the client, by the environment, or by a combination of the two? The chemically dependent client's dependence on alcohol and drugs has developed in a complex fashion, as discussed in Chapter 2, and a simplistic approach to problem identification can be unproductive. Identifying a few common characteristics of dependent individuals and recommending a general treatment plan may be effective occasionally. But this "shotgun" approach leaves out many other hurting clients. It is necessary to thoroughly explore the client's problem areas, helping the client to formulate what he perceives as his primary problems.

Every client deserves the right to try to explain his behavior or his destructive use of alcohol and drugs. This may not help the person recover, but it will help formulate a clear understanding of how the dependency developed. If the counselor is willing to explore every possible cause, both environmental and individual, then the client may feel satisfied that all options have been explored. If this is not done, the client will always have some doubts about his dependency that will make staying abstinent even more difficult.

Frequently, the counselor needs to redefine for the client the problems presented early in counseling. The client is likely to be out of touch with his feelings and may avoid responsibility for problems. It is the counselor's job to help the client restate problems in a more concise, responsible, and behaviorally oriented fashion. It is also helpful to attach some feeling words to the problems if the client hasn't already done so. As the counselor expands upon and clarifies the presenting problem, the client learns to take a broader view of himself and his environment, possibly expanding his area of potential problem solutions.

This process can be tedious, particularly when the client is uncooperative and denies the existence of a problem with alcohol or drugs. Here again, it is important to consider your frame of reference. Also, consider the client's attitude toward seeing a chemical dependency counselor. If the client expects you to label him as alcoholic, he may resist your effort. It is best, early on, to avoid the issue of labeling clients. Take the time to get to know them; ask about their job, family, social life, hobbies, what makes them laugh, and what makes them angry. Gradually move towards posing the question of why the client is in counseling and what it is he wants to accomplish. What are the client's needs? If the client says he needs to avoid going to court on another drunk driving charge, you might ask, "How is it that I can be of help?" The problem statement phase is a negotiating phase where the counselor and client check out boundaries and value systems.

For instance, if the client says, "I just want you to write the judge and tell him I'm not an alcoholic so that I can keep my license," you might respond, "Well, I won't do that because I'm not sure you are not an alcoholic. What could we do together to find out if you are?" Here the question is reframed to offer the client an option that the counselor is more willing to accept. Some counselors may find this negotiating unproductive and frustrating. Yet, to ensure the client's cooperation and trust on major issues, you must also secure cooperation and trust on minor issues. If the client learns from the beginning that you will not try to exert control over him but are willing to negotiate, you may have more success. Mutual respect of each other's needs is essential in developing the client-counselor relationship.

How Many Problems Are Enough?

Every novice counselor could uncover a multitude of problems in a client if allowed to dig around enough. But this tends to slow the process down. It is best to settle on a few specific issues and get to work. In doing this it is important to develop a clear sense of how to prioritize and organize problem statements. With the client's help the counselor can begin to establish what issues should come first. The first issue is frequently the client's anger and resentment over having to see a counselor. Or the client may realize he has a drinking problem yet not be ready to discuss abstinence. One rule of thumb is to *begin where the client is at*. If the client wants to talk about fears of losing a job and you want to talk about how many times a week he drinks, there is a problem in priorities. If you want a client to enter residential treatment immediately and she has no way of arranging child care for her five-year-old, then, again, there is a problem in establishing priorities.

The counselor's most frequent difficulty with the chemically dependent client is the client's refusal to recognize his problem. The heavy use of alcohol and drugs tends to insulate a person from his feelings as well as the rest of the world. If the facts indicate a real problem with alcohol or drugs, the counselor must push for some kind of recognition by the client. The next phase of counseling (work phase) will be fruitless if the client does not recognize his dependence.

Identifying and Accepting the Problem Statement

In this process the counselor needs to sort out the facts carefully and bring them into the open. Again it is important to avoid accusatory statements. It is more helpful to politely but firmly probe for as much information as possible about the use of chemicals and any other related issues. Part of the counselor's role is to "paint a picture" for the client, identifying life patterns that may or may not be harmful. It is important not to present the attitude of "I know you're a drunk and I'm going to prove it to you." It is more helpful to present a neutral attitude, to deal with the concrete facts and "manipulate" the client into proving to you that he has problems with drugs and alcohol.

Manipulate tends to carry a negative connotation, but all counselors manipulate their clients. Counselors use manipulation to positively motivate clients and thus to increase the potential for successful therapy. It is best to encourage the client to articulate the problem statement in his own words. The problem statement must be believable to the client given his current level of understanding. For example, in the early stages of chemical dependency counseling the client may be reluctant to see the value of remaining abstinent for a lifetime. The need for lifetime abstinence would in any case be a premature conclusion. Problem statements are not intended to be problem solutions. We merely want the client to recognize and accept some clearly identified problem areas to work on.

Jon Weinberg offers a helpful method of identifying and phrasing a client's drinking problem. In this approach the client is simply asked to summarize the facts in a statement that outlines the problem but does not box him into only one solution. The statement would go something like this: "Drinking often produces results I dislike, and I cannot consistently drink without those results occurring"

(Weinberg, 1977). This sort of statement establishes the boundaries of counseling and provides the client and counselor a focus for future work. There could be many variations to this statement to fit the circumstances at hand, yet the process of arriving at any such statement must involve the client and be in his own words.

Work Phase

This phase involves matching a particular counseling style, technique, or method to the problem already identified. Regardless of the approach, the client and counselor work together to generate new ways of looking at problems, potential answers, and new issues to work on later.

We recommend that the counselor's attitude be one of flexibility and resourcefulness. Our experience has shown that counselors will be more successful if they can adapt their approach to fit the needs and personality of the client. Chemical dependency is a complex problem and counselors find clients at all levels and degrees of dependence. A client's position on this continuum will dictate the counselor's course of action. Someone at the chronic stage requires more confrontation and determination than someone with a minor problem at the other end of the continuum.

Guidelines for Selecting a Counseling Method

To match the client to a specific counseling approach, it is necessary to compare the client's needs against what the various approaches have to offer. Here are some general guidelines.

- *Clarification and Reflection of Client Feelings.* Chemically dependent clients are frequently detached from and unaware of their feelings. Their recovery will, to a degree, be determined by how well they identify and express their feelings. Many clients must be taught how to know what they feel and how to express themselves appropriately. Before counseling can proceed smoothly, the counselor may need to consider if education about feeling identification and expression is necessary.
- *Confrontation and Encounter.* Frequently, chemically dependent clients have not learned an appropriate way to confront others when they feel strongly about something. Also, some chemically dependent clients never hear anything said to them that is not strong and direct. Assessing your client's ability to communicate is essential to selecting your counseling method.
- *Psychological Boundaries.* The chemically dependent family has particular difficulty in establishing and maintaining clear ego boundaries among its members. Thus it is important for the counselor to explore with the client his sense of self. Is it well established or is it entangled with other people's egos?

- *Illogical Thoughts*. Many clients have difficulty changing their behavior because the new behavior does not match their underlying thoughts about themselves. Here it is important for the counselor to explore the client's thinking process and self-image. Again, clients may need to be taught new ways of thinking about themselves.
- *Role Reversal*. If relationship problems are of primary importance, the client may wish to try reversing roles with the counselor. This will provide practice in interacting in new ways, with the counselor serving as a model.
- *Value Systems*. It is not uncommon (particularly among young clients) for counselors to find that the client has never established a value system to live by. The client may need help in learning about values and in selecting those that will work for him.
- *Knowledge of Drugs and Alcohol*. Finally, it is essential to include education about drugs and alcohol. An understanding of the psychologic, physiologic, and social effects of drugs and alcohol will be helpful in recovery.

Decision for Action

In this phase the client and counselor generate alternative solutions for problems that have been identified, consider advantages and disadvantages, select a solution, and try it out. It is particularly valuable for the chemically dependent client to learn this process. Chemically dependent people frequently have difficulty thinking out problem solutions and acting intentionally. Even when the client intends to drink only 2 beers he ends up drinking 10 or 12. New solutions are necessary as well as new processes for selecting solutions.

If the client insists that he can control his drinking, the counselor might work out a plan of how this could be done and the consequences if the plan fails. If the client is unsuccessful, the counselor would return to the problem statement phase, redefine the problem, and select a different work phase approach.

The counselor cannot always accurately predict which solutions will work for the client. A process of trial and error may be necessary, and the counselor is always free to begin again the three phases of the counseling process. Too many times the authors have seen the counselor blame the client because a plan failed. The plan may have failed because it was not realistic for the client and not well thought out in advance. The process described above helps the counselor ensure flexibility and responsiveness to client needs.

STRUCTURING THE COUNSELING RELATIONSHIP

Counselors need to possess a clear sense of how to organize the counseling relationship. Counselors and clients should have a mutual understanding with respect to (1) time limits, (2) beginning and ending the session, (3) counselor versus client agendas, (4) role limits, and (5) process limits.

Time Limits

Depending upon the setting, a minimal time frame, which counselor and client regard as a trial period, should be agreed upon initially. Usually, at least six sessions should be sufficient to determine if continued counseling is necessary or would be fruitful. It is important that clients believe they have the option to discontinue counseling and that they will not be punished by the counselor for doing so. Counseling, even if court ordered, should be regarded by clients as a useful expenditure of their time.

There are some counseling settings where the time limit is predetermined by an outside authority. Even so, the counselor needs to make some clear statements about the time limit. In a court-ordered counseling relationship the clients' ability to adhere to the time responsibilities can be one of the important measures of success (as measured by a judge, for instance). Courts do not always expect major changes in chemically dependent clients' use habits, but they do expect them to follow the rules.

Emphasizing to clients the importance of agreeing on how long you are to work together sets the stage for getting down to serious work, and makes clients realize that they do not have unlimited time to work on their problems. The counselor needs to consider three aspects when setting time limits:

1. the time limit of each session;
2. the total length of the counseling relationship; and
3. agency-imposed limits.

A chemical dependency counselor working in an outpatient clinic has a very different set of time limit considerations than an inpatient counselor. The time limits imposed by inpatient treatment must be very specifically spelled out for the client. Furthermore, the counselor needs to take into consideration the limited amount of time available to accomplish treatment goals. It is best not to set goals that cannot realistically be accomplished within the short stay in treatment. And, since an inpatient counselor has only so many hours a day to work with a client, the counselor must teach the client to make the best use of this time.

The outpatient counselor has a much more flexible set of alternatives when setting time limits. Yet, even with this flexibility, the counselor needs to be specific about time limits. Setting a time in the future for an evaluation of the relationship is a good idea. The client needs to know that the relationship will have a specific end point, as well as criteria (i.e., goals), that will determine the successful completion of counseling.

Beginning and Ending the Session

This is often a difficult task for the new counselor. At the beginning of the session the counselor should state exactly how much time has been set aside for the client. Simply saying "We have one hour to spend together today so let's get started" is a good way to begin. As the session develops and the client unfolds his story, a new counselor may feel embarrassed at mentioning that time is nearly up. Our suggestion is to directly and firmly announce, "Our time today is up, so why don't we pick up here next time." Or, "Our time is nearly over, so let's summarize some of what we discussed today." It is not recommended to end a session by stopping in midsentence; telling the client that there are only a few more minutes is a better way. Of course every counselor hates to end a session feeling that something was left unfinished. But it is an unhelpful habit to begin stretching out sessions until there is complete closure. Both the counselor and client need to work together to reach conclusions as soon as possible and then move on to deeper levels. Allowing the client to ramble forever on any subject can become a way of avoiding intimacy and depth in the relationship.

Remember, you are the master of the process and it falls upon you to use the counseling session efficaciously. Part of your role is to help bring closure to issues raised by the client. The client may not know how to do this or even see a need to do so. Without rushing the client, try and use your time to bring closure to issues. If you realize there are only minutes remaining, begin summarizing what has been said and invite the client to help bring the session and the issue to a close.

Counselor versus Client Agendas

There is a common tendency among inexperienced counselors to expect a client to progress at a rate that meets the needs of the counselor. Clients do not always resolve problems when we think they should even after we have done our best for them. Clients progress at their own pace and if we push them to do so at ours, we tend to get only empty compliance.

Frequently, a client's resistance to change is partially motivated by perceived unrealistic counselor expectations. The chemically dependent client complicates this problem further by an inherent tendency to deny that his dependence is causing a problem. This denial tends to wash over into other areas such as relationships, marriage, and work. The anxious counselor who is impatient with a slow-moving, resistant client is further impaired by this denial of reality. The chemically dependent client may need considerable time to explore, excuse, and rationalize the use of alcohol and drugs before honestly considering another way to live. Simply stating to the client that he is an alcoholic or an addict will not necessarily convince him that this is so. In any case, a ready agreement may indicate nothing more than empty compliance with a rigid agenda.

Individual counseling sessions must be structured around the time that is set aside for this purpose. Similarly, the counselor must also structure the entire counseling relationship around a time frame that will be realistic given the goals to be accomplished—realistic in terms of how many weeks or months there are to work with a client and how the client can be expected to change during that time.

Role Limits

Another aspect of structuring the counseling relationship is determining the expectations and limitations of roles. A client entering counseling has a set of expectations of the counselor. It is valuable to question clients as to what their expectations are. What are their beliefs about counselors? Do they have any preconceived notions? If this is not discussed in the beginning, there is a possibility of conflict arising later on.

The chemically dependent client may have a variety of role expectations for the counselor. Some might be:

- The counselor will simply tell me what to do, and if I do it I'll get better.
- The counselor is an adversary and must be resisted at all costs.
- Counselors don't know anything anyway, but I will pretend to listen.
- Counselors sometimes give good advice and if I cooperate things may get better.
- The counselor is going to have to prove to me he can help me before I will come back.

What are the limits of the counselor's role? An honest discussion of this subject is essential when initiating the counseling relationship. Statements such as the following may be helpful.

- As the counselor I refuse to do anything for you that you are able to do on your own.
- I see this relationship as one of equal responsibility and I expect you to put forth an effort equal to mine.
- I will make suggestions, give you feedback, and support you, but I will not tell you what to do.
- I hope that you can see me as a resource that you can utilize to resolve your own problems.
- My primary concern is to see that you are successful in meeting your goals.
- Chemical dependency can be life threatening and I will always be honest with you about my fears and concerns.

These statements help the client know what to expect from you. Discussing roles also helps the client know what it is you expect of him, that is, how you see his role in the relationship. Some *unhelpful* expectations of the client would be:

- If you aren't willing to admit that you are a drunk, you might as well leave now.
- I only work with people who are motivated to change.
- I hope you understand that this is a serious illness and that few people ever recover.
- If you want to get well I will expect you to do what I tell you.
- Don't think you are somehow unique; I have worked with a lot of junkies and they are all alike.
- I don't like to set appointments; just come in when you want to.

Some *helpful* expectations of the client would be:

- We will meet regularly at this time; I will be here and I expect you to be here too.
- If at any point you should have doubts about the value of counseling, please feel free to talk with me about it.
- It will be important for you to do your best at helping set goals for counseling.
- Once we have agreed upon goals, I expect you to work toward fulfilling them.
- At no time will I expect you to do anything against your will; your participation is always voluntary.

Role limits and expectations are not necessarily static and can be renegotiated periodically if required. It is helpful to let clients know they can discuss anything without fear of punishment. However, it is also advisable to remain firm in those roles and expectations you believe are essential to successful counseling. Role limits maintain clear boundaries of responsibility and help you and the client to remain directed.

Process Limits

Clients frequently enter counseling with misconceptions about what is likely to happen. It is the counselor's responsibility to carefully explain the limitations of counseling and put to rest any unfounded fears. It is not uncommon for clients to view counseling as a mysterious and potentially threatening experience. Chemically dependent clients may fear counseling because of the possibility that it will interfere with their usage pattern. Also, the client who is in the chronic stages of a chemical dependency and suffering from delusions may fear loss of sanity. Consequently, counseling can arouse fears of commitment to a mental hospital. It is important to explain the limits of counseling—what will and will not happen.

In this process it is prudent to accurately represent yourself to the client. State your training and educational background, what degrees you hold, your level of experience, any licenses or certificates you possess, etc. Do not, for instance, represent yourself as a clinical psychologist if your role is that of a chemical dependency counselor. Do not represent yourself as a hypnotherapist because you once watched your uncle hypnotize someone. Also, do not apologize for yourself and your perceived limitations. State what you can do in positive terms.

Maintaining Client Confidentiality

One of the most common fears a client has in coming to see a chemical dependency counselor is that someone he knows will find out. The counselor must clearly spell out the rules of confidentiality. These are:

1. protection of the client's identity;
2. protection of the content of counseling sessions;
3. refusal to release any information without the client's written permission; and
4. respect for the client's right to withhold specific information from members of his family.

The issue of anonymity varies in importance from client to client: some are extremely nervous about anyone knowing they are seeing a chemical dependency counselor; others are rather indifferent. However, do not base your efforts at maintaining confidentiality upon the attitude and wishes of the client alone. It is best to maintain the same strict code of confidentiality for every client. This attitude will protect the client and you as well. One effective way to help the client become desensitized to letting others know he is chemically dependent is to encourage attendance at AA and Narcotics Anonymous meetings. It is not necessary to identify oneself at these meetings, but it does defuse the issue, to a degree, simply to be seen there.

Maintaining Client's Sense of Control

Another fear clients have about counseling is that they are relinquishing control of themselves. The counselor needs to clearly state that this is not so. Again, emphasize that counseling is a cooperative effort and not coercion. However, coercion is sometimes necessary in life-threatening situations. For instance, if an intoxicated client must be placed in detoxification for his own safety, strong tactics are sometimes required.

Involving others in counseling is another fear of clients. It is not uncommon to hear, "I don't want my wife involved, just leave her out of this." Or, "If my boss finds out I am here, he will fire me." Or, "I see no reason for you to call my physician, that is none of your business." Generally, the client's efforts to exclude someone from the counseling process are protective in nature. It is important to express your reasons for wanting others involved in counseling and to confront the client's attempts to prevent this involvement. If your efforts to break down the client's resistance fail, it is better to respect those wishes and try again later. Any strategic moves made by the counselor require the cooperation of the client or they may prove to be counterproductive.

Reassuring the Anxious Client

Finally, it is helpful to take the time to reassure clients who exhibit apprehension about entering the counseling process. As the counselor, you can help the client simply by saying that you understand his apprehension, that it is normal, and that as you get to know each other he will feel more comfortable. On rare occasions you may meet a client who exhibits a genuine phobic reaction to counseling. This reaction may be characterized by sweating, nervous twitching, rigid posture, brief answers, or an unwillingness to communicate. There are several things that you can do to help the client through this frightening time. For instance:

• Ask the client to take long, deep breaths.
• Have the client recall a pleasant event and tell you about it.
• Talk about yourself, your family, your hobbies, what you like about your job.
• In some cases you might move toward the client just to touch his hand and make a reassuring comment.

Regardless of how you choose to help the overly anxious client, putting the person at ease will pay off in improving the chances he will return to continue therapy.

THE COUNSELOR'S PERSONAL DEVELOPMENT

Within every profession there exist standards for maintaining proficiency of skills necessary to perform a given job. Professionals should also have a commitment to improve their personal lives (their relationships, economic status, community standing, etc.). We all have differing needs regarding these issues and meet our goals in ways compatible to our own values and needs.

The chemical dependency counselor is also concerned with growth and personal development. In this section we will explore how to set goals for your own development, how to evaluate your progress, how to approach career planning, and how to give and receive supervision. Not everyone will pursue the same course of growth; we wish only to suggest options and strategies for planning your own future.

Skill Maintenance

When you begin working as a counselor, regardless of what kind of learning environment you came from, you terminate one type of learning and begin another. This requires a new orientation toward yourself as a learner and a practitioner. Now you need to select your learning experiences based upon what will be of immediate use to you as a counselor as well as what will enhance your sense of self-worth. The payoffs for continued learning have changed somewhat from when you were a trainee or student. Some reasons for counselors to continue learning and upgrading skills are to:

- maintain current certification and licensure
- fulfill employer expectations
- expand knowledge and skill in specific areas
- fulfill personal career planning goals
- learn new ways of resolving personal conflict
- increase potential for job advancement

Another motivation to upgrade skills is to maintain a fresh, interested, and excited attitude toward one's work as a helping professional. As trainers, the authors have encountered counselors who are "burned out" after only a few years. Frequently these are people who have lost interest in their work and want to do something else. This is an unfortunate situation, which in many cases can be prevented if individuals take a serious look at their motivation prior to entering the field and maintain an active interest by continually seeking new learning experiences and expanding their repertoire of skills. You owe it to yourself, your clients, your colleagues, and your family to do all you can to maintain the highest possible standards of professional performance and to enjoy doing it. It should be fun to go to work and feel challenged each day.

Assessing Your Learning Needs

Most of us have experienced the majority of our learning in rather traditional environments (e.g., schools, colleges, etc.). In these environments we typically find ourselves being taught by someone who knows more than we do. This arrangement makes some practical sense, particularly for children. But it may not be logical for adults in the role of learners. Research has shown (Tough, 1971) that adults learn best on their own initiative and in a natural (nontheoretical) manner. When adults learn in this way, what they learn has a deeper and more relevant meaning to them than learning acquired in a more traditional manner.

Learning that is engaged in for purely personal development can be planned by an individual on his own terms and with only a loose structure. But learning that has as its purpose improving one's competence to perform a job must take into account the needs and expectations of organizations, professions, and society. Learning is best when it is fun but selecting learning experiences on the basis of enjoyment may not always meet your learning needs as a developing professional. When assessing your learning needs, it is important to take an honest look at what you expect of yourself, what your employer expects, and what your clients need. Ultimately, any learning plan needs to be satisfying to you. By participating in the process of determining your own learning needs, formulating your own objectives, identifying resources, choosing strategies, and evaluating your accomplishments, you develop a sense of commitment to the plan.

A learning need is the gap between where you are now and where you want to be, in regard to a particular set of competencies. You may already be aware of certain learning needs as a result of a personal appraisal process.

The first step in beginning this process is to construct a model of the competencies required to perform the role of a chemical dependency counselor. A competency can be thought of as the ability to do something at a certain level of proficiency and is usually composed of some combination of knowledge, understanding, skill, attitude, and values. For example, the basic procedures for conducting an individual counseling session require specific knowledge and abilities. The ability to conduct a family counseling session is a more complex process and requires a more refined expertise in basic counseling skills as well as knowledge of how families work, awareness of your own family values, and knowledge of human development. It is useful to produce a competency model, even if it is crude and subjective, because of the clearer sense of direction it will provide.

Having constructed a competency model, your next task is to assess the gap between where you are, and where the model says you should be, in regard to each competency. You can do this alone or with the aid of people who have been observing your performance. You may discover that you have already developed some competencies to a level of excellence and that you can concentrate on those you do not have.

An example of this process could be as follows:

Assessing Ability to Express Empathy

Empathy is the ability to enhance communication and understanding by accurately responding to the emotional state of the client in a way that expands awareness and acceptance of self.

After determining this component of a model, you would plot your learning gap. "R" represents where you want to be and "P" represents where you are now. This process helps assess how much of a given skill or knowledge you possess.

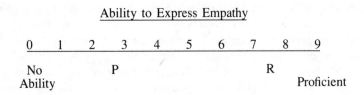

Ability to Express Empathy

0   1   2   3   4   5   6   7   8   9

No   P   R
Ability   Proficient

After determining your learning needs, translate them into objectives that describe specifically what it is you want to learn. Objectives can come in any form as long as they are clearly defined and are measurable when completed. Decide how to fulfill these objectives. (What learning resources and strategies will you use?)

How To Select a Learning Experience

When preparing to select a particular learning experience, ask yourself, "How do I learn best?" Some people learn best by classroom listening; some, by watching someone else perform a task. Others prefer a combination of both kinds of learning. Some people can see the entire picture from understanding just one part; others do better by fully mastering each component of a skill one at a time.

Chemical dependency counselors can choose from academic classroom environments, short-term, extended, or intensive workshops, broadly based conferences, colloquiums, or the mentor learning model. It is helpful to choose a learning environment that matches your own learning style. The following is a brief discussion of each learning environment.

Academic Classes

Academic classes provide a structured experience with clear expectations and standards. They are thorough and offer in-depth knowledge on a given subject. Usually this approach focuses more on academics and less on practical skill application. A course that offers an even blend of both can be a very valuable learning experience.

Workshops

The title implies that participants are going to work; it is best to investigate in advance to learn the facilitator's plans. It is not uncommon to find that a "workshop" is in fact a lecture, with little opportunity to practice skills. However, workshops can be one of the best ways to learn a specific skill or procedure. If you need only a brief introduction, the short-term workshop may meet your needs. In this environment you will be given some basic concepts and a few brief demonstrations. The extended, intensive workshop offers opportunities to learn the basics, practice them under supervision, and get feedback on your performance. This format tends to ensure more comprehension and longer retention.

Conferences

At a conference, a large number of people come together to share information on a broad subject area. Generally, it is not a good environment for learning and developing skills. It is an opportunity to meet and exchange ideas with your peers.

Colloquiums

A colloquium is usually a short presentation by a recognized expert in a given field. There is usually an opportunity to ask questions but rarely time for practice. Generally, there is little opportunity to interact with peers. This experience very much resembles a lecture with specific beginning and end points.

Mentors

It is valuable to have a mentor regardless of whether or not you attend learning events. The mentor is someone working in your field whom you respect and perceive as having more skill and knowledge than you. The mentor must be able to effectively knowledge and facilitate your growth in a way that you believe is helpful. This learning model is valuable to help you further refine your abilities while pursuing a specific objective.

Evaluating Your Development

It is advisable to build an evaluation method into your personal growth program that responds directly to your learning needs and objectives. There are a number of ways to do this: timelines, performance appraisals, consultants, or a qualitative/ quantitative systematic evaluation. However you choose to evaluate your progress, be specific in what it is you want to know. Consultants can be helpful in initially establishing evaluation standards. However, be clear in your own mind as to what standards are acceptable.

To effectively evaluate ourselves we must know what it is we are striving for. Small, observable improvements are usually the most realistic and easiest to accomplish. Total transformations are next to impossible. If you are completely dissatisfied with your ability as a counselor, it may be best to consider another field. If you feel basically competent but need some improvements, stay in the field and gradually work towards those changes. It is natural to feel less than competent if you are just starting out. Additional training can help; however, you need to allow yourself more time to become adept at what you have already learned. Referring back to what was said in Chapter 1 will help in determining your personal standards of performance.

SUPERVISION: HOW TO USE IT AND HOW TO DO IT

Supervision is a valuable resource for the chemical dependency counselor. Unfortunately, not everyone has had a positive experience with supervision, and some may view it as an unnecessary burden. We would suggest that this process is an essential component to any professional counseling service.

Supervision is the process by which the work of one individual can be planned, directed, monitored, and evaluated by another individual or individuals who have authority to perform those designated tasks. Generally, supervision occurs in the context of a hierarchically ordered relationship between two or more individuals in a work organization. The purposes of supervision are to ensure (1) a level of quality in the delivery of services and (2) the conformance of workers to the standards of conduct and performance that are reflected in the established policies, procedures, and rules of a given organization or agency. The role of supervisor refers to the responsibility and authority given to an individual to plan, direct, control, coordinate, and evaluate the work activities of others. The responsibility and authority that are associated with the role of supervisor, in the ideal sense, are inherent in the role rather than in the person who occupies the role.

When supervision is effectively utilized, it protects not only the agency and the client but also the individual counselor. By maintaining frequent contact with the supervisor you minimize the possibility of jeopardizing your position. A supervisor who does not know what you are up to cannot support you in a difficult situation where you are unsure how to proceed.

Supervisors must be clear about their own motivations and have a realistic perception of their relationship with the staff. If counselors perceive your purpose as helping them to more effectively do their jobs, you are off to a good start. But, if counselors perceive your role as one of watchdog, meddler, or adversary, there is a fundamental problem in the way supervision is handled in your agency.

To further clarify the purposes of supervision we have identified three basic aspects of the process for application in chemical dependency programs.

1. *Administrative.* Those supervisory activities related to the general direction, monitoring, oversight, and evaluation of performance against agency policies, procedures, and rules.
2. *Clinical.* Those supervisory activities related to the direction, monitoring, teaching/learning, and evaluation of the direct service activities of counselors against a stated standard of effectiveness.

3. *Evaluation*. Those activities specifically designed to evaluate the performance of counselors and determine levels of efficiency and effectiveness.
Clearly set policies, standards, and expectations are essential to successful
supervision. It is difficult to follow, as well as enforce, vague and sketchy
guidelines. Everyone in the supervisory process needs a clear sense of what
is expected.

CAREER PLANNING

When considering a particular field as a career, it is always advisable to look at
its future as well as what will be required of you to achieve your career objectives in
the field. The chemical dependency field is still young and going through many of
the growing pains any new field goes through. Given current economic conditions,
it is difficult to predict where the field is going. In the latter half of the seventies it
appeared that the chemical dependency field was going to become a profession
characterized by rapid growth and unlimited potential. This is no longer true.

During the seventies the federal government was the primary funder of drug and
alcohol programs in this country; now the responsibility is being picked up by state
or local governments or not at all. Many states simply cannot afford to replace
millions of dollars in federal grant monies. Taxpayers, who already feel overbur-
dened, are unwilling to support raising taxes to generate revenue to underwrite and
maintain existing programs. Fortunately, the private sector is moving into the
chemical dependency field because it is a relatively open market. Unfortunately,
private corporations charge higher rates, and unemployed and poor citizens who
used to be eligible for federal programs are now finding it difficult to find low- or
no-cost programs.

These realities need to be considered when planning a career in the chemical
dependency field. Ten years ago the number of programs did not begin to meet the
need. Now the need is worse than ever, and some programs are having to close
down due to the loss of public funding. One of the effects has been to create a
temporary surplus of treatment personnel on the market. The existence of a greater
number of formal training programs is making it even more difficult for established
but minimally trained counselors to compete. The obvious advice for anyone
entering the field now is to get as much quality training as possible.

The authors are confident the field will rally soon and continue its growth.
However, there must be a radical change in attitude regarding the funding of
chemical dependency programs. One thing that may help is that more insurance
companies are recognizing chemical dependency as a treatable medical problem
and offering coverage for both inpatient and outpatient care. Some state legisla-
tures have been successful in pressuring insurance companies to make chemical
dependency coverage a standard part of every major medical policy. The reorienta-

tion of funding sources will take some time to occur. However, we believe this is still an excellent field and encourage interested people to pursue it. Plotting a course that will eventually lead to a realization of one's career goals requires careful planning, patience, a realistic attitude, and knowledge of the field. Some important questions to begin with are:

- What are your purposes in entering the chemical dependency field?
- What do you find reinforcing: money, status, competency, being helpful, security, or respect? How would you rank your reinforcers?
- Where do you want to be in 2, 5, 10, and 20 years?
- What do others expect of you (e.g., family, friends, employers)?

Thinking of a job merely as a way to make money and spend your time can lead very quickly to frustration and disappointment. Your career is an investment in yourself and your future and deserves every bit of consideration as well as commitment.

Career goals are best accomplished through small steps. For instance, starting out as a treatment technician may seem a far cry from your eventual goal as program director. To achieve it will require several years of preparation and the accumulation of varied experiences. The first step is to consider what it takes to become a good program director. What skills, knowledge, experience, and abilities do program directors need? Then look for opportunities to learn what you need to accomplish your goal. During the first few years you may concentrate solely on learning all you can about counseling and the chemically dependent person. Then you might want to gain experience in program development, budgeting, and so on until you feel prepared to apply for the position of program director.

Every goal is generally made up of several smaller subgoals. Patience is a necessary ingredient to achieving your goals. Understanding the field you work in and what can go wrong in it can also help. Chapter 7 offers some useful information on survival skills in the chemical dependency field.

REFERENCES

Rosenthal, R., & Jacobson, L. *Pygmalion in the classroom: Teacher expectations and pupils' intellectual development*. New York: Holt, Rinehart and Winston, 1968.

Tough, A.M. *The adult's learning projects: A fresh approach to theory and practice in adult learning*. Ontario: Institute for Studies in Education, 1971.

Weinberg, J. Counseling the person with alcohol problems. In Estes, N., and Heineman, M. (Eds.), *Alcoholism, development, consequences and intervention*, St. Louis, Mo.: C.V. Mosby Co., 1977.

SOME QUESTIONS TO CONSIDER

1. Am I ready mentally to see my first client?
2. What is my frame of reference?
3. What do I hope to do with my clients?
4. What is my theory of counseling?

Chapter 5

Basic Counseling Techniques

Dan C. Ellis

This chapter will focus upon the actual process of counseling, that is, the different techniques to be employed by the chemical dependency counselor. Chapter 4 helped to establish your frame of reference; your frame of reference will, in turn, have an impact on how you utilize specific counseling methods.

COUNSELOR LEAD-INS

Once you have structured the counseling relationship, it becomes necessary to get to work on the client's expressed problems and concerns. Getting information and deepening the relationship becomes the focus of counseling; counselor lead-ins can enhance this. Lead-ins are simply invitations to the client to go further and say more about a particular issue. Lead-ins can also help the counselor and client clarify where to proceed next.

Restatement of Content

Frequently the content of what a client presents is confused, disorganized, and lacking in insight. The counselor can help by restating in a clearer manner what the client has said. For instance:

> CLIENT: "Drinking doesn't cause me problems, and I don't know why I am here anyway. It is my wife that can't handle it, and you should really talk to her, not me."
>
> COUNSELOR: "I understand you are reluctant to talk about yourself. How could my talking with your wife help you?"

Here the counselor recognizes the client's resistance to talk about his drinking and challenges him to explain how talking with his wife will help. In restating the content, it is important to organize the client's comments in order to provide new insight.

Another name for this process is *paraphrasing*. When you paraphrase what the client has said you use your own words but feed back essentially the same content. This process lets the client know you understand what he has said and that you are able to repeat it back in new or different words. The phenomenon of simply being heard and understood has great therapeutic value for the client.

Questioning

Questioning can be an effective method, but it can also be an irritant in the counseling process as well as a way of covering up a counselor's lack of skill. Asking questions when you don't know what else to do is not helpful. Silence is better than asking numerous, inane questions. However, asking the right questions at the right time can be very helpful and can take counseling to a deeper level. A good question shows that you can see deeper into the client than he thought. A good question can disrupt the denial process, especially if the question is unexpected. The "why" question is generally the most unhelpful one to ask a client. For instance: "Why do you drink so much?" or "Why do you think you lost your job?" This kind of questioning is of little help to the client, and for the actively using person it is an invitation to lie or rationalize. The "why" question also tends to put the client on the defensive and implies that there is a right or wrong answer to the question. We recommend using "how" and "what" questions in place of "why" questions whenever possible. For instance, a rewording of the original questions: "How is it that you drink as much as you do?" "How was it that you lost your job?" Here the counselor is asking for information on how certain events happen; he is not asking for a causal explanation. There is less implied value judgment in the "how" question than in the "why" question. "How" suggests that you simply want to know the way something happened; "why" implies to clients that they should have an acceptable reason for what they did.

"What" questions have a somewhat similar function as "how" questions. The "what" question limits the client to telling you the facts, while withholding any judgments about the client's behavior. Example: "Tell me what you did last night when you were drunk." Here the counselor is not asking for a justification or rationalization, simply for an account of the events that took place. However, clients have learned that they must justify their behavior in order to make it acceptable and may not fully understand the "what" or "how" questions at first. When the chemically dependent client begins to justify his behavior, it is necessary to remind him that you only want to know about the how and the what. For instance:

COUNSELOR: "Tell me what happened when you lost your job."

> CLIENT: "Well, if my boss hadn't been on my back all the time it wouldn't have happened. It was really all his fault. Nobody can get along with him."
>
> COUNSELOR: "I don't want you to tell me who is to blame, just tell me *what* happened that led up to your losing your job."

The chemically dependent client frequently has difficulty separating his sense of identity from his behavior. Clients may believe that the things they do well make them acceptable to others and to themselves. This model of the world tends to encourage considerable defending of self. Your questions, in this case, need to be posed in a way that does not allow the client to continue this self-protective approach to communicating. You may have to repeat your "what" and "how" questions many times as you teach clients to change their responses.

Another kind of helpful question is the open-ended question. This type of question tends to focus the client's thinking into a specific arena but leaves open how he will answer. As an example, a man is depressed over the death of his wife, and the counselor responds in the following way:

> "Tell me about how you might be able to focus on other parts of your life so as to give your life new meaning."

The phrasing of this question does not allow for a yes-or-no answer but forces the client to expand on the subject. An open-ended question invites the client to explore a given area further, without boxing him into a corner with few alternatives. Continuing with the same client, let us look at a few examples of a closed question.

> "Do you think you could focus on other parts of your life and thereby feel more hopeful?" "Do you think killing yourself will solve anything?"

Both questions are getting at important material; however, the way they are phrased does not demand much more than a yes-or-no answer.

Reflection of Feeling and Content

When reflecting feelings and content in client communications, the counselor is attempting to:

1. encourage the client to continue talking;
2. let the client know the counselor understands him; and
3. subtly lead the client to a deeper level of communication.

Reflecting the content of what a client has said is somewhat easier than reflecting the feelings involved in the communication. Content reflection is generally straightforward and demands that you simply repeat or paraphrase what the client has just said. Reflecting feelings is harder because clients are not always able to clearly express what they are feeling. In this case the counselor may have to expand on what was said in order to get to the feelings implied. For instance:

CLIENT: "I want to kill myself. Ever since Marge died I have nothing to live for. She was the center of my world and now she is gone. I just don't want to go on."

COUNSELOR: "I guess you have been feeling depressed and hopeless since Marge died."

In this interchange, the counselor gives words to the client's feelings as well as reflecting the content of what he said. It may seem to be an obvious process, yet it is essential in developing the counseling relationship. Counselors need to perform this function to help keep the client in reality, by saying, "This is how you appear, feel, sound, etc." The counselor becomes the other half of a feedback loop for the client. Getting this feedback helps give the client a sense of what is real, that his experience has been confirmed and understood. If you don't think this is important, try talking about an intimate feeling to someone who says nothing in reply, does not nod his head, and in no ways acknowledges what you have said.

To further clarify the difference between the reflection of feeling versus content, consider the following examples:

CLIENT: "How long does he think I am going to put up with this? Every
(wife)   night he comes home drunk and I will not stand for it anymore. He is tearing this family apart, and yet I feel like I'm supposed to be at fault."

Reflecting feeling

COUNSELOR: "You seem angry at your husband and resent feeling that you are somehow responsible for the problems the family is having."

CLIENT: "What am I supposed to do? Every time I go home she nags me
(husband)   and complains about my drinking. She isn't the least bit concerned about my problems."

Reflecting content

COUNSELOR: "I hear you saying that your wife nags at you, complains about your drinking, and is not concerned about your problems, and that you don't know what else to do."

Empathy

Empathy, which was discussed in Chapter 1, is a process similar to reflection. We are able to distinguish between two different levels of empathy: primary level empathy and advanced empathy. With primary level empathy, the counselor is combining feeling and content reflection in response to what the client has directly said. Advanced empathy helps the client take a larger view of his problem, identify patterns, and see deeper implications. For example:

CLIENT: "It's really hard for me to admit that Sue can't handle it. She is so competent in other ways. I don't know what she will say about treatment; she really won't want to be away from the kids and her friends. I'm really anxious about what she will do. Also, she will really object to having to admit her problem in front of my parish members. You know, all that stuff about a religious image and what would people say."

Primary Level Empathy Response: "It is hard for you to think of Sue being incompetent. You are also anxious about how she will react to the idea of going into treatment. And you expect she will resent her friends finding out about her problem."

Advanced Empathy Response: "You seem so worried about how Sue is going to handle all this, but I am wondering about you. My hunch is that you are ashamed of your wife's chemical dependency and are worried about how this will reflect upon you. Also, I expect you are concerned about how you and the kids will cope while Sue is away for treatment."

Primary empathy simply reprocesses the basic content of what the client has said. This allows both the client and the counselor to be sure they are understanding each other. The advanced empathy response goes beyond what the client has shared and expands it in a way that pinpoints the client's personal concerns for himself. It is good practice to precede the advanced level response with the primary level response: this ensures that you have a clear understanding of the content being shared before trying to take it to a deeper level.

Reassurance and Self-Disclosure

It is not uncommon for clients to experience apprehension about the counseling process and their potential for getting better. Maintaining a positive attitude is generally very helpful to clients even if they do not seem affected by anxiety. As counseling lead-ins, reassuring comments can facilitate the process. For example:

> "We are out of time today, and I want to say that you did quite well and I feel we made good progress."

Reinforcing statements such as these are necessary so that the client is aware of your feelings when he is making progress. Nonverbal gestures can also be reassuring to the client (headnodding, leaning forward, eye contact, touching, etc.).

Another way to reassure a client is through the use of self-disclosure (Jourard, 1971). This process allows the client to know you as a person and confirms for him that other people have had similar experiences. Self-disclosure can have a very powerful effect upon the client and can deepen the counseling relationship. However, self-disclosure used haphazardly can prove to be unhelpful. The counselor who makes a habit of telling stories about himself during each counseling session can greatly inhibit the counseling process. Obviously, the client is a captive audience and generally feels an obligation to be polite and defer to the counselor's implied control. However, just because clients seem to be interested in our stories does not mean they are not bored stiff!

If, after working with a client for several sessions about some destructive behavior pattern related to his chemical dependency, you still find he believes he is the only one with that problem, self-disclosure might be very appropriate. Here the recovering chemical dependency counselor has an advantage over the non-chemically dependent counselor. The recovering counselor is more likely to have some actual experiences similar to those of the client. When these experiences are shared at the right time, the insight to the client can be quite helpful. If sharing the experiences demonstrates that you are human, and experience problems just as others do, then your efforts will probably be successful. But, if your self-disclosure makes you seem superior to the client, you should question your motivation.

Interpretation

Interpretation is an essential lead-in for the chemical dependency counselor. Yet, like self-disclosure, it must be used with caution. Part of the counselor's role is to reflect the client's image back to him in a helpful way. Interpretation of what the client presents is one more way of doing this. Effective interpretation helps the client link up disjointed bits of information in order to form a new, more accurate image of self or of others. There are two ways of interpreting client communication: content interpretation and process interpretation.

Content interpretation involves focusing upon what the client has actually said and then decoding the message into a more meaningful form. When interpreting the content of a client's communication, it is important not to come across as dogmatic or righteous. Example: A client tells you that his drug use is OK because it is under control. Earlier, the client said to you that he feels that there are too many rules in society and that people are not free to make their own choices. An interpretive response to the content of the client's statements might be:

> "It seems that your belief that you can control your use of chemicals gives you a sense of power over your own life. Yet I wonder if you are not again just being controlled by other forces, such as your friends. Is this truly free choice on your part?"

The counselor's response is not demanding nor does it imply that the counselor's interpretation is correct. The counselor is simply connecting two bits of seemingly related information and attempting to present the client with a pattern. If the interpretation of the content is not presented in a judgmental manner, the client will be more willing to consider its merits. However sound the insight of the counselor, the client may still reject it. The chemically dependent client is particularly inclined to do this as part of the denial system. The counselor must not be discouraged, but keep at it until the denial begins to crack.

Process interpretation focuses upon what is actually happening during a counseling session. Here the counselor is attempting to interpret the hidden, and not so hidden, meanings of interpersonal dynamics. The counselor's goal is to help clients fit together the meaning of their interactional processes and their model of themselves and the world. Continuing with the same example, the counselor might make the following process interpretive response:

> "When you discussed your feelings about others controlling you, I could sense your anger, your fists were clenched, your voice was raised, and your eyes opened wider. I remember noticing the same things going on when you talked about your father last week. My hunch is that you feel powerless when around your father and this makes you feel angry and controlled by him. Am I right about this?"

Here the counselor noticed a similarity in the feelings the client was presently expressing and the feelings expressed earlier about another issue. The counselor then made the connection between this anger and the client's father. Again, the counselor was tentative in his interpretation and checked its validity with the client.

When making interpretations, the counselor must take care that he is on relatively solid ground. Random guesses can tend to stall or misdirect the entire counseling process. Also, if the client is not prepared to hear the interpretations, it is best to wait. Arguing over the accuracy of interpretations is pointless when the client is not ready to hear them. When the timing seems right, it is helpful to use familiar terms, relating them to events and attitudes already discussed. Finally, the counselor is wise to consider his own ability to be objective with a given client in a given situation. How do your values and attitudes compare with those of your client? What kinds of social environments do both of you come from? How might your relative ages and life styles affect the relationship? Knowing "where you are coming from" can help you maintain a more objective point of view when interpreting client communication.

Confrontation

Confrontation is one of the chemical dependency counselor's most potent tools, and it is also one of the most dangerous. Confrontation tends to be a loaded word, meaning different things to different people. Egan (1970) states that confrontation takes place when one person either deliberately or inadvertently does something that causes or directs another person to reflect upon, examine, question, or consider changing some aspect of his behavior. The purpose of confrontation is *not* to cause people to change their behavior. (This is not likely to happen, in any case.) Thus, if we dislike something a client is doing, we must be careful how we communicate this. Venting our personal frustration through confrontation can lead to a destructive and counterproductive relationship. The purpose of confrontation should be to bring the client into more direct contact with his own experience and any discrepancies or distortions in that experience.

Preconditions for Successful Confrontations

Counselor Requisites. Confrontations are more helpful if the counselor:

- has a good relationship with the client or at least is sensitive to the quality of their relationship;
- accepts the client and is willing to get more involved with him as a person;
- phrases his confrontations as suggestions or requests rather than demands;
- directs his confrontations toward concrete behavior rather than to motives;
- makes his confrontations positive and constructive rather than negative;
- states his confrontation succinctly and directly; and
- represents facts as facts, hypotheses as hypotheses, and feelings as feelings.

Client Requisites. A client will benefit more from a confrontation if he:

- accepts it as an invitation to explore himself;
- is open to knowing how he is experienced by others;
- is willing to tolerate the temporary disorganization that may result from a confrontation; and
- responds differently to different modes of confrontation rather than responding in a stereotyped way (such as accepting every confrontation as truth or dismissing all confrontations as worthless).

Group Situations. Confrontation that takes place in a large group situation can be facilitated by a high degree of acceptance and trust. It is difficult to face a confrontation without being defensive if you do not trust or feel accepted by the group members. Confrontation is also better received if it fits the goals and purposes of the group. Interpersonal confrontation at a faculty meeting or at a social gathering, for example, can have disruptive effects. These groups are meeting for different purposes than the typical growth group, and the confrontation comes as a surprise.

Methods of Confrontation

Berenson and Carkhuff (1968) have distinguished five major types of confrontation (here, *confronter* refers to the counselor, and *confrontee* to the client):

1. *Experiential*. A response to any discrepancy perceived by the confronter between the confrontee's statements about himself and his own experience of the confrontee.
2. *Strength*. Focused on the confrontee's resources, especially if he doesn't realize them himself.
3. *Weakness*. Focused on the confrontee's pathology or liabilities.
4. *Didactic*. Clarification of misinformation or lack of information.
5. *Encouragement to action*. Pressing the confrontee to act on his world in a constructive manner and discouraging a passive attitude toward life.

Research has shown that effective helpers use experiential and strength confrontation more frequently; less effective helpers tend to confront a client's weaknesses. It is important to consider the conditions first and then how best to help clients recognize the differences between their experience of their behavior and the reality of their behavior. This can be a time-consuming process, and, some would say, the primary goal of the inpatient counselor.

Chemically dependent persons in need of inpatient treatment generally suffer from a gross distortion in their ability to discern between the real world and their reaction to their environment. This presents the counselor with a great challenge. This distortion also relates to why the first step of AA ("We admitted we were powerless over alcohol—that our lives had become unmanageable") *is* the *first* step as well as so difficult. Only by continuously confronting clients' distortions can we ever help them see the gap between reality and their experience of reality.

TECHNIQUES THAT FACILITATE COMMUNICATION

The chemical dependency counselor also needs to be aware of, and able to utilize, fundamental communication skills when working with a client. This section will discuss some basic techniques that can facilitate communication and keep the counseling session moving.

Acceptance

Carl Rogers (1967) has coined the phrase "unconditional positive regard," which simply means accepting clients as they are. We may not always particularly like our clients nor agree with their value systems. Yet we are obliged by our professional ethics to try and accept clients as they present themselves to us. To do this unconditionally, we must resist placing our own value judgments on the client's behavior and attitudes.

Acceptance can be communicated both verbally and nonverbally. When communicating acceptance verbally, it is not always necessary to make statements such as "I accept and care for you just as you are." Acceptance can be just as effectively communicated by implication. For example:

> CLIENT: "When I got drunk last night, I totally lost control and beat up my wife. I have never done that before, and wouldn't have if she hadn't nagged me like she did."
>
> COUNSELOR: "You feel bad that you lost control and did something that hurt your wife. Let's talk some more about your responsibility in this incident and how you might change your behavior."

The counselor's response reflects understanding without being judgmental. The counselor urges the client to look deeper into the problem his drinking has caused and isn't sidetracked by the client's attempt to blame his wife. The counselor's intent is not to condone his client's wife-beating; rather, he hopes to redirect the client in a way that allows him to vent his violent feelings without danger to himself or others. In contrast, an unhelpful counselor response would have been:

> COUNSELOR: "Beating up your wife won't solve anything, and it only shows me just how sick you really are."

Although this statement may be true, it does not help the client understand himself and probably would create a block between client and counselor. This kind of response also decreases the possibility of sharing any such information again in the future.

Acceptance can be communicated nonverbally by headnodding, smiling, maintaining an open posture, and other reassuring gestures. The way you look to the client as he is talking to you lets him know whether you accept what is being said. Frowns and a closed posture can tell the client you do not like what he is saying. To some clients, a neutral expression can also communicate nonacceptance. Therefore, it is important to consider how you look to the client and whether the image you present will facilitate communication.

Acceptance is sometimes very difficult to achieve but as counselors we must remember that it is not our responsibility to judge our clients. Our responsibility is to facilitate clients' understanding and acceptance of themselves; for clients, it is to evaluate what they like and dislike and want to change. The counselor who continually evaluates and judges his clients is doing work that the clients should be learning to do for themselves. The counselor must always try to maintain open and honest communication with clients; acceptance will enhance this as well as show clients our trust in them.

Clarification

Clarification has to do with making sure that counselor (and client) understand what the client has said. Clients frequently speak in vague and incomplete ways and thus need assistance. The counselor can use his own words to clarify what has been said or attach the statement to an earlier one in order to make more sense out of it. Do not hesitate to interrupt a client to ask for clarification; much can be gained from this. Asking for clarification also helps clients learn to be specific in their communications.

General Lead-ins

General lead-ins help when clients are capable of expressing themselves but need some encouragement. Such statements as "Tell me more," "Could you say more about that?" are helpful in getting clients to elaborate on short, unenlightening comments.

Feedback

Providing feedback lets clients know how they are coming across and enhances the entire communication process. There are some specific guidelines for giving feedback that will make it more likely that the client will make the best use of it. Feedback is most often heard by the client when:

- it is requested by the client.
- it is given as promptly as possible after the observed behavior.
- it is given in nontechnical language.
- it is concise—that is, it does not contain more detail or information than was present in the individual's observed behavior.
- it focuses on the individual's specific and observable behavior as opposed to his character. For example: "You don't look at me when you talk to me" rather than "You are strange or distant."
- it is given in a personal, helpful, nonthreatening manner and avoids value or moral judgments. For example: "When you look away from me, I feel you are being insincere" as opposed to "Nobody likes people who don't look at people."
- it concentrates only on behavior over which the individual has some control. For example, it would be inappropriate to tell a client you don't like the color of his eyes.
- it focuses on the individual's strengths as well as his weaknesses. For example: "I like the way you look at me when you talk" is effective feedback focusing on the client's strengths.
- it is discussed by the counselor and client until they both can agree on what each is communicating.

Advice Giving

Giving advice to a client is generally a practice that the effective counselor avoids. Giving advice tends to prevent clients from making decisions for themselves. However, there are rare occasions when it is appropriate, as well as necessary, to give advice. When you give advice at the right time and on the right issue, it can enhance communication because clients learn to count on you to tell the truth and protect them from making unnecessary mistakes. It is appropriate to give advice on such subjects as client rights and privileges, referral sources in the community, and life or health risks as well as when the client is obviously misinformed on a particular issue affecting his life. In most cases, when the client asks "What do you think I should do?" we recommend placing the responsibility for the decision back on the client.

Silence

For the beginning counselor, silences during the counseling session can be agonizing and are usually avoided at all costs. The counselor's primary fear is that the silence may not end or that the client may think he does not know how to continue. Silence may also be interpreted as rudeness or boredom.

Silence, however, can be a valuable tool of the effective counselor who knows when and how to use it best. Here are some ways that silence can be beneficial to the counseling relationship.

- The client may pause to think over what he has just said or is planning to say next. It is best to let the silence continue until the client is ready to go on.
- Silence can be used to punctuate a particular thought or interaction that has just occurred.
- Silence during the initial session is common, and the counselor can help by simply saying, "It's hard to get started, isn't it?" It is best to avoid punishing the client when he is silent.
- Sometimes silence can mean that the client is experiencing painful emotions and may need your assistance and encouragement to go on.
- At other times, silence can be an invitation by the client to be drawn out further. The client may wish to tell you more but is looking for your support.
- Finally, silences can come immediately after some particularly emotional event, when both the client and counselor need some time to consider the event quietly.

Silence can be used in ways that are unhelpful to the counseling process. The unskilled counselor may use silence in an almost sadistic manner as a way to provoke the client into some kind of meaningful outburst. Our experience has been that counselors use silence in this way to cover up their own inadequate skills. A prolonged silence, which is intended to manipulate the client, generally has the effect of threatening the client's self-worth—this can be catastrophic with the chemically dependent client whose sense of self-worth is already in bad shape.

A careful use of silence can encourage clients to take responsibility for their feelings and actions, particularly if they know this is the purpose of the silence. Silences can also be used to pace counseling when it seems to be moving too fast. Silence can be helpful to the inarticulate client who is more comfortable with regular pauses between interchanges in order to prepare for his next statement.

The Counselor Verbal Response Scale

Kagan (1966) and his associates at Michigan State University have developed a verbal response scale to describe the counselor's communications in four dimensions: affective-cognitive, understanding-nonunderstanding, specific-nonspecific, and exploratory-nonexploratory. Kagan uses this scale to evaluate counselor responses and thereby help counselors gain an understanding of which domain their responses fall into most frequently. If counselors learn that their responses fall into one or two dimensions too often, they have a clear sense of where and how to initiate changes. We will offer a brief description of the four dimensions mentioned above.

Affective-Cognitive Dimension

This dimension indicates whether a counselor's responses refer to feelings or to thoughts. Affective responses tend to focus attention upon the emotional aspects of a client's communications. Examples might be:

- Referring to an implied feeling of the client. Example: "It sounds like you were really angry at him."
- Encouraging an expression of affect by the client. Example: "How does it make you feel when your parents argue over Dad's drinking?"
- Approving an expression of affect by the client. Example: "It really does help to let your feelings out once in a while, doesn't it?"
- Presenting a model for using affect to the client. Example: "If somebody treated me like that I would be really mad."

Cognitive responses deal primarily with the content of a client's communications. Frequently such responses are seeking information of a factual nature. Examples might be:

- Referring directly to the cognitive component of the client's statement. Example: "So you're thinking of leaving your husband if he won't enter treatment?"
- Seeking further information of a factual nature from the client. Example: "How many DWIs have you had?"
- Encouraging the client to continue to respond at the cognitive level. Example: "When did you begin drinking?"

Understanding-Nonunderstanding Dimension

This dimension indicates whether a counselor's responses communicate an understanding of, or a willingness to understand, the client's basic communications, thereby encouraging the client to continue to gain insight into the nature of his concerns. Examples might be:

- Directly communicating an understanding of the client's communication. Example: "In other words, you want to be treated like a man."

- Seeking further information to facilitate a better understanding of the basic problem. Example: "What does being a man mean to you?"
- Reinforcing client communications that exhibit understanding. Example:

CLIENT: "I guess when people criticize me, I'm afraid they'll leave me."

COUNSELOR: "I see you're beginning to make a connection between your behavior and your feelings."

Nonunderstanding responses are those in which the counselor fails to understand the client's basic communication or makes no attempt to obtain appropriate information. Examples might be:

CLIENT: "When he called me a jerk, I just turned red and clenched my fists."

COUNSELOR: "Some people don't say nice things."

- Seeking information that may be irrelevant to the client's communication. Example:

CLIENT: "I seem to have a hard time getting along with my brothers."

COUNSELOR: "Do all your brothers live at home with you?"

- Squelching client understanding or moving the focus to another irrelevant area. For example:

CLIENT: "I guess I'm really afraid that other people will laugh at me."

COUNSELOR: "We're the butt of other people's jokes sometimes."

CLIENT: "Sometimes I really hate my mother."

COUNSELOR: "Will things be better when you go to college?"

Specific-Nonspecific Dimension

In this dimension, the counselor's responses indicate whether he is able to focus on the client's concerns with increased clarity. Nonunderstanding responses are also nonspecific since they do not help the client clarify his concerns. However, understanding responses may not always be specific. The responses may reflect understanding in a general way without necessarily providing more clarity. Specific responses focus on the core concerns being presented by the client. Examples might be:

- Delineating more closely the client's basic concerns. Example: "This vague feeling you have when you get in tense situations—is it anger or fear?"
- Encouraging the client to discriminate among stimuli affecting him. Example: "Do you feel scared in all your classes or only in some?"
- Rewarding the client for being specific. Example:

CLIENT: "I guess I feel this way most often with someone who reminds me of my father."

COUNSELOR: "So, as you put what others say in perspective, the whole world doesn't seem so bad. It's only when someone you value, like your father, doesn't pay any attention to you that you feel hurt."

Nonspecific responses indicate that the counselor is not focusing on the basic concerns of the client and, if anything, is adding to the confusion. The counselor does not help the client distinguish between various stimuli. Also, the counselor may try to reach some vague conclusions even though he lacks the necessary facts. Examples might be:

- Failing to delineate the client's concerns or bring them into focus. Example: "You seem very confused about your drinking. Can you tell me more about it?"
- Missing the basic concerns being presented by the client even though the counselor may ask for specific details. Example:

CLIENT: "My business has done very well this year and I still feel lousy."

COUNSELOR: "What was your business like in the years before this one?"

- Discouraging the client from bringing his concerns into sharper focus. Example: "You and your wife argue all the time. What do other people think of your wife?"

Exploratory-Nonexploratory Dimension

This dimension indicates whether a counselor's responses permit the client to explore further his concerns in the cognitive and affective domains. Exploratory responses encourage the client and permit him freedom in his responses. The counselor may focus clearly on either the cognitive or affective; nevertheless, the counselor's questions are open-ended. Examples might be:

- Encouraging the client to explore his own concerns. For example:

COGNITIVE: "You're not sure if this is the right time for you to go into treatment, are you?"

AFFECTIVE: "Maybe you are really mad at yourself. What do you think of that?"

- Providing the client with possible alternatives designed to increase his range of responses. For example:

COGNITIVE: "Besides leaving home, what other alternatives do you have?"

AFFECTIVE: "In these situations, do you feel angry, sad, helpless, or how?"

- Rewarding the client for exploratory behavior. For example:

COGNITIVE: "It seems that you have considered a number of alternatives. That's good."

AFFECTIVE: "So you're beginning to wonder if you always want to be treated like a man."

Nonexploratory responses give the client little opportunity to explore his concerns or express himself freely. For example:

COGNITIVE: "So you are not going into treatment at all."

AFFECTIVE: "You're angry because your wife does not respect you."

When assessing your own counseling within the framework of these four dimensions, it is important to understand that a healthy balance is necessary. No one can ever completely avoid making responses that indicate nonunderstanding, and no one can always make specific responses. We strive to achieve a balance in our responses that is both realistic and at the same time helpful. This scale can help you evaluate your responses. If you find that they tend to fall into one category most of the time, you may wish to work on expanding your repertoire.

REFERRALS

All counselors, at some time or another, encounter a client or situation that they feel less than capable of handling. When this happens to you, it is your professional responsibility to help that person secure the help he needs through the referral process.

Determining When Referral is Necessary

It is safe to assume that every client entering your agency has a perceived need for help. The need may or may not be a real need, but in all likelihood it is real to the client. As the counselor, your task is to attempt to understand what the client's need is and in what way you can be of help.

In agencies serving the chemically dependent, counselors often assume that every potential client has a serious alcohol or drug problem. This would seem a safe assumption, yet it may be entirely or partially inaccurate. It is not uncommon to find, after an hour of talking with a client, that he is in the wrong place. If your agency is listed in the phone book and somewhere in the listing the word *counseling* is used, almost anyone may show up at your door seeking help. This can happen even when the client is referred by another well-intentioned professional in the community. One of the authors had a family referred for chemical dependency counseling by a mental health counselor because she assumed there was alcoholism in the family. This assumption was based on the wife's description of the husband's behavior at home. Unfortunately, the referring counselor failed to ask the wife if her husband did in fact drink. After a lengthy interview with both the wife and the referring counselor, the author asked how much the husband drank and the wife replied, "Why, he has never touched a drop of alcohol in his life."

On other occasions the authors have seen clients who in fact presented bona fide chemical dependency problems; however, there were other issues that took precedence over the presenting problem. Issues such as food, housing, health, child care, and law enforcement can be of more immediate concern. If these fundamental life issues are not dealt with first, no amount of chemical dependency counseling will be of much help. In these circumstances a referral to another agency for specific services may be called for. It is generally beyond the scope of the chemical dependency counselor's resources to assist clients with basic survival issues. Thus, it is important for chemical dependency counselors to be knowledgeable of all the social services available in their community or region.

Assessing Counselor Limitations

Part of the process of determining when a referral is necessary calls upon the chemical dependency counselor to assess his own limitations as a professional. You cannot be everything to everybody, but you can know where to find help when you need it. This requires that you be honest with yourself and utilize your peers to help you assess your limitations. The following are some of the conditions that could cause counselors to consider referring their clients to someone else for services.

- Counselors must feel they can be objective with their clients and not let personal interests interfere in any way. Thus, it is not advisable to counsel friends, relatives, fellow employees, neighbors, or students in training within the agency.

- The presenting problem may touch on an area that the counselor feels is too close to a current problem he is experiencing. For instance, a counselor currently going through a divorce should not do marital counseling.
- Counselors should not work with clients presenting problems with which they have had no prior experience. Incest is a good example of a common problem presented to chemical dependency counselors. If the counselor has no experience in this area and is aware of some confused prejudices about it, it may be best to refer the client to an expert.
- Counselors are generally people who wish very much to be helpful to others who are hurting. Because of this, counselors sometimes find it difficult to say no to clients in need, and their caseloads can quickly become unmanageable. This is a situation that often necessitates referral.
- Sometimes counselors impose specific limitations upon themselves because they do not feel comfortable working with certain kinds of cases (e.g., groups, families, children, sexual abuse cases). In such instances, it is perfectly acceptable to make a referral to someone who could do a better job. The key is to be honest with yourself and your colleagues; you can't be everything to everybody.

Agency Restrictions

In addition to personal limitations, agency restrictions can sometimes necessitate a referral. Each agency must determine its own set of standards for serving clients. These standards help the agency decide what kind of presenting problems it wishes to treat, the geographic area to be served, client eligibility criteria, and how the agency fits into the larger community's human service resources. State, local, and federal funding sources will also dictate what kind of services the agency can provide. When confined by specific programmatic guidelines, individual counselors must limit their services to those determined by agency policy and/ or law. This sometimes means turning away clients whom you are qualified to serve but are not allowed to due to program restrictions.

When you encounter any of these restrictions, it is part of your professional responsibility to provide a referral to another helping professional. A careful and respectful explanation of why you must refer the client is always helpful. Generally, clients understand the limits of an agency's ability to serve the public. However, some clients may not accept your explanations and may wish to speak with a supervisor. Do not hesitate to refer the client to a supervisor for a final determination and/or explanation. It is important to help clients realize they have alternatives and to explore them. Simply saying, "I am unable to help you and I have other people waiting to see me" is unhelpful and needlessly rude.

The chemical dependency counselor is a specialized practitioner who must also be aware of the multitude of other personal problems a client may experience. You may not necessarily know how to resolve all the problems the client presents to you, but you can be prepared to help the client select the proper resource.

Specific Referral Sources

Financial Counseling

In the eighties, a time of apparent recession, many people are experiencing tough times making ends meet. Frequently, alcohol and drugs become one way to turn off all the tension and anxiety of not having enough money. Unfortunately, the user's dependency becomes just one more drain upon the budget. It is not uncommon for chemically dependent persons to be thousands of dollars in debt due solely to their extravagant use of alcohol and drugs. Generally, as the chemical dependency counselor, it is not your job to help your clients straighten out their financial difficulties. (Few counselors are actually trained as financial consultants and/or advisors, in any case.) However, you must always consider all the factors that may impede the client's successful recovery in order to develop an appropriate intervention strategy. If one of the issues that led the client to using abusively in the first place was money problems, then you can be relatively sure that things have not improved now that the client has sought counseling. Clients need to know that successful recovery is contingent upon changing many aspects of their life.

When counseling on the issue of finances, it is best to help clients clarify what their needs are as well as their resources. Also, the client must determine what expenses have priority and which can wait for a while. Clients rarely have the money to hire a financial consultant, so you will need to search for economical resources in the community. Here are several options:

- Most community colleges offer courses in personal budgeting at a low cost.
- Frequently, the client's banker will be willing to help straighten out the client's budget.
- There may be other recovering alcoholics in the community with expertise in finance who would be willing to donate their time as advisers.
- Your own agency's finance officer may be able to arrange classes in budget management.
- Community organizations frequently make financial counseling available at no cost.
- College students in business or finance may be willing to donate time or offer counseling at a small fee.

In order to make these kinds of referrals successful, the chemical dependency counselor needs to actively direct the client toward the appropriate referral. Simply recommending financial counseling may not always be sufficient; some phone calls or personal contacts may be required to get the process started.

Sex Therapy

One of the most debilitating consequences of chemical dependency can be the inability to achieve satisfactory sexual functioning. This raises several difficult issues for the chemical dependency counselor.

Generally, the counselor is not well prepared to help the client experiencing sexual dysfunction. Whatever help the counselor may be able to offer cannot be considered on the same level as that offered by the professional sex therapist. The complexities of this subject can be identified in three ways:

1. Determining what is satisfactory sexual functioning can be the counselor's first frustration. Without adequate training we tend to rely upon our own personal experience in determining what is satisfactory. Thus our own biases and prior learning can cloud our judgments. It is best not to try to judge what is appropriate for the client based upon what has worked for us.
2. An inadequate professional knowledge of human sexual functioning can also be a handicap to the chemical dependency counselor. It is counterproductive to supply clients with information that later turns out to be false.
3. Finally, the socially debilitating consequences of chemical dependency upon sexuality can have a profound effect on the client's recovery. When clients have had previous unfortunate sexual experiences due to the use of alcohol and drugs, they are likely to feel insecure about new relationships. We attach our self-worth to many things, including our sexuality. If every time we had sex in the past it turned out badly, we will tend to fear what it will be like while sober. This becomes a very delicate and sensitive stage of recovery and is best handled by a professional when it appears to be necessary.

Marriage Counseling

Somewhat related to the issue of sexuality, marital counseling is an area that the chemical dependency counselor is usually not trained in. Obviously, the spouse of a client must be involved in treatment if it is to be successful, and the chemical dependency counselor is well experienced in helping spouses understand their role in the chemical dependency problem. However, other issues not related to chemical dependency may arise, usually after recovery has begun, that may require professional marriage counseling. Marriage counseling can require techniques different from traditional chemical dependency counseling. Hence, it is wise to utilize existing resources in the community either for a referral or consultation. Establishing communication with a good marriage counselor and sex therapist in your community can be very valuable.

Legal Aid

A knowledge of the law and how it may affect clients is a very useful tool for the chemical dependency counselor. However, the counselor's legal knowledge should never be used to take the place of a lawyer. For your own protection and your client's, always refer the client to a lawyer for a legal opinion. Knowing which lawyers specialize in what kind of law, what they charge, and their general reputation can be helpful when making a referral.

Job Placement Assistance

It is not uncommon for the chemically dependent person to have had a history of unsuccessful work experiences and be in need of either new employment or job training. With the constant change in our economy, the counselor is wise to keep up to date on the employment field, changing job training programs, and future employment potentials. Again, your client may need the services of some other community professional experienced in job placement and training. Keeping up to date can help avoid frustration due to referring clients to programs that have no placements available or that have been unreliable in placing applicants in the past.

Physicians

Chemically dependent persons tend to exhibit multiple medical problems if they have been using heavily for a long period of time. Obviously, the chemical dependency counselor is not trained in medicine and cannot attempt to diagnose a client's illness even if the symptoms seem quite specific. One symptom can frequently cover up other, undetected symptoms, and it is always best to refer to a physician whenever there are any physiological symptoms of concern to the client. Also, chemically dependent clients have generally degenerated into a habit of neglecting their health, and, as a counselor, you may need to help clients regain or establish new health maintenance activities. Regular visits to the doctor may need to be encouraged as part of the client's recovery program.

Another issue that the counselor can overlook is the presence of physical dysfunctions inhibiting the client's progress in counseling. Heavy use of alcohol and drugs can, in some cases, cause specific types of brain damage, central nervous system dysfunction, and damage to the endocrine system and other vital body functions. These kinds of medical problems can have an adverse effect upon the client's ability to fully participate in a treatment program and/or limit the kinds of therapeutic goals that are achievable. If you suspect medical problems, do not hesitate to refer the client for medical consultation. If a client complains of physical discomfort and does not attend sessions regularly because of this, do not jump to the conclusion that he is simply avoiding counseling. The client deserves the benefit of the doubt and should be urged to check out any physical ailments immediately.

As with other referral procedures, it is helpful to know the kinds of medical services available in your community. Are there community health clinics for those clients without health insurance? Do you have a list of physicians who are sensitive to chemical dependency and have worked with addicted clients in the past? Does your agency have a consulting physician or at least a physician on its advisory board?

Psychiatrists

Many chemical dependency counselors are hesitant to refer clients to psychiatrists if in the past clients have only returned with a bolstered supply of drugs and a new rationalization for using them. Providing referrals to psychiatrists should be done with care. First, visit with the doctor to discover his attitude regarding chemical dependency. Then, when you make the referral, be sure to maintain contact with the client and the psychiatrist to see how things are going. The psychiatrist is an important component of any chemical dependency program, and every effort should be made to develop a good working relationship with the psychiatrists in your community.

There are a multitude of issues that can come up for your clients that may demand psychiatric care. It is not uncommon to find chemically dependent persons beginning to exhibit previously unnoticed psychotic symptoms when they discontinue use of alcohol or drugs. When this occurs, it is best to arrange a consultation with the psychiatrist. If the case is serious, an actual transfer of the case is recommended. Another issue that frequently comes up with chemically dependent clients is suicide. A patient who seems suicidal should be referred for psychiatric assistance. Suicide management can be very difficult and only the well-trained professional should handle such cases.

Community Recreation Groups

Another reason for the counselor to make referrals is to help clients learn to use their leisure time in healthy, constructive, nondrug-oriented ways. This can be a tremendous adjustment for people who are used to depending on drugs or alcohol to get them through every social situation. If your agency does not have a recreation program or a recreation therapist, we suggest referring the client for help in learning new ways to utilize leisure time. Generally, the local office of the United Way can help you locate programs in the community. The YMCA and YWCA are also good resources.

Support Groups

Recovery from chemical dependency is difficult even with the help of friends but next to impossible when done alone. There are, of course, isolated cases of individuals who simply stopped using one day and have never had any trouble since. But these are rare cases. More commonly, it takes the help of many other concerned people to begin and maintain a successful program of recovery. The chemical dependency counselor can be a part of this process but is only one component. The client cannot live day in and day out with his counselor; he needs other people to pick up where the counselor leaves off. These people will be around long after the counselor is gone and will continue to be a support to the chemically dependent person well into the future. This is why the support group can be so critical to the client's recovery. A support group can be almost anything as long as one of its functions is to help the client maintain a drug- and alcohol-free life. AA is one of the most well-known and popular support groups. Yet many recovering people find the help they need through church groups, Narcotics Anonymous, Emotions Anonymous, Overeaters Anonymous, Alanon, Alateen, growth groups, and a variety of other informal support groups. As a counselor, you need to know what groups are in your community and how to refer your client to such groups.

How to Make a Referral

The referral process is relatively easy if you have done your homework and have selected the proper resource. We recommend following these four steps when making a referral:

1. Share what you know about the referral agency with the client. What do they do there? What will it cost? Will it be confidential? are all questions clients are likely to ask.
2. Offer to make the initial contact in order to ensure that the client sees the right person, that the referral counselor knows he is coming, and that the client knows exactly where to go, on what date, and at what time. The referral process is more efficient if you take care of these details yourself; however, if you feel clients need to learn how to do these things, coach them but let them make the contact themselves.
3. The client should sign a confidential information release before following through with a referral. The release should indicate that you can release information regarding the client to another specific agency or individual. Upon arrival at the other agency, the client should sign another release in order to ensure the easy flow of information back and forth. Exhibits 5-1 and 5-2 are examples of release forms.
4. Always follow up on the referral to see if your client arrived at the agency, if he received the service needed, and what the outcome was. It is pointless to make referrals if you don't know what happens after the client leaves your office. It is best to talk with both clients and the agency they were referred to. This is one way to ensure that you are referring people to the right places.

Exhibit 5–1 Authorization for Release of Information

I, the undersigned, hereby authorize _____

(Name of Agency)

_____

(Address)

to disclose to _____

(Name of Agency/Person to receive information)

_____

the following information from records in its possession:

____ Treatment/Discharge Summary   ____ X-Ray Reports
____ Psychological Testing and   ____ Laboratory Reports:
     Evaluation   ___ All Laboratory Reports
____ Psychiatric Consultation   ___ Specific Laboratory Reports
____ ECG Reports   _____
____ EEG Reports   ____ School Transcripts and Grades
____ Social History   ____ Other (specify) _____
____ Medical History and Physical   _____

The purpose or need for such disclosure is _____

_____

This authorization to disclose information may be revoked by me at any time except to the extent
that action has been taken in reliance thereon. This authorization shall expire upon:

_____

(Specify date, event, or condition upon which it will expire)

_____   _____

(Signature of client)   (Date)

_____   _____

(Signature of legal guardian)   (Relationship of legal guardian)

_____   _____

(Signature of witness)   (Signature of witness)

NOTICE TO WHOMEVER DISCLOSURE IS MADE: This information has been disclosed
to you from records whose confidentiality is protected by Federal Law. Federal regulations (42
CFR part 2) prohibit you from making any further disclosure of this information without the
specific written consent of the person to whom it pertains, or as otherwise permitted by such
regulations. A general authorization for the release of medical or other information is NOT
sufficient for this purpose.

When the client is unwilling to cooperate in the referral process, it is important
to proceed slowly but firmly. Explain at length and in detail the need to seek some
other professional or service within the community. If you are certain that you
cannot help the client or are restricted by agency policy, do not let a client talk you
out of the referral. When a client is resistant to the referral, it is usually because of

Exhibit 5–2 Authorization and Consent for Disclosure of Patient Records

Patient: _____

Number: _____

I hereby authorize, direct, and consent to the disclosure of records held by the Chemical Dependency Unit concerning _____,
with the following limitations and conditions to be observed:

1. The name of the program that is to make the disclosure is _____;
2. The name or title of the person(s) or organization(s) to which the disclosure is to be made is _____, and such disclosure is strictly limited to such person(s) or organization(s);
3. The purpose or need for this disclosure is _____
_____
_____
_____;
4. The disclosure is to be limited to such extent and in such manner so that only the following is disclosed: _____
_____
_____;
5. This consent is revocable at any time, except as to actions taken specifically in reliance thereon. In addition, this consent will automatically terminate without express revocation as of _____, 19 __, or upon the occurrence of the following event or condition: _____
_____.
In no case shall this consent be effective longer than that reasonably necessary to effectuate the purpose for which it is given.

I hereby agree to idemnify and hold the Chemical Dependency Unit, its employees, agents, and officers harmless from all legal liability for all claims that may arise from the release of such records as specified above.

DATE: _____
PATIENT: _____
REPRESENTATIVE: _____
    RELATIONSHIP TO CLIENT: _____
WITNESS: _____

the fear of going somewhere new. Be patient and explain what the other agency is like, and if necessary, offer to go with the client for the visit. Following up on such arrangements is critical. It is very easy to lose a client who is reluctant to be referred, and you must be sure to check on whether he made it. If you find the client did not make it to the new agency, try and start the process over again.

TERMINATING THE COUNSELING RELATIONSHIP

Ending the counseling relationship can be difficult for both the client and the counselor. As you work with someone for weeks, maybe months, an attachment develops that can be painful to break when it is time to terminate. This is why it is helpful to establish specific treatment goals at the beginning that will allow you and the client to clearly evaluate when it is time to end the relationship. When it seems to you that the goals are nearing completion, it is helpful to begin discussing termination. Do not spring termination on clients at the last minute and not allow them any time to prepare. We would recommend that you consider the following steps when preparing for termination:

- It is best to end counseling in a positive way, when the client is feeling confident and seems to be making independent decisions.
- Have the original goals of counseling been achieved? If so, does the client wish to renegotiate new goals? If the client seems uncertain, it may be time to initiate the termination process.
- Be positive, tell clients how much you have appreciated them, and encourage them to continue their growth.
- Develop an aftercare plan focusing on areas of needed growth that clients can pursue on their own.
- Suggest options for the client in case other problems arise in the future. Be sure there is a solid support system available for the client to lean upon during the hard times.
- Tell the client that other problems will come up and not to expect a bed of roses. Explain to the client that having problems does not mean he has failed or is a bad person but that he will have to work out solutions using what he learned from counseling.
- Leave the door open for clients to return if they feel a need to and encourage periodic phone contacts just to let you know how they are doing. It helps to try and be specific about the conditions under which clients may choose to reenter counseling, as well as any specific prerequisites you may have for initiating counseling again.
- Sometimes counseling ends negatively, with clients terminating before reaching completion of their goals. We would not recommend punishing clients for one more failure. (They have experienced enough of this.) Comment on your concerns for them, that you respect their right to make this decision, and that they can come back at a later date if they want to. When terminating in this manner, it is best to stick to the "facts" and avoid value judgments on the client's commitment, sincerity, or morality.

One final consideration about initiating the termination process: sometimes it is difficult for us to let go of our clients, and we do not always see when it becomes necessary. Our need to stay involved with clients—to keep them needing us—can blind us to their need to be on their own. If you feel you are overinvested in a particular client, discuss the situation with a supervisor or a colleague. It would be helpful to discover if there are certain kinds of clients you have difficulty letting go of. Our own fear of failure sometimes motivates us to keep a client longer than we should in the hope of making him perfect. This is an unhealthy need and can only be destructive to the client and the counselor. Consider again what was said in Chapter 1 regarding the motivations for becoming a counselor.

REFERENCES

Berenson, B.G., & Carkhuff, R.R. Beyond counseling and therapy. New York: Holt, Rinehart and Winston, Inc., 1967.

Combs, A.W., Avila, D.L., & Purkey, W.W. Helping relationships: Basic concepts for the helping professions. Boston: Allyn and Bacon, 1971.

Egan, G. The skills helper. Monterey, Calif.: Brooks/Cole, 1975.

Glasser, W. Reality therapy: A new approach to psychiatry. New York: Harper Row, 1965.

Jourard, S. Self-disclosure: An experimental analysis of the transparent self. New York: Wiley Interscience, 1971.

Kagan, N. Interpersonal process recall. East Lansing: Michigan State University, 1965.

Maslow, A. Toward a psychology of being. New York: Van Nostrand, 1967.

Moustakas, C. Personal growth: The struggle for identity and human values. Cambridge, Mass.: H.A. Doyle Publishing Co., 1969.

Rogers, C., Gendlin, G.T., Kiesler, D.J., & Truax, C.B. The therapeutic relationship and its impact: A study of psychotherapy with schizophrenics. Madison: University of Wisconsin Press, 1967.

Twelve steps and twelve traditions. Alcoholics Anonymous Publishing, Inc., 1953.

SOME QUESTIONS TO CONSIDER

1. What is the technique that I will use most often?
2. How will it get me where I want to be with the client?
3. Are there some techniques that I am not good at? What are they?
4. How can I improve them?

Chapter 6

Group Counseling in the Treatment of Chemical Dependency

Gary W. Lawson

INTRODUCTION

Perhaps the best way to begin this chapter is with a statement of what it is not: it is not all you have ever wanted to know, or will ever need to know, about groups. It would be impossible, in one short chapter, to provide the reader with the knowledge and skill to be an effective group leader (that is, a group leader who consistently produces therapeutic results when leading a group). Needless to say, it takes study and practice to develop into a first-rate group facilitator. There have been hundreds of books and articles written about groups; so why should a chemical dependency counselor read this particular chapter about groups?

First, unlike much that has been written about groups, this chapter was written specifically with the chemical dependency counselor in mind. Second, it provides a structure for the future study and practice of group counseling in the treatment of chemical dependency. This chapter may be best viewed as a map for the chemical dependency counselor to use to help him along toward a greater understanding of group process and, in turn, toward improved skills as a group leader. The point is to encourage *you*, as a chemical dependency counselor, to continue your study of group counseling far beyond the scope of this chapter—and to have you recognize that group counseling is not just individual counseling done with more than one person. The dynamics and usefulness of group counseling go far beyond those of individual therapy in the treatment of the chemically dependent client. However, like individual therapy, groups used inappropriately can be harmful to the group member and can detract rather than add to movement toward the individual group member's treatment goals. This negative effect will be discussed in more detail later. For now a brief description of what *is* covered in this chapter is in order.

WHY USE GROUPS?

The first question that should be addressed is one of major concern for all chemical dependency counselors, and that is, why use groups at all? This leads to many other questions. For example:

- How is group therapy different from individual therapy?
- What kinds of groups are there?
- What makes a group therapeutic?
- Are there general rules and goals for a group?
- How much should a group leader structure the group session?
- What are the qualities of a good group leader?
- Who are appropriate group members?
- What are some specific models for alcohol or drug groups?
- What are some group dynamics that can make a member feel worse rather than better?
- What are the ethical issues involved in groups?

These and other questions will be discussed in the following pages. Read these pages not from the perspective of "at last I have found the answers" but rather, "at last I have begun to understand the question!"

So why *should* the chemical dependency counselor use groups as a treatment approach? This can be answered from many different perspectives. First and foremost in the heart of the program administrator, groups make sense economically. A counselor who can see 6 individual clients per day can run 3 groups instead and see over 20 clients. In a field such as chemical dependency, where there are many more clients than counselors, group counseling may be the only way for counselors to effectively handle their caseload. This would not be an acceptable solution to the time bind if there was evidence that those attending groups received significantly less therapy than those who attended only individual sessions; this, however, is not the case. Although most treatment programs include both group and individual therapy, often it is in the group that the client or patient makes the most progress toward significant therapeutic movement. Why is this? Essentially because man is an indivisible, social, decision-making being whose actions have a social purpose (Dreikurs & Sonstegard, 1968). This is also true for chemically dependent clients; however, they have often had very poor experiences in social relationships and desperately need positive social interaction to enable them to give up the self-destructive patterns of chemical use that have developed over a lifetime.

Fulfilling Individual Needs Through the Group

To be more specific, individual needs that can potentially be fulfilled in the group include:

- The need to belong, to find a place, and to be accepted as one is.
- Affection needs—to be loved and to be able to provide love; the opportunity to have a therapeutic effect on others.
- The opportunity to engage in the give-and-take that is required for the maturing of social interest and altruistic feelings.
- Help in seeing that one's problem is not unique but perhaps is universally experienced in the group.
- The opportunity to develop feelings of equality, to be part of a group regardless of what one brings to it in terms of intellect or affect.
- The need to develop one's identity and work out an approach to the various social tasks of life (Dinkmeyer & Muro, 1979).

Each theoretical approach to group counseling (e.g., transactional analysis, rational emotive therapy, behavioral therapy) provides its own rationale for using groups as a therapeutic technique. Each type of group (e.g., encounter groups, t-groups, educational groups) has separate reasons why it should be used. It is not appropriate in this chapter to detail when, and why, each different type of group or theoretical model should be used. However, it is important to note that the reason a counselor chooses to use groups as part of a treatment plan should be congruent with the type of group chosen. For example, if one of the major individual treatment goals is to build self-esteem, a group that involves a great deal of personal confrontation might not be the most appropriate type of group to reach this goal; a more supportive group would be more appropriate.

The answer to the original question becomes this: the chemical dependency counselor should consider the use of group therapy as part of an overall treatment plan because it is economically the best use of his time, and groups are often the best method for reaching many of the social goals of a complete treatment plan for the chemically dependent client.

ADVANTAGES OF GROUPS

Therapeutic groups have certain distinct advantages over other intervention strategies. As listed by Corey and Corey (1977) these advantages include:

- Participants are able to explore their style of relating to others and to learn more effective social skills.

- The group setting offers support for new behavior and encourages experimentation.
- There is a re-creation of the everyday world in some groups, particularly if the membership is diverse with respect to age, interests, background, socioeconomic status, and type of problem. When this occurs, a member has the unique advantage of being in contact with a wide range of personalities, and the feedback received can be richer and more diverse than that available in a one-to-one setting.
- Certain factors that facilitate personal growth are more likely to exist in groups. For instance, in groups, members have the opportunity to learn about themselves through the experience of others, to experience emotional closeness and caring that encourage meaningful disclosure of self, and to identify with the struggles of other members.

LIMITATIONS OF GROUPS

While there are some distinct advantages to group methods, there are some limitations to the effectiveness of therapeutic groups.

- Groups are not "cure-alls." Unfortunately, some practitioners and participants view groups as the exclusive means of changing people's behavior. Worse yet, some hope that a brief and intense group experience can remake people's lives. Counseling and therapy are difficult forms of work, and we believe that shortcuts are not necessarily fruitful.
- There is often a subtle pressure to conform to group norms and expectations. Group participants sometimes unquestioningly substitute group norms for norms they had unquestioningly acquired in the first place.
- Some people become hooked and make the group experience an end in itself. Instead of using the group as a laboratory for human learning and as a place where they can learn behavior that will facilitate their day-to-day living, they stop short, savoring the delights of the group for its own sake.
- Not all people are suited to groups. The idea that groups are for everybody has done serious harm to the reputation of the group movement. Some people are too suspicious, or too hostile, or too fragile to benefit from a group experience. Some individuals are psychologically damaged by attending certain groups. Before a person is accepted into a group, the factors need to be carefully weighed by both the counselor and the client to increase the likelihood that the person will benefit from such an experience.
- Some people have made the group a place to ventilate their miseries and be rewarded for "baring their soul." Unfortunately, some use groups as a vehicle

for expressing their woes, in the hope that they will be understood and totally accepted, and make no attempt to do what is necessary to effect substantial change in their lives (Corey & Corey, 1977).

The chemical dependency counselor who knows the most about the different types of groups and the different theoretical approaches will be the most effective at helping chemically dependent persons reach their treatment goals.

TYPES OF GROUPS

There are many different types of groups, as well as many different theoretical approaches to groups. It would go beyond our purpose here to list and describe all of them, but we will mention a few. One of the major types of groups that the chemical dependency counselor is likely to become involved with is the treatment group, often used during an inpatient treatment program in conjunction with individual therapy. Sometimes these groups are used to "break the denial" of the patient, using heavy confrontation by the group leader and other group members: sometimes this is called the "hot seat method." Often this simply leads to compliance rather than to the individual actually getting in touch with the reality of his chemical dependency; it becomes easier for the patient to falsely admit to alcohol or drug dependence than to be confronted by the group. This might be one reason for a high dropout or recidivism rate among chemically dependent clients in treatment. An alternative to the "hot seat" model might be a less threatening, more supportive group that would allow patients to explore their life situations with honest and open feedback. Certainly not all therapy groups that use confrontation conclude with high dropout rates and recidivism; the majority are supportive as well as confrontational and end with a positive result. It is important, however, to remember that groups can be harmful as well as helpful, and that extremes, whether in confrontation or support, are subject to negative results.

Educational Groups

The second type of group often used in the treatment of chemical dependency is the educational group. This is a modified lecture format, where patients learn about new ways to look at old problems. For example, a group topic might be sex and recovery. The facilitator or group leader might make several remarks about the importance of sex and its relationship to the recovery process and then lead a discussion among group members about the topic. These groups are often very meaningful to the members, both from the perspective of the information they provide and from the feeling of having shared problems with other group members. Members often find they are not, as they thought, the only ones with a particular problem.

Self-Help Groups

Another type of group that helps members not to feel alone with their problem is the "self-help group." The "self-help group" has a long and successful history in the field of chemical dependency. Many people are sober and leading productive lives as a result of groups such as AA and Narcotics Anonymous. If these groups are so successful, why should the chemical dependency counselor bother with any other type of group? There are several reasons. First, it is unclear just how many people respond to the self-help group. It would be safe to assume that there are people who attend one or more of these groups but who do not get sober or lead productive lives. It would also be safe to assume that some members of these groups are sober yet not happy or fully functioning. The group members themselves have coined a name for such people—"the dry drunk." Self-help groups are self-selective; that is to say, the membership is made up of people who want to be members and who are willing to follow the guidelines of the group. Those who are not successful at doing either of these usually do not maintain attendance or membership. Therefore, only those who are successful remain members, which accounts for the high degree of success reported among members. The reality is that in the United States there are over 10 million alcoholics and drug dependent individuals, and, thus far, only about 1 million of those have been successful in self-help groups. Self-help groups should be an adjunct to, not a substitute for, therapy groups. For a discussion of why self-help groups work for some and fail to work for others, see Lawson, Peterson, and Lawson, *Alcoholism and the Family: A Guide to Treatment and Prevention*, Aspen, 1983. For further information see Ward, *Alcoholism: Introduction to Theory and Treatment*, Chapter 9, Kendall/ Hunt, 1980.

Aftercare Groups

Perhaps a blend of the qualities of the self-help group and the therapy group has been reached in the aftercare group. These groups are used to support the chemically dependent person after inpatient treatment and are sometimes offered in conjunction with individual outpatient counseling. Unlike the self-help groups, they usually have a trained group leader and an identified goal, possibly stated in the client treatment plan. The aftercare group can be run using any number of theoretical models. For example, social therapy as conceptualized by Rudolf Dreikurs would seem an excellent approach. A brochure from the Dreikurs Institute for Social Equality* lists these goals of social therapy:

---

*This brochure is available from the Rudolf Dreikurs Institute for Social Equality, 725 Emerson Ave. South, Minneapolis, MN 55403.

- to develop a sense of belonging, not isolation
- to learn to consider alternative solutions to problems
- to learn to function as a decision-making person
- to learn to express frustration or annoyance without blaming someone else
- to rediscover your strengths, learn to build upon them, and help others do the same
- to learn to take feedback about yourself
- to gain perspective on your own life style
- to rediscover your sense of humor

The Behavioral Approach to Groups

Some good reasons have also been presented to use a behavioral approach in groups. According to Varenhorst (1969, p. 131), the behaviorist use of learning principles in group process makes groups more effective than individual therapy because:

- There is a greater variety of models within a group.
- There are greater numbers of sources of reinforcement within the group.
- There are more opportunities for creating realistic social enactments whereby role rehearsal can be practiced, changed, and strengthened.
- There is an immediate situation in which generalization as well as discrimination can be learned with greater efficiency.
- Membership in the group itself can be utilized as a powerful reinforcing agency.

The behaviorists suggest that persons in groups need to perform certain specific behaviors. They are:

- Share feelings openly.
- Suggest ideas and actions.
- Reinforce others as the need occurs.
- Give feedback.
- Participate in demonstrations or role playing of alternative actions.
- Be willing to accompany group members on assignments outside of the group.
- Make a commitment to one's goals and the purposes of the group.

These are only a few of the many possible theoretical approaches to groups. Whether the chemical dependency counselor leads a treatment group, an educational group, an aftercare group, or another type of group, several theoretical approaches should be explored in an attempt to find the one most compatible with the group goals and the skills and style of the facilitator. Besides the ones mentioned above, a chemical dependency counselor might consider these additional theoretical models:

- Transactional analysis (TA) groups
- Group-centered or humanistic groups
- Gestalt groups
- Rationale emotive therapy groups
- T-groups
- Reality therapy groups

WHAT IS THERAPEUTIC ABOUT GROUPS?

In one of the most widely read and quoted books ever written about groups, Yalom (1975) has identified 11 curative factors of groups: they are presented here with regard to the chemically dependent client. The first of these is the instillation of hope. This is a crucial factor in the treatment of chemically dependent clients because, so often, they have given up all hope. They have tried many things to deal with their condition, without success. The family doctor, their minister or priest, self-control, and all manner of internal and external assistance for the problem have been sought and tried. Hope is important for several reasons: it keeps the patient in therapy, and fosters high expectations, which have been shown to correlate highly with success. In other words, the more a person believes in a treatment approach the more likely it is to work. By observing the improvement of other group members, each member draws hope from the other members: thus, hope can be enhanced in chemical dependency groups by including beginning patients in groups that also include patients more advanced in treatment.

The second curative factor is universality, that is to say, a sense of shared problems. Often chemically dependent persons enter therapy with the disturbing thought that they are the only ones alive with their particular problem; they are plagued with the thought that what they have experienced is unacceptable. Usually, just realizing they are not unique in their problems is a powerful source of relief. After hearing others disclose problems similar to their own, group members report feeling more in touch with the world and, simply put, the feeling "we are all in the same boat" is very comforting. Statements reinforcing this by the group leader are effective in chemical dependency groups.

The next curative factor (the third) is imparting of information. This includes information about chemical dependency (the dynamics involved in the chemical dependency condition as well as advice to clients about how to cope with their problems) offered by the group facilitator or other group members. It is important for the group leader to be aware of the group member who seeks advice from other group members, only to reject their advice: this should be pointed out to that member. Other dynamics include making a bid for attention and nurturance by constantly asking for group suggestions for a problem that is insoluble or that has already been solved. Other types of groups give advice and guidance directly through slogans (for example, "one day at a time," asking that the person remain sober for only the next 24 hours). There is much misinformation and myth regarding chemical dependency; the counselor should have accurate facts in this area.

The fourth curative factor is altruism. Simply put, you receive through giving. When a group member is able to help another group member, it is hard to distinguish who receives the most benefit from the exchange. There is nothing that does more to build self-esteem than the act of unselfishly giving help to another. This wisdom has long been shared and proven by AA, with the 12th step—"We try to carry this message to alcoholics." Many an alcoholic has maintained a high level of sobriety by helping others. In short, people need to feel needed; the group can fulfill this need.

The fifth curative factor is described as the corrective recapitulation of the *primary family group*. Without exception, chemically dependent persons enter group therapy with a history of a highly unsatisfactory experience in their first and most important group—their family of origin. Over half of those who enter treatment have parents who themselves are chemically dependent. For many patients, working out problems with therapists and other group members is also working through unfinished business from long ago. The role of the family is explained in more detail in Chapter 5.

The development of a socializing technique (the sixth factor) includes the development of basic social skills. Many chemically dependent persons either never learned basic social skills or lost them sometime during their period of chemical abuse. For these people, the group often represents the first opportunity for accurate interpersonal feedback. The changes gained in the level of social skills are not an end in themselves, but they are often exceedingly instrumental in the initial phases of therapeutic change.

It is often apparent that senior members of a group have acquired some highly sophisticated social skills. They are aware of group process and have learned how to be helpfully responsive to others. They have also acquired methods of conflict resolution and are less prone to be judgmental. They are more capable of experiencing and expressing accurate empathy. These skills cannot but help to improve their future social interactions; these members should be pointed out and offered as models of behavior for newer group members.

Initiating behavior (the seventh factor) is an important therapeutic force. The healthy behavior of the group leader often becomes the model for the rest of the group. Imitating another group member, even it turns out that the role doesn't fit, is a therapeutic process. Learning what one is not is often progress toward learning what one is.

The next two curative factors as listed by Yalom are interpersonal learning and group cohesiveness (the eighth and ninth factors); he includes an entire chapter on each of these concepts. Interpersonal learning involves the corrective emotional experience involved in a group as well as the therapeutic value of experiencing the group as a social microcosm. Group cohesiveness includes the source of stability that one feels from being a part of a cohesive group. This has been described as a "oneness" with the group.

Catharsis (the tenth factor) has assumed the role of a therapeutic process from the early time of Freud. This is the purging of oneself to cleanse away excessive emotions. But this expulsion alone is not enough; it is the process of "learning how to express feelings" that is the most therapeutic aspect of catharsis, not the expulsion itself.

Finally, the existential factors of group therapy (the eleventh category) are considered. This is basically a compilation of factors not included in the categories above. There are five of them, and they seem particularly important for the chemically dependent client. They are:

1. Recognizing that life is at times unfair and unjust;
2. Recognizing that ultimately there is no escape from some of life's pain and from death;
3. Recognizing that no matter how close I get to other people, I still face life alone;
4. Facing the basic issues of my life and death, and thus living my life more honestly and being less caught up in trivialities;
5. Learning that I must take ultimate responsibility for the way I live my life, no matter how much guidance and support I get from others.

This has been a brief discussion of the concepts discussed in detail by Yalom; it is highly recommended that the chemical dependency counselor read his book in its entirety.

Other Therapeutic Factors in Groups

The ideas of Corey and Corey (1977), who have also addressed the issue of therapeutic factors that operate in groups, bear mentioning here. Although there is some overlap between these factors and the ones listed above, they are worthy of listing again:

- *Hope*. This is a belief that change is possible—that one is not a victim of the past and that new decisions can be made. Hope is therapeutic in itself, for it gives members confidence that they have the power to choose to be different.

- *Commitment to change*. A resolve to change is also therapeutic in itself. If one is motivated to the point of becoming an active group participant, the chances are good that change will occur. This commitment to change involves a willingness to specify what changes are desired and to make use of the tools offered by group process to explore ways of modifying one's behavior.

- *Willingness to risk and trust*. Risking involves opening oneself to others, being vulnerable, and actively doing in a group that which is necessary for change. The willingness to reveal oneself is largely a function of how much one trusts the other group members and the group leader. Trust is therapeutic, for it allows persons to show the many facets of themselves, encourages experimental behavior, and allows persons to look at themselves in new ways.

- *Care*. Caring is demonstrated by the listening and involvement of others. It can be expressed by tenderness, compassion, support, and even confrontation. If members sense a lack of caring from either group members or the group leader, their willingness to lower their masks will be reduced. Clients are able to risk being vulnerable if they sense that their concerns are important to others and that they are valued as persons.

- *Acceptance*. This involves a genuine support from others that says, in effect, "We will accept all of your feelings. You do count here. It's OK to be yourself—you don't have to strive to please everyone." Acceptance involves affirming a person's right to have his own feelings and values and to express them.

- *Empathy*. A true sense of empathy involves a deep understanding of another's struggles. In groups, commonalities emerge that unite the members. The realization that certain problems—such as loneliness, the need for acceptance, fear of rejection, fear of intimacy, and hurt over past experiences—are universal, lessens the feeling that one is alone. And, through identification with others, one is able to see oneself more clearly.

- *Intimacy*. People are able to experience closeness in a group, and from this intimacy develops a new sense of trust in others. Participants may become aware, after experiencing this feeling of closeness to others, that there are barriers in their outside lives that prevent intimacy.

- *Power*. This feeling emerges from the recognition that one has untapped reserves of spontaneity, creativity, courage, and strength. In groups, personal power may be experienced in ways that were formerly denied, and persons can discover ways in which they block their strengths. This power is not a power over others; rather, it is the sense that one has the internal resources necessary to direct the course of one's life.

- *Freedom to experiment.* The group situation provides a safe place for experimentation with new behavior. After trying new behavior, persons can gauge how much they want to change their existing behavior.

- *Feedback.* Members determine the effects of their behavior on others from the feedback they receive. If feedback is given honestly and with care, members are able to understand more clearly the impact they have on others. Then it is up to them to decide what to do with this feedback.

- *Catharsis.* The expression of pent-up feelings can be therapeutic in that energy can be released that has been tied up in withholding certain threatening feelings. Catharsis may allow a person to realize that negative and positive feelings toward others may coexist. A woman may be suppressing a great deal of resentment toward her mother, and, by releasing it, may discover a need for her mother's affection and a feeling of love for her mother.

- *The cognitive component.* Catharsis is even more useful if a person attempts to find words to explain the feelings expressed. Some conceptualization of the meaning of intense feelings associated with certain experiences can give one the tools to make significant changes.

- *Learning interpersonal skills.* Participants in groups can discover ways of enhancing their interpersonal relationships. Thus, a woman who feels isolated from others may come to understand concrete things she does that lead to these feelings and may learn to lessen this isolation by asking others for what she needs.

- *Humor.* Laughing at oneself can be extremely therapeutic. This requires seeing one's problems in a different perspective. Thus, a man who sees himself as stupid may eventually be able to laugh at the stupidity of continually convincing himself he's stupid. People who are able to laugh at themselves are better able to cope with seeing themselves clearly.

- *Group cohesion.* A group is characterized by a high degree of "togetherness" at times, providing a climate in which participants feel free to share problems, try new behaviors, and in other ways reveal the many dimensions of themselves. Group cohesion is influenced by many variables, a few of which are the attraction of the group for its members, the enthusiasm of the leaders, the trust level of the group, and the extent to which the members identify with one another.

To further conceptualize what is therapeutic about group therapy, Corey and Corey have asked group members what they had learned through the group process. Their responses were:

- Others will care for me if I allow them to.
- I'm not alone in my pain.
- I'm not helpless, as I had convinced myself I was.
- I don't need to be liked by everyone.
- It's not too late to change if I want to.
- The choice is mine if I want more from others.
- Experiencing intense feelings will not make me crazy.
- There are others close to me, and I need not feel isolated.
- I alone am responsible for my misery.
- I can trust people, and this trust can be freeing.
- I do have options.
- Whether I change or not depends on my decisions.
- Being spontaneous is fun.
- I'm a lot more attractive than I gave myself credit for.
- I'll never be truly accepted unless I'm willing to risk rejection.
- I get from a group what I put into it.
- My greatest fears did not come true when I revealed myself.
- I'm more lovable than I thought I was.
- I need to ask others for what I want and need.
- I'm hopeful about the future, even though it may involve struggle.
- Some degree of risk and uncertainty is necessary—there are no guarantees.
- I'm able to identify with the emotions of others; regardless of age, there is a common bond linking humanity.
- Intimacy is frightening, but it's worth it.
- Decisions about my behavior must come from within and not from the group members or leaders.
- Making changes takes sustained effort.
- People can be beautiful and creative when they shed their masks.
- It takes a great deal of effort to maintain a facade.

It can be concluded that the goal of a group is to provide its members with the therapeutic factors discussed above. But, to maximize the use of these therapeutic forces, it is wise to be even more specific about group goals.

GROUP GOALS AND OBJECTIVES

For the chemically dependent client the group provides a chance for self-exploration that can lead to a reassessment of one's values and behaviors. This process should be an invitation to examine seriously a segment of one's selfhood or behavior. It is up to the group member to decide what, how much, and when he wishes to explore and change; if this invitation becomes a command, the likelihood of real self-exploration is diminished. Far too many chemical dependency counselors believe that clients need to be coerced or forced to look at themselves before they will avail themselves of this opportunity. Chemically dependent clients are in a great deal of pain—emotionally, physically, and spiritually. Given the opportunity of self-exploration and change by a group leader who is accepting and permissive, and at the same time confronting and encountering, the chemically dependent person will most often welcome the opportunity to change.

Goals for Group Members

Some specific goals that are appropriate for any type of group and are universal to all group members have been listed by Corey and Corey (1977). They include:

- becoming more open and honest with selected others
- decreasing game playing and manipulation, which prevent intimacy
- learning how to trust oneself and others
- moving toward authenticity and genuineness
- becoming freer and less bound by external "shoulds," "oughts," and "musts"
- growing in self-acceptance and learning not to demand perfection of oneself
- recognizing and accepting certain polarities within oneself
- lessening one's fear of intimacy and learning to reach out to those one would like to be closer to
- moving away from merely meeting others' expectations and deciding for oneself the standards that will guide one
- learning how to ask directly for what one wants
- increasing self-awareness and thereby increasing the possibilities for choice and action
- learning the distinction between having feelings and acting on them
- freeing oneself from the inappropriate early decisions that keep one less than the person one could or would like to be
- recognizing that others struggle too
- clarifying the values one has and deciding whether and how to modify them
- becoming able to tolerate more ambiguity; learning to make choices in a world where nothing is guaranteed
- finding ways of resolving personal problems
- exploring hidden potentials and creativity

- increasing one's capacity to care for others
- learning how to give to others
- becoming more sensitive to the needs and feelings of others

All of these are appropriate goals for the chemically dependent person.

Goals for Group Leaders

Dinkmeyer and Muro (1979) have listed ten specific goals for group leaders. They are:

1. To help each member of the group know and understand himself and to assist with the identity-seeking process.
2. As a result of coming to understand self, to help individuals develop increased self-acceptance and feelings of personal worth.
3. To develop social skills and interpersonal abilities that enable members to cope with the developmental tasks in their personal and social areas.
4. To develop increased self-direction, problem-solving, and decision-making abilities, and to help members transfer these abilities to use in regular work and social contacts.
5. To develop sensitivity to the needs of others, resulting in increased recognition of responsibility for one's behavior. To help members become able to identify with the feelings of significant others as well as to develop a greater capacity for empathy.
6. To help members learn to be empathic listeners who not only hear what is said but also recognize the feelings that accompany what has been said.
7. To help members develop the ability to be congruent with self, able to offer accurately what they think and believe.
8. To help members formulate specific goals that can be measured and observed behaviorally, and to help them make a commitment to move toward those goals.
9. To help members develop a feeling of belonging and acceptance by others that provides security in meeting the challenges of life.
10. To help members develop courage and the ability to take rational social risks and to show them that it is rewarding to risk and grow through sharing.

Guidelines for Group Leaders

At this point it will be helpful to list some guidelines for chemical dependency counselors to follow when leading a group. Corey and Corey (1977) have listed these:

- It is important to teach group process to the members. This need not involve giving a lecture; rather, issues can be discussed as they arise in the course of a group.
- The issue of confidentiality should be emphasized in the group. The dangers of inappropriate sharing of what occurs during a session need to be highlighted, and members need to have an opportunity to express their fears or reservations concerning the respect of the rest of the group for the disclosures that are made.
- Instead of talking about a group member, the leader and other members should speak directly to the person in question.
- Each member is free to decide for himself what issues to work on in the group, and each person may decide how to explore a problem. A person's right to say "I pass" should be respected. It is the member who is responsible for the decision to disclose or not to disclose.
- Confrontation is an essential ingredient in most groups, but members must learn how to confront others in a responsible manner. Essentially, confrontation is a challenge from another to look at the discrepancy between what one says and what one does, or to examine the degree to which one is being honest.
- Questioning is more often a distraction than a help in group process, and members should be warned of this. Generally, questions of a probing nature have the effect of pulling the questioned participant away from the experience of feeling. Asking questions can generate a never-ending series of "whys" and "becauses." It is an impersonal way of relating that keeps the questioner at a safe distance.
- If members are to engage in any personal work, it is imperative that a climate of trust and support be established. If people feel they can be themselves and be respected for what they feel, they are far more inclined to take the risk of sharing intimate aspects of themselves than if they expect to be harshly judged.
- Members need to learn how to listen without thinking of a quick rebuttal and without becoming overly defensive. We don't encourage people to accept everything they hear, but we do ask them to really hear what others say to them and to seriously consider these messages—particularly those messages that are repeated consistently.
- The issue of how what is learned in a group can be translated into out-of-group behavior should be given priority. Contracts and homework assignments can help members carry the new behaviors they develop in a group into their daily lives.

By following these guidelines the counselor should achieve the group's goals. It is worth mentioning here that just reading this material will not make a person an excellent group counselor; practice and experience, along with the supervision of a well-trained supervisor, are essential. However, there are certain individuals who learn group counseling more readily than others (those who are almost naturally therapeutic and who have very little problem learning the group model). There are also those who find it difficult to lead a successful group.

THE GROUP LEADER

It is oversimplistic to say that a good group leader is one who has good leadership skills. But the fact remains that this is true; what separates those who are therapeutic from those who are not is their leadership skills level. This discussion, then, becomes one of what are good leadership skills, not what is a good leader. In terms of such factors as client satisfaction, smooth group operation, and positive client change, the following skills are offered by Dinkmeyer and Muro (1979). They are discussed here in terms of the chemical dependency counselor.

- *Effective group counselors are able to develop trust in the group.* Without a sense of trust, no group can be successful. A trusting counselor invites trust in the group members. If the counselor does not trust the group members to make decisions in their own best interest, they will not do so. Trust also means that the counselor and group will not use results of their interaction to hurt each other. The cohesion that develops in a group is not a license for manipulating others to fit the mores of a culture or subculture. The counselor who earns the confidence of the group can, in turn, help each member gain the self-confidence necessary for positive growth.
- *Effective group counselors are skilled listeners.* The term "active listeners" can be applied here. This means that the counselor hears not only the words but also the emotional tone in which the words are spoken; this is more than what happens in a day-to-day conversation. Counselors who listen actively are interested in group members and are willing to give of themselves to those who need help.
- *Effective group counselors are able to develop mutual group and idiosyncratic goals.* If a group member has as a goal the exploration of the possibility of controlled drinking in the future, and a major goal of the group leader is total abstinence for all members, neither the group leader nor the group member is likely to meet his goals. In group counseling, as in individual counseling, the goal is not necessarily first and foremost to change behavior; this is difficult for chemical dependency counselors to accept. When it is obvious to all but a

particular group member that chemical use is causing that group member continued problems, it is easy for the group leader and members to insist on abstinence as the primary goal for this individual. However, unless the individual has accepted this goal, it is likely that he will leave the group feeling out of place, and identified by other group members as not ready to work on his problem. This person may have been ready to work on "his problem," as he saw it. In this instance the group might have been able to influence an attitude change and thus a change of goals and behavior. But if the original goals are not accepted by the group and the member does not return to the group, there will be no continued group influence. It is essential for the group leader and the group members to be flexible and to come to mutually agreeable goals.

• *Effective group counselors are spontaneous and responsive.* Responses should be natural and direct, yet they must not harm any member of the group. In individual counseling the counselor can take time to ponder and speculate about a comment or technique; the group rarely allows time for this. The group counselor must rely on an immediate, intuitive, honest reaction. Those who lack spontaneity will likely find group counseling difficult.

• *Effective group counselors can be firm.* The counselor's firmness lies in encouraging the group to recognize him as the leader and the central figure in the group. As such, the leader must minister to the needs of all members, challenging some, encouraging others, and blocking or reducing the potential impact of harmful interaction. The counselor must not use the group to meet personal needs but must be willing to change, grow, and learn. By combining firmness with spontaneity, humor, and empathy, the group leader becomes a real person rather than a manipulator of desired behavioral norms.

• *Effective group counselors have a sense of humor.* The treatment of the chemically dependent person is often perceived as a somber, serious business. Indeed, at times it is, but there are other times in the life of the client that call for appropriate laughter. The ability to laugh shows that the counselor is a genuine individual who is capable of expressing a full range of emotions. This is an appropriate model for group members.

• *Effective group counselors are perceived by group members as being with them and for them as individuals.* Successful group counselors are able to convey an attitude of care and concern for each group member. Group members should not see the counselor as ranking them as better or worse along any given dimension. For example, group members cannot be told that they have complete freedom to discuss whatever they wish and then find that the counselor is more interested in Helen's sex problem than in Bob's drinking problem. Success in group counseling is a product of strong, mutual liking and respect between the counselor and each group member and among the various members. No counselor who cares little for the group members will earn their respect or care.

EVALUATING GROUP COUNSELING SKILLS

The skills mentioned above (and, in fact, all the group counseling skills) should be thought of as existing in various degrees rather than on an all-or-none basis (that is, they may be highly, or only minimally, developed). Corey and Corey (1977) have developed rating scales for counselors to rate themselves and for group members to rate group leaders. These scales are most beneficial for counselors who wish to improve their skills and are included here with that purpose in mind.

Self-Rating Scale

Rate yourself from 1 to 7 on the following items:

$$1 = \text{I am very poor at this.}$$
$$7 = \text{I am very good at this.}$$

1. *Active listening:* I am able to hear and understand both direct and subtle messages.
2. *Reflecting:* I can mirror what another says, without being mechanical.
3. *Clarifying:* I can focus on underlying issues and assist others to get a clear picture of some of their conflicting feelings.
4. *Summarizing:* When I function as a group leader, I'm able to identify key elements of a session and to present them as a summary of the proceedings.
5. *Interpreting:* I can present a hunch to someone concerning the reason for his behavior without dogmatically stating what the behavior was.
6. *Questioning:* I avoid bombarding people with questions about their behavior.
7. *Linking:* I find ways of relating what one person is doing or saying to the concerns of other members.
8. *Confronting:* When I confront another, the confrontation usually has the effect of getting the person to look at his behavior in a nondefensive manner.
9. *Supporting:* I'm usually able to tell when supporting another will be productive and when it will be counterproductive.
10. *Blocking:* I'm able to intervene successfully, without seeming to be attacking, to stop counterproductive behaviors (such as gossiping, storytelling, and intellectualizing) in the group.

11. *Diagnosing:* I can generally get a sense of what specific problems people have, without feeling the need to label people.
12. *Evaluating:* I appraise outcomes when I'm in a group, and I make some comments concerning the ongoing process of any group I'm in.
13. *Facilitating:* In a group, I'm able to help others openly express themselves and work through barriers to communication.
14. *Empathizing:* I can intuitively sense the subjective world of others in a group, and I have the capacity to understand much of what others are experiencing.
15. *Terminating:* At the end of group sessions, I'm able to create a climate that will foster a willingness in others to continue working after the session.

Rating Scale for Group Counselors

The following evaluation form can be used in several ways. Group leaders can use it as a self-evaluation device, supervisors can use it to evaluate group leaders in training, group leaders can use it to evaluate their coleaders, and group members can use it to evaluate their leader.

Rate the leader from 1 to 7 on the following items:

1 = to an extremely low degree.
7 = to an extremely high degree.

1. *Support:* To what degree does the group leader allow clients to express their feelings?
2. *Interpretation:* To what degree is the group leader able to explain the meaning of behavior patterns within the framework of the theoretical system?
3. *Confrontation:* To what degree is the group leader able to actively and directly confront a client when the client engages in behavior that is inconsistent with what he says?
4. *Modeling:* To what degree is the group leader able to demonstrate to members behaviors he wishes them to emulate and practice both during and after the session?
5. *Assignment:* To what degree is the group leader able to direct clients to improve on existing behavior patterns or to develop new behaviors before the next group session?
6. *Referral:* To what degree is the group leader able to make available to clients persons capable of further assisting clients with personal concerns?
7. *Role direction:* To what degree is the group leader able to direct clients to enact specific roles in role-playing situations?

8. *Empathy:* To what degree does the group leader demonstrate the ability to adopt the internal frame of reference of a client and communicate to the client that he is understood?

9. *Self-disclosure:* To what degree does the group leader demonstrate a willingness and ability to reveal his own present feelings and thoughts to clients when it is appropriate to the group counseling situation?

10. *Initiation:* To what degree is the group leader able to initiate interaction among members or between leader and members?

11. *Facilitation:* To what degree is the group leader able to help clients clarify their own goals and take steps to reach these goals?

12. *Diagnosis:* To what degree is the group leader able to identify specific areas of struggle and conflict within each client?

13. *Following through:* To what degree is the group leader able to implement (and follow through to a reasonable completion) work with a client in an area that the client has expressed a desire to explore?

14. *Active listening:* To what degree does the group leader actively and fully listen to and hear the subtle messages communicated by clients?

15. *Knowledge of theory:* To what degree does the group leader demonstrate a theoretical understanding of group dynamics, interpersonal dynamics, and behavior in general?

16. *Application of theory to practice:* To what degree is the group leader able to appropriately apply a given theory to an actual group situation?

17. *Perceptivity and insight:* To what degree is the group leader able to sensitively and accurately extract the core meanings from verbal and nonverbal communications?

18. *Risk taking:* To what degree is the group leader able to risk making mistakes and to profit from mistakes?

19. *Expression:* To what degree is the group leader able to express thoughts and feelings directly and clearly to clients?

20. *Originality:* To what degree does the group leader seem to have synthesized a personal approach from a variety of approaches to group leadership?

21. *Group dynamics:* To what degree is the group leader able to assist a group of people to work effectively together?

22. *Cooperation as a coleader:* To what degree is the group leader able to work cooperatively with a coleader?

23. *Content orientation:* To what degree is the group leader able to help group members focus on specific themes in a structured type of group experience?

24. *Values awareness:* To what degree is the group leader aware of his own value system and of the client's value system, and to what degree is he able to avoid imposing his values on the client?

25. *Flexibility:* To what degree is the group leader able to change approaches— to modify style and technique—to adapt to each unique working situation?

26. *Awareness of self:* To what degree is the group leader aware of his own needs, motivations, and problems, and to what degree does the leader avoid exploiting or manipulating clients to satisfy these needs?
27. *Respect:* To what degree does the group leader communicate an attitude of respect for the dignity and autonomy of the client?
28. *Care:* To what degree does the group leader communicate an attitude of genuine caring for the client?
29. *Techniques:* To what degree is the group leader knowledgeable of techniques and able to use them well and appropriately to help clients work through conflicts and concerns?
30. *Ethical awareness:* To what degree does the group leader demonstrate awareness of, and sensitivity to, the demands of professional responsibility?

CHOOSING GROUP MEMBERS

In reality the chemical dependency counselor often has very little choice about what clients or patients become group members. Inpatient drug and alcohol treatment programs routinely include patients in group therapy as a part of the total treatment program. All of those in treatment attend groups. Whenever possible, however, the chemical dependency counselor can maximize the group's effectiveness by carefully selecting group members. Referrals to self-help groups after, or in conjunction with, treatment should also be done in a selective manner.

For example, despite the widespread recognition that AA has enjoyed an exceedingly fine success rate (and AA itself has spread widely throughout the world), it must also be recognized that the traditional precepts of AA as spelled out in the 12 steps have no appeal for, and may even antagonize, the patient in some populations. More specifically, the traditional AA group may be problematic for some people. Heath (1981) has reported that some years ago a Navajo Indian made the simple, but eloquent, point that "it's not right to tell all them personal things, about what I did to my wife and how I argued with her father, and all that." And by contrast, in a Costa Rican community many problem drinkers were willing, even eager, to publicly confess the injuries they had caused others but could not accept the principle of surrender. As one Costa Rican put it, "Damn, I'm not about to admit that alcohol is stronger than I am. What kind of a man would say that? . . . One's purpose should be again to be strong like a man, to overcome this alcohol with one's own forces."

In instances such as these, routine referrals to self-help groups might be unwise. Who belongs in what group? How does one determine what combinations of individuals produce optimal conditions for maximum effectiveness? The first approach one might take is to decide whom to *exclude* from the group. All manner of individuals have been recommended for exclusion from the group: these include psychotics or prepsychotics, those who are brain damaged, paranoid, extremely narcissistic, hypochondriacal, or suicidal, and even those addicted to drugs or alcohol. For obvious reasons it would be impossible for the chemical dependency counselor to exclude all of these as group members.

The best approach might be to include individuals who meet the following criteria:

1. They have a sense of reality;
2. They can be related to interpersonally;
3. They have sufficient flexibility to help reduce, or to heighten, intragroup tensions; and
4. They can serve, at times, as a catalyst for the group.

Motivation is another factor to consider; however, many seemingly unmotivated persons have become motivated as a result of their group experience. It would be a mistake to assume that because people do not admit to being "alcoholic" or "drug dependent" they do not desire or value personal change. (It may be that they are unwilling to pay the price of *admitting* to chemical dependency.) They may also view themselves as deficient in understanding their own feelings or the feelings of others. Admitting one's problems is a step toward solving those problems, but it is not the only step or necessarily the first step. The first step may be examining those problems, and this can be effectively done in a group. It is important for group members to express satisfaction with their group if they are to continue membership. Members continue membership if:

- They view the group as meeting their personal needs.
- They derive satisfaction from their relationship with group members.
- They derive satisfaction from their participation in the group task.
- They derive satisfaction from group membership vis-à-vis the outside world.

Heterogeneous vs. Homogeneous Groups

There is another factor that should be considered here: should the group be homogeneous, or heterogeneous, in makeup? That is, should groups be made up of members with similar problems and backgrounds or different problems and backgrounds? With regard to the chemically dependent client there are some definite advantages to homogeneous groups. They include:

- Group identification takes place rapidly.
- Reeducation takes place rapidly, and insight develops quickly.

- Psychodynamics are laid bare more rapidly.
- Duration of treatment is lessened.
- Attendance is more regular.
- Interferences, resistances, and interactions of a destructive nature are lessened.
- Intragroup cliques are uncommon.
- Recovery from symptoms is more rapid.

There are advantages to heterogeneity within groups as well, but for the chemically dependent client the advantages of a homogeneous group are far greater. Yalom (1975) has also cited alcoholics as an example of a population that does poorly in mixed intensive outpatient group settings. This is not because of their drinking but because of their interpersonal behavior; he cites excessive nurturant needs and a low tolerance for frustration as possible reasons for this.

Yalom (1975) sees selection of group therapy members with specialized goals such as obesity, alcoholism, or addiction as relatively uncomplicated. The admission criterion, he states, may simply be the existence of the target symptom, "in this case chemical dependency."

We would again remind chemical dependency counselors that there are many different reasons why people become chemically dependent and that chemical dependency manifests itself in numerous behaviors. The counselor who remains constantly aware of this and who meets each client's needs on an individual basis (including what group to refer a client to) will have the most success. The point is, some kind of screening and selection process is necessary; counselors who don't pay attention to this phase of group work unnecessarily increase the psychological risk for the group members.

ETHICAL AND PROFESSIONAL ISSUES

The group leader is the one who is primarily responsible for the direction the group takes with regard to ethics. The group leader sets the tone and models behaviors for group members. Some issues and responsibilities that a group leader should consider are these:

- What does a group leader need to tell potential members about the group?
- Were members screened? How?
- Is group membership voluntary or involuntary?
- What does a group member need to do if he wishes to leave the group?
- Are there any consequences attached to leaving the group?

Confidentiality

Confidentiality is a major issue for the group leader. It is not only that the group leader must keep confidences but that he must get the group members to do so as well. Group leaders should emphasize the importance of confidentiality at various stages of the group's development. If, at any time, any member gives an indication that confidences have been broken, the group leader should explore this matter with the group.

Group leaders owe it to their clients to specify at the beginning of a group the limits on confidentiality. For example, a group leader should let the members know that he may be required to testify against them in court unless the leader is entitled to privileged communication. In general, licensed psychologists, psychiatrists, and licensed clinical social workers are legally entitled to privileged communications. This means that these people cannot break the confidence of a client unless in their judgment, the client (1) is a danger to himself or others or (2) may do serious harm to someone else (Corey & Corey, 1977). Many an AA meeting place has a sign that sums up confidentiality. It says: "Let what is said here stay here." That is generally good advice for group members in any group.

Psychological Risk

Another ethical and professional issue is that of psychological risk to the group members. The therapeutic forces at work in a group are powerful ones, and their unleashing involves a certain amount of risk. These forces have the potential to be just as harmful as they are helpful. The leader must not assume that the members of a group are aware of them. Members of a group may be subject to scapegoating, group pressure, breaches of confidence, inappropriate reassurance, and hostile confrontation; the group process may even precipitate a crisis in the group member's life. These hazards should be discussed and examined during the initial session, focusing on ways that these hazards can be avoided.

Evaluating Oneself As Group Leader

Another issue that the group leader must confront is that of his own competence as a group leader. Counselors should ask themselves questions such as: What kind of clients am I capable of dealing with? What are my areas of expertise? What techniques do I handle well? How far can I safely go with clients? When should I refer? Truly competent group leaders have answers for why they do what they do in a group. They can explain the theory behind their group work. They can express the goals of their group. They can provide a relationship between the way they lead a group and the goals they hope to achieve. And, finally, they know how to evaluate how well these goals are being met.

As you might imagine, one does not become an effective group leader without extensive training and experience; that is the idea that we began this chapter with and the one we will end it with. The group experience can be one of the most therapeutic tools that the chemical dependency has to work with. But it takes time and effort for the counselor to learn to maximize the group experience for the therapeutic movement of its members. However, it will be time and effort well spent.

REFERENCES

Corey, G., & Corey, M.S. *Group process and practice.* Monterey, Calif.: Brooks/Cole, 1977.

Dinkmeyer, D., & Muro, J. *Group counseling: Theory and practice.* Itaska, Ill.: Peacock Publishers, 1979.

Dreikurs, R., & Sonstegard, M. Rationale for group counseling. In D.C. Dinkmeyer (Ed.), *Guidance and counseling in the elementary school: Readings in theory and practice.* New York: Holt, Rinehart and Winston, Inc., 1968.

Heath, D.B., Waddell, J.D., & Topper, M.D. (Special Eds.). Cultural factors in alcohol research and treatment of drinking problems. *Journal of Studies on Alcohol,* 1981 Supplement, No. 9.

Varenhorst, B. Behavioral group counseling. In G.M. Gazda (Ed.), *Theories and methods of group counseling in the schools.* Springfield, Ill.: Charles C Thomas, 1969.

Ward, D. *Alcoholism: Introduction to theory and treatment.* Dubuque, Iowa: Kendall/Hunt, 1980.

Yalom, I.D. *The theory and practice of group psychotherapy.* New York: Basic Books, Inc., 1975.

SOME QUESTIONS TO CONSIDER

1. How do I feel in a group situation?
2. What are my group skills?
3. What are my personal group experiences?
4. How would they affect my group leadership style?

Chapter 7

How To Survive in a Chemical Dependency Agency

P. Clayton Rivers

Each year, new counselors enter the alcoholism treatment field. Each counselor has survived some selection process, some type of training experience, and other stress-related activity. However, many will discover that the field of alcoholism counseling is filled with experiences they did not anticipate, for which they were poorly prepared by their training. Most alcohol counselor training programs give little attention to the types of system-level problems that exist in all agencies, and they spend a minimal amount of time dealing with the system issues peculiar to alcoholism treatment agencies.

As a result of the failure to deal with these issues and to help prepare the counselor for the adjustment needed to work effectively within a given job setting, many counselors experience anxiety, frustration, and anger as they attempt to adjust to their jobs. While most of these counselors survive the process of adjustment from the idealism of training to the reality of the job place, many are unaware that the frustrations, anxieties, and self-doubts they experience are also occurring in their colleagues and thus they lose a valuable opportunity to share their feelings with others. As for those who do not survive the intensity and work demands of the alcohol work place, some leave without doubting that the job change was the correct vocational decision for them. Some leave because they cannot deal with the ambiguity or the mixed messages so frequently given in caregiving systems. Others leave with anger and, due to their frustration, display hostility toward the system. Still others leave with the feeling that they have failed in some basic and personal way, both as a human being and as a professional.

Survival is defined here as the ability to adjust to job demands without being overwhelmed by stress, i.e., avoiding burnout. It is of course possible to "survive" in an agency by simply becoming less involved with clients and disengaging from the agency, i.e., by suffering burnout. This latter condition is defined as *existence*.

This chapter addresses some of these problems and raises issues that the author has observed in his work as a staff member, an outside consultant, and a trainer of personnel in the alcoholism treatment field. The chapter will focus on issues common to most social service agencies, e.g., dealing with internal staff relations and roles, as well as those specific to alcohol agencies, e.g., dealing with the potential problems that can develop between staff members who are themselves recovering from chemical dependency (referred to here as recovering counselors) and staff members who are not (referred to here as nonrecovering counselors). Counselors should be aware that many of the specific issues they will confront may be ignored or treated too briefly in this chapter. A complete coverage of all the possible issues substance abuse counselors will confront in the job place is clearly beyond the scope of this chapter. However, it is hoped that some of the issues raised here will be helpful to counselors by making more public, and explicit, issues that were previously experienced but not articulated. Making these issues a labeled part of the experience of counselors makes it possible for much of the frustration, anxiety, and anger generated by these experiences to be shared with colleagues and dealt with as real staff maintenance issues. This awareness will improve counselors' morale and help them focus on the job of providing better services to their clients.

SOME INITIAL CONSIDERATIONS

This chapter deals with issues applicable to most social service agencies and some that are specifically relevant to the alcohol service system. We shall first turn to a consideration of issues that are applicable to most service agencies, including those in the substance abuse field.

Problems of Social Service Agencies

One of the things that you, as a counselor, may not be initially aware of is that like your clients, the agency you work in has its own ability to adjust and meet its problems or to behave in irrational and destructive ways. There are several reasons why social service agencies may have more problems than agencies not dealing with the personal problems of people. These considerations are discussed below.

Daily Demands of Clients

Frequently clients attempt to set one staff member up against another either to get something they want or to vent unresolved hostility. Because clients may have dealt with many agencies in the past, they frequently have developed a highly manipulative style of dealing with agencies. For example, they may have found that being demanding or extremely dependent is an effective tactic for dealing with bureaucracies. They may have also learned that setting one counselor against another can keep the pressure off them when they enter treatment. It is possible for counselors to react negatively to these behaviors rather than to see them as a part of the clients' problems. In an agency where there is not adequate communication among staff members these problems can escalate and lead to deterioration in staff relations.

Communication Breakdowns

Client demands can cause problems when there is poor communication in an agency. In fact, like a marriage relationship, an agency rapidly begins to show serious difficulties when there is a breakdown in communication. While breakdowns in communication frequently occur, they are usually corrected if the basic structure and process of communication are in place. However, we are talking here about chronic problems in communication. These may occur as vertical communication problems (e.g., a supervisor with a counselor) or as a horizontal problem (e.g., between two counselors doing the same type job). Left unchecked, these problems can develop into distrust, with the result that communication exists only in smaller cliques, and a type of war can break out between these cliques. Regardless of the pattern, the efficiency of the agency is seriously affected, and the functioning of the agency can be distorted in drastic ways. Like a family, agencies will adjust to communication breakdowns and may well continue to function for considerable periods of time. However, both work efficiency and the morale of many of the agency's workers are lowered when these adjustments are made.

Emotional Involvement with Clients

One of the factors that is involved in most social service agencies is the need for counselors to become emotionally involved with clients. Emotional investment in individuals is a characteristic usually found in the effective caregiver. However, when a caregiver invests himself in a client, there is a potential that the client will disappoint or frustrate the caregiver. This frustration can lead to a drop in self-esteem and general morale of the staff member. This is particularly true in the substance abuse field, where chemical dependency counselors work with clients who show a pattern of frequent relapse. Therefore, working with these clients can be particularly frustrating to new counselors, who are already concerned about their ability to become competent counselors. In this situation, new counselors are constantly seeing clients relapse and asking themselves if they are doing all they can for their clients. In many cases, novice counselors blame the failure on themselves and, consequently, suffer self-doubt and a loss of self-esteem. An interesting consequence of emotional investment and caring is that, generally speaking, the counselor who is able to empathize with the client, and project warmth and concern, is usually the most effective counselor. In other words, being concerned and caring leads to more effective treatment in most caregiving situations. However, it is frequently the most committed and caring counselors who suffer counselor burnout. Conversely, many of the people who are not emotionally invested in their clients may well be survivors in the agency, but at the cost of the clients. (Many individuals may be people who had originally been very caring but, due to disillusionment, have become cynical and less caring about their clients.) Another danger for substance abuse workers is that they may vent all of their job frustrations on the client, who is the most visible source of their frustrations. Therefore, a balance between the ability to emotionally invest in a client and to maintain some emotional distance is basic to survival in caregiving agencies.

Ambiguity of Tasks

Another issue faced by staff in social service agencies is the general ambiguity of the tasks they are asked to perform. Few therapists, for example, can ever say that their counseling was the major factor (or sometimes, even a minor factor) in a given client's recovery. In fact, a counselor who does carry out a specific intervention will only know if the intervention led to a positive outcome by waiting to see how the client changes. Frequently these delays between intervention and outcome are quite lengthy and even very effective therapists can feel they have done little to help the client.

Conflict Between Recovering and Nonrecovering Staff

One of the most important differences between substance abuse agencies and other caregiving agencies is that in many, perhaps most, chemical dependency agencies, both recovering and nonrecovering personnel are employed. There are very few caregiving systems, outside the substance abuse field, where people who are recovering from the problem become therapists. While many agencies manage the relationships between people with differing entrance credentials quite well, some agencies do not spend enough time or energy dealing with the potential problems that may ensue. Some of the potential problems are discussed below.

Staff Motivation

Recovering staff in chemical dependency agencies are frequently suspicious of the motivation of the nonrecovering staff, particularly in alcoholism agencies. For example, recovering alcoholics may wonder why a person who has not suffered through an alcohol problem would care anything about the welfare of alcoholics. (Many alcoholics, despite their own recovery, still view the active alcoholic in a moralistic way. They assume that other people also have this viewpoint.) And while they seldom voice their concerns to the nonrecovering counselors, the recovering counselors frequently wonder if the nonalcoholic counselors are working in the agency simply because the jobs were available, or if they plan to "rip off the agency by drawing their pay and doing little to earn it." In some cases, they may see the nonalcoholic as a con artist who is trying to gain control of the agency, i.e., become the head of the agency. In general, recovering staff may see non-recovering staff as less dedicated than they are and may resent their equal or superior status in the agency.

Education Differential

Recovering staff can sometimes be threatened by the fact that the nonrecovering staff have more training. Because many recovering counselors enter the alcoholism treatment field through on-the-job-training/workshop experiences, they do not receive the academic credentials that go with formal education. Many of these counselors are extremely sensitive about their lack of formal education and seem to fear that, someday, the better educated, nonalcoholic counselors will reveal the alcoholic counselors' ignorance to the world in one fell swoop of intellectual ambush. Obviously, this fear makes the counselor who is a recovering alcoholic very cautious and circumspect in his dealings with the better educated, non-alcoholic counselor. While this attitude may seem quite irrational to the casual observer, it is better understood when one remembers the problems with self-esteem and lowered self-worth that many alcoholics must struggle with for an extended period of their life following the achievement of sobriety.

A regrettable consequence of these first two points of friction is that although the recovering alcoholic counselor has much to offer the nonaddicted counselor, because of the suspiciousness and hostility generated between the two groups, a beneficial exchange between them may not be possible. It is also true that the degreed counselor may have skills and points of view that might benefit the recovering counselor. Unfortunately, the frequent antagonism between the two camps may not allow for constructive dialogue—a dialogue that might eventually lead to better care for both types of counselors' clients.

Formation of Cliques

The nonalcoholic counselor may resent the in-group cliquishness of the recovering counselor. The fact that the alcoholic counselors have a built-in bond of AA association and some experiences they perceive as shared can make the non-alcoholic counselor feel excluded. Another aspect of this same issue is that the nonrecovering staff member may see alcoholic staff members as exercising a reverse sort of snobbery. That is, the alcoholic counselor may insist that the only way you can really understand an alcoholic is by being one yourself and that, as a result, the nonrecovering counselor can never really be effective.

Differing Attitudes Toward Alcoholism

There may be differences in the way the recovering and nonrecovering alcoholic view alcoholism. In many cases, the counselor who is a recovering alcoholic will see alcohol problems in less differentiated ways than the academically trained counselor who, through education, has been exposed to widely differing models of alcoholism. For example, the recovering counselor may see alcoholism as an either/or issue, i.e., either you're alcoholic or you're not. The notion of alcoholism as a disease may have been fundamental in the alcoholic counselor's training history and close ties with the philosophy of AA may be seen as the sole basis for treatment.

On the other hand, the academically trained counselors may have been exposed, through university training, to a multicausal model of alcohol abuse and may see differing types of interventions as appropriate where there are differing developmental histories for the alcohol abuse. It goes without saying that these differing approaches can frequently become the basis for a communication breakdown and neither group really appreciates that a major part of the problem is in the model they are using to treat alcoholism and alcohol abuse.

Academic versus Craft Training

Another difference exists in the source and philosophy of training for the degreed professional and the recovering alcoholic counselor. Kalb and Propper (1976) have characterized the differences between these two types of substance abuse professionals as science versus craft training, respectively. The scientist-professional background of the degreed counselors usually means that they have learned their caregiving skills not only experientially, as an apprentice to a skilled counselor, but that through didactic training they have been exposed to the teachings of many others regarding alcohol problems. In this type of training, counselors will normally be exposed to a wide range of differing viewpoints and are encouraged to exercise independence in establishing their conceptualization of the issues. The ability to engage in original, independent thinking and to critically evaluate the work of one's teachers and peers is the highest calling of the scientist-professional model.

On the other hand, craftsmen obtain their qualifying skill or knowledge primarily through observing and experiencing the actual tasks required under the tutelage of a master craftsman. The knowledge they acquire is a product of the experiences of their teacher, and the acquisition of the craftsman's skills is demonstrated by the ability to consistently replicate the performance of the master craftsman. In mastering these skills only limited elaborations of style are allowed, and critical examination of the traditions of the craft are actively discouraged. In fact, shared agreement on the traditions of the craft is the criterion for loyalty in a craft-like organization.

In the past, paraprofessional preparation in the alcoholism treatment field has primarily followed the craft model. Trainees are usually indoctrinated in the philosophy and principles ("the 12 steps") of AA by trainers who are themselves recovering alcoholics and who have used this approach in their own recovery. These students are expected to emulate their teachers' thinking and actions. Their goal is to one day be like their teachers and teach others what they have learned. As a result, most paraprofessionals in the alcoholism treatment field are committed to traditional concepts and are resistant to alternative views of alcoholism. The steadfast refusal to question their own premises, despite conflicting evidence, helps to create and maintain an intense loyalty and unity among these recovering counselors. While this problem between the recovering and nonrecovering counselors has been an ongoing one, it could become more severe in the next few years as more alcohol counselors complete training in more formal settings and are exposed to competing models of alcohol use and abuse.

Appropriate Modeling Behavior versus Emotional Catharsis

The nonrecovering counselor may sometimes view the recovering counselor as having as many psychotherapy needs as the clients he is trying to help. Of course, lay counselors may very well tie their recovery to helping other people, particularly since twelfth stepping is a tenet of AA. Frequently there is a close tie between the treatment philosophy of an alcohol treatment program and the philosophy of AA. Therefore, alcoholic counselors may use their own histories with alcohol abuse extensively to teach other patients how they managed their personal recoveries. There is, of course, a fine line between illustrating appropriate recovery behavior and experiencing some emotional catharsis that may be useful to the mental health of the alcoholic counselor. It is also probable (and possibly necessary, in order to appropriately model the desired behavior) that the recovering alcoholic will use a group or individual session to deal with his own personal problems. It is imperative, however, that counselors, whether alcoholic or nonalcoholic, remember that they are there to help the people in treatment, not themselves. Whenever a counselor's problems become the predominant, ongoing focus of treatment, then the concern of fellow counselors is justified, and it may be necessary to intervene, in some way, to find outside therapy for the counselor having difficulty.*

---

*The reader is referred to Knauert and Davidson (1979) and to Wegscheider (1981). The latter author has generated a checklist so that people working with substance abusers can evaluate their own levels of adjustment at a given point in time. Wegscheider (1981, pp. 248–253) has introduced what she has labeled "The Whole Person Inventory." This inventory covers both personal and job-related issues and may be helpful to counselors who are experiencing difficulty.

Alcohol Counselors and Other Mental Health Professionals

Problems for new alcohol counselors may be especially pronounced when it becomes necessary for them to work with people from other disciplines. It may be particularly difficult, for example, for those substance abuse counselors working in mental health agencies. There one must relate to disciplines such as psychology, psychiatry, and social work, which have different ideological and philosophical training histories. Bridging the gap to form a collegial relationship may be very difficult for the substance abuse counselor, for a number of reasons. First, the philosophical and ideological differences among the above training disciplines are great, and these differences are even more pronounced between the substance abuse counselors and these professions. For example, the center of client motivation for most mental health professionals is in the client, i.e., the client must want to change before therapy can be effectively instituted. In working with the alcoholic and drug abuser, considerable external coercion may be used to get persons to enter treatment and to get them involved in the initial stages of treatment. Second, many mental health personnel view individuals who are working with alcoholics as "paraprofessionals." As Kalb and Propper (1976) have noted, the paraprofessional has operated as an adjunct to, and under the supervision of, the professional in mental health settings. On the other hand, the paraprofessional in the alcohol field has been a teacher or colleague rather than a student. These differences in expectations about roles add to communication difficulties. Finally, a considerable amount of hostility toward, and avoidance of treatment of, alcoholics has historically been present in all of these disciplines. Many of them see alcoholics as a lower level of client, and may see the alcohol counselor, regardless of level of training, as a person who is competent only to deal with these hopeless clients. Many mental health agencies insist on both physical and administrative separation of the two caregiving systems. Frequently, very little communication is maintained between these two groups, and considerable resentment and hostility can develop.

As noted above, this is not an exhaustive list of the potential problems that may exist between recovering and nonrecovering counselors. It is hoped that it will alert alcohol counselors to some of these issues and lead to the issues being discussed between staff members.

Inter-Agency Conflict

Because the alcohol field began as a grass roots movement, primarily through AA and the National Council on Alcohol,* it has developed as a highly person-

---

*A fact frequently overlooked by the alcohol field is that the field actually had considerable professional/scientific input at its inception and that the founder of the National Council, Marty Mann, actually received considerable support from Jellinek and his group at Yale (see Jellinek, 1960).

alized, very politicized system. In particular, there has been a major concern with protecting one's turf against competing agencies, both in and out of the alcohol field. Part of this "paranoia" is historically justified, since alcohol treatment has traditionally been underfunded. Individuals in the field have had to fight for scarce resources with other caregiving systems (e.g., mental health agencies) and even with competing alcohol agencies. As a result, the system has not only become paranoid toward agencies outside the alcohol field, but within the field one agency may become suspicious of other agencies that might be competing with it for patients. With this view of internal and external agencies as threats to their survival, alcohol agencies are frequently susceptible to rumor, internal fantasy generation, and the distortion of facts. While all of these problems can be present in human service agencies generally, the degree of severity seems to be greater in the alcohol field. Of course, this means that some forum for open discussion of issues and some mechanism for resolution of differences must be rigorously maintained. When clear channels of communication are not maintained, then alcohol agencies can engage in very destructive behaviors.

Inter-Agency Conflict and Client Care

None of the above issues would be of much importance if they had little bearing on the care of clients. However, relationships within and between agencies can directly and indirectly affect the quality of care provided to the clients of these agencies. We will consider only a few of the more important consequences of disrupted internal and external agency relationships. The main point to remember here is that agency functioning is not an abstract event, unrelated to day-to-day client care. As we shall see, there are rather direct tie-ins between some of the above issues and the quality of client care provided by an agency.

One example of the direct impact of problems between agencies is that appropriate referral of clients can be disrupted. For example, if you do not have good relations with a long-term care agency and a client discharged from your treatment center needs this care, the probability of adequate referral is lowered. The reader could doubtless supply many other illustrations of how poor relationships with other agencies can potentially affect client care, ranging from referral to aftercare.

Indirect effects of internal and external agency conflict are more difficult to observe (and frequently more difficult to correct). However, if you concentrate on a given agency, you can readily see how many of the indirect effects discussed here are operating in that agency. Whenever there is internal or external strife within an agency, the amount of emotional energy left to caregivers to do their daily counseling is reduced (and thus their effectiveness is reduced). In addition, the frustration, anger, and anxiety felt by the counselor are communicated to the clients under his care. Therefore, in agencies where staff are spending considerable time and energy dealing with internal or external conflict, clients receive less effective treatment. The clients frequently begin to show acting out behavior in response to the caregiver's emotional reactions being transmitted to them. This trickle-down effect usually occurs about two weeks following the initiation of the caregiver's conflict and for the same amount of time following the resolution of the conflict.

These problems indicate that the frequently held notion that inter- and intra-agency planning meetings are a waste of valuable treatment time is not necessarily accurate. The provision of structure (e.g., regularly scheduled meetings) to discuss issues, and the existence of an ongoing process (an openness and honesty between staff members in communication) are important for substance abuse agencies. Ensuring open communication can lead to more effective treatment of clients and a reduction of acting out behavior on the part of the people in treatment.

EARLY JOB ADJUSTMENT IN AN AGENCY

Most counselors would agree that alcohol agencies are not unchanging, static organizations. However, one of the things caregivers frequently overlook is the fact that they themselves also change in a number of ways in the course of their careers. The ability to manage psychological and philosophical adjustments is crucial to survival in caregiving agencies. In this section we shall examine some of the adjustments that caregivers entering an agency may need to make over a period of time. We will also suggest some strategies that can be helpful in dealing with these issues. A cautionary note: the sequence of adjustments described here is typical, but may not occur for all counselors in all settings. The timing of each of the following phases is also highly variable, both across settings and for caregivers in the same setting. Therefore, the phases described should not be perceived as automatic procedures that will be experienced by all alcohol counselors or all caregivers.

The Honeymoon Period

Part of the problem new counselors face is that they simply do not know the agency very well. Another factor is that the new counselor may approach the job in an idealized way. If we were to have an organizational chart of the agency drawn from the new counselor's perspective, we would expect much of the agency would be left out, and the counselor's role in the agency would be much larger than it would be from the perspective of an objective observer. The new counselors' egocentric behavior is initially reinforced, since in the early days and weeks people in the agency usually welcome them in and attempt to be very supportive. Additionally, the counselors are, ideally, not yet swamped with a heavy caseload and have time to interact with their new colleagues. None of this is necessarily maladaptive since we would hope that a new counselor would enter the job with enthusiasm and excitement. However, this period, sometimes called the "honeymoon" period, is not generally characteristic of the experiences the counselors will encounter once they become fully involved with their job in the agency.

One reason for highlighting the honeymoon period is that some counselors suffer early severe doubts about whether they have chosen the right job, right career, etc., because of the contrast between this period and the emotional letdown they experience following it. After the honeymoon period, some counselors may feel that they have chosen the wrong job or even the wrong career. While these feelings may be correct, leaving the agency at this point may be a serious mistake simply because the counselor may not have enough information on which to base a rational decision. The point for counselors to remember, if they suffer some early disillusionment within the first three to six months, is that other very competent, committed, and dedicated counselors in the same agency may have had the same feelings and stayed with the job until the initial adjustments were made.

Mastering Routine Tasks

Several other adjustment phases in caregiving agencies have been described (Sarata, 1979). These phases are usually filled with ambivalence and uncertainty for the caregiver. We will call the first of these phases "mastering standard operating procedures." This stage is usually overlapped by the "honeymoon period," described above. In mastering procedures, the counselor is preoccupied with learning things such as the clerical demands of the agency, e.g., how to fill out the necessary forms correctly, how to get progress notes typed up, and procedures for setting up an interview with the family. Many counselors may experience this period as a time when there are an overwhelming number of things to learn. Many fear they will never learn it all. Generally, counselors at this point in this phase are so busy with the nitty gritty functions of the agency that they have relatively little concern about their comparative job performance. To their disappointment, new counselors discover that a portion of the work they will be doing is routine, monotonous, and uninteresting. The boring routine of learning the right forms to use, the appropriate channels to get things done, etc., may be tasks that the new counselors did not anticipate. In addition, they learn that their general training in counseling did not provide many of the technical details needed in their new job. Close relationships with a more experienced counselor or their supervisors are needed to handle the adjustments in this phase. However, novice counselors must be mature enough (and assertive enough) to seek out this technical advice and support in order to reduce the stress of this period.

Comparing Work Attitudes and Philosophies

In the third phase, counselors may begin to compare their work attitudes and philosophies with those of co-workers and superiors. Each interaction seems to provide an opportunity for the new workers to compare their ideas to those of relevant others in the job place. While some counselors may be concerned with what supervisors think, more often counselors are interested in what their fellow counselors are thinking and doing. The sharing of experiences with fellow counselors is important because new chemical dependency counselors face what has been called the "crisis of competence" (Cherniss, 1980). The comparison of their performance with those of their peers allows feedback about the relative quality of their performance. Being able to share experiences and receive support from their peers provides several benefits for the neophyte counselors. Colleagues can offer the neophyte counselors a sympathetic ear when they want to talk about work problems, resulting in an emotional release of tension and anxiety. A better perspective and understanding of the problem is frequently possible after sharing job problems with colleagues. Supportive colleagues are particularly important when the novice counselors find themselves in conflict with administrators or agency policy. Colleagues also offer a readily available resource for the large amount of technical information that must be acquired. Colleagues offer feedback on one's performance, feedback that is important for the feeling of professional competence. Finally, colleagues can help the new counselor confirm or disconfirm his perception of his performance on the job.

Self-Doubts About the Caregiver Role

Eventually, the fourth phase is reached. This phase involves a preoccupation by the caregivers with their fitness for, or commitment to, the caregiver role. Counselors may begin to examine how far their clients have progressed and to question whether or not they are doing an effective job. Counselors may also begin to reflect on the stresses and satisfactions experienced in the job. The paramount question that seems to be asked during this phase is "Are the job and I suited for each other?" Moving to another agency is one way to resolve the uncertainties of this issue. However, the counselor should be aware that working through the above phases and learning to pace oneself seem to be necessary adjustment procedures for assuming the caregiving role.

The above adjustments are frequently experienced by the counselor as a lonely, internal struggle. It is frequently lonely because caregivers find it difficult to request assistance for themselves and often relegate their own cares and concerns to another time. It is important, then, for counselors to seek out peer and supervisor support as they progress through these phases. The question "Should I share my concerns with others in the agency?" is one that must be answered by counselors based on their perception that other staff will be supportive and on their own ability to be open. If the counselor does decide to risk asking for support, a potential long-range advantage is that, even if specific questions are not answered, the counselor has built a network of support that can be utilized in the future.

An awareness of the above phases should be helpful in a number of ways to new counselors entering an alcohol agency:

- Like their clients, it is better if counselors have some preliminary understanding of some of the things they may experience. Daily adjustment requires the ability to label and understand experiences. If neophyte counselors are aware that the above experiences are relatively common, they are less likely to be hesitant in sharing their experiences with coworkers. In particular, if other counselors at the same level are present, it may encourage the counselors to form a mini-support and discussion group. Support from peers may be readily available in the agency.

- If a particular job situation is not going well, an awareness of the existence of ongoing work place adjustments may allow the counselor to more readily put things in perspective. For example, when the above phases are being worked through, the occurrence of a frustrating event can have a heavier impact on the counselor's morale. An awareness that experiences may have a greater impact on people when they are already feeling perplexed and confused (something counselors tell their clients all the time) can be helpful in maintaining a more objective and long-range perspective. Both of these points can be useful in surviving the initial adjustments necessary in the work place.

COMMUNICATION ISSUES WITHIN AN AGENCY

One of the factors frequently overlooked in assessing the quality of care provided to clients in an alcohol agency (or any caregiving agency) is the degree to which an agency communicates internally and externally. This section will focus on internal agency communication; external communication (communication with other agencies) will be considered in the following section.

Open Communication

One of the most obvious advantages of open communication within an agency is that if counselors talk to each other, then clients are likely to get better and more appropriate care. This function is frequently (but certainly not always) appreciated by alcohol caregivers and can be seen in daily staffing meetings, where lively discussions of client progress and what types of interventions may be needed occur. What is often ignored is that adequate communication regarding clients requires clear communication between staff in that agency.

This staff communication network frequently involves a highly personalized series of interactions. When these personalized interactions are characterized by openness, sensitivity to other colleagues, candor, and trust, then the agency is more likely to perform well tasks such as evaluating client progress and planning treatment. However, when the communication network is characterized by defensiveness, insensitivity, dishonesty, and mistrust, even basic client evaluation and treatment planning sessions become distorted by the overall breakdown in communication within the agency. The breakdowns can occur for a number of reasons. Some examples include the following: competition for what may be considered a more ideal job assignment; distance that may be created because coworkers have little in common in terms of outside interests; or a situation where one person may be perceived as the favorite of the supervisor and the rest of the counselors scapegoat that person. Whatever the reason, jealousy, envy, or simple lack of interest can create communication gulfs in an agency (Cherniss, 1980).

As implied above, the lack of sensitivity on the part of counselors toward colleagues can lead to defensive behavior and to closing down communication between counselors and their colleagues. Much of what has previously been discussed would apply in the area of defensive behavior; however, one additional point should be made. All people have vulnerable points. If they are attacked at these points, they will overreact and behave in irrational ways. Counselors should become aware of these vulnerabilities in their colleagues and avoid arousing defensiveness whenever possible. However, if they do make a fellow counselor defensive, counselors should remember that their colleague is likely to behave in an irrational manner. Frequently, it is better to apologize for making the person angry and then to try another tack in communicating with the individual about the issue.

Personal Insensitivity and Communication

Personal insensitivity within an agency can have a powerful impact on communication. There will be times when counselors do not get the support and concern they need from their fellow counselors simply because the other counselors are so preoccupied with their own job responsibilities. Also, it is frequently forgotten (or overlooked) that it is the small, sensitive things that count in day-to-day interaction. Being human and humane with colleagues can reduce emotional and psychological distance and make communication both easier and more open. Since counselors are human, they tend to talk more to the people who are sensitive to their needs and to become more defensive (and so, less communicative) toward those people who are not sensitive to their needs. A common error for counselors is to attend so much to the needs of their clients that they ignore entirely the needs of their peers. Counselors frequently show sensitivity, warmth, care, and concern with their clients, then leave the counseling session and greet their colleagues as if they had been trained in the Attila the Hun school of therapy. Again, the empathy and warmth shown to patients is not transferred to counselors' interactions with colleagues.

Areas of Potential Insensitivity

One area of potential insensitivity comes out of the differing training histories of the personnel typically employed in an alcohol agency. The degreed, professional counselor may be insensitive to factors such as the role that AA plays in the lay counselor's life. Professional counselors may, in the beginning, be insensitive to the fact that for people using AA as a support group, an attack on AA's principles is similar to an attack on a person's religion (i.e., they are touching on an area that is a central value for these people). New counselors will quickly be made aware that for the counselor who is a recovering alcoholic, the strengths and weaknesses of using AA as a support group is not a topic for academic discussion. Obviously, an early encounter of this type can lead to anger, defensiveness, and less effective communication between the two groups.

Recovering counselors, on the other hand, sometimes are insensitive toward the professional counselors. For example, the recovering counselor may make caustic remarks about the degreed counselors' lack of a true understanding of the problem they are trying to treat. Attempts to belittle the utility of education also reflect insensitivity and defensiveness on the part of the alcoholic counselor when such comments are directed at their academically trained peers. These patterns of interaction affect the degree and level of communication and lead to the formation of cliques within an agency.

Communication Structures

In order to better understand communication breakdowns, counselors need to understand or make explicit some factors that are so much taken for granted that they are never really looked at closely. To begin with, there are format and form issues involved in communication within any agency. For example, setting up daily meetings implies that some format has been provided within which communication can occur.

New counselors must learn the format of communication in their agency. This structure can vary from highly formalized meetings, with someone acting as chairman, to a casual hallway meeting system where things are decided in a very informal way. In some cases, a highly formal system may be set up, but this system is not really involved in how things get communicated (e.g., things may be communicated and decisions consensually agreed upon prior to the formal meeting). The issue is not which one of the above formats is most effective (both can be effective or ineffective) but rather which one or which combination is used in the agency. When counselors first enter an agency, part of the "honeymoon" period described earlier should be spent studying how things are communicated and how tasks are accomplished in the agency. If counselors are initially aware that two systems of communication and decision making can coexist, they may be less frustrated when they discover that issues they bring to the more formal session are not extensively debated or considered before a decision is made.

The Communication Process

In addition to understanding the structure of communication, it is also important to recognize and monitor the process of communication. As noted earlier, if people in the agency are basically honest, open, sensitive, and supportive toward their colleagues, then there is likely to be a relatively free and easy exchange of information. If the members of an agency cannot talk to one another, then the best series of structured meetings will not lead to effective communication. While the structure of communication patterns may provide the vehicle for communication to occur, open, trusting communication with colleagues will determine whether the communication patterns will be clear and effective.

In some agencies, disagreements between staff are avoided or played down in order to maintain a surface harmony. Inevitably, this results in distortion in the process of communicating, and dealing with some issues between counselors is avoided at all cost. For example, feelings toward one staff member may be so intense that some or all of the counselors avoid confronting that staff member about issues where there is disagreement. Again, not only communication processes, but also decision-making procedures, can be distorted.

Communication Breakdown and Mistrust

Mistrust in an agency is frequently a byproduct of a breakdown in communication, but, obviously, it also can contribute to communication problems once it is present. Sometimes mistrust occurs because an individual has dealt with personal confidences in a destructive manner. At other times an individual (or the agency hierarchy) has not followed through on promises or supported staff members in the agency when a difficult issue is being dealt with. Mistrust is a threat to the fabric of intra-agency communication and, once established, can seriously erode the quality of staff interaction. The question that is sometimes asked is "Can anyone be trusted or is everyone out for number one?"

Mistrust, like communication, can either be vertical or horizontal, or it can be present at all levels when the entire agency has problems with trust. When there are problems throughout the agency, an easy way out is to make some outside threat a greater problem than the problems that need to be dealt with internally. While such a strategy may be effective for a short period of time, it does not provide a long-term solution. Like the marriage relationship, relationships within agencies can only be assured by continually dealing with issues as they arise. As with other communication issues, a common mistake is believing that only a single intervention is required to deal with mistrust. It is an agency maintenance issue that can be dealt with routinely where communication and trust levels are high, but which becomes difficult to deal with when they are not. Some strategies that seem to be helpful here include the following:

- Keep messages between counselors and their peers clear and deal with interpersonal problems as they occur rather than putting them off. Reducing ambiguity in communication with peers is an important goal in this respect.

- Remember that personal fantasy and rumor are like gas on a burning fire when trust is an issue. Counselors should attempt to confirm or disconfirm rumors as soon as they hear them. They should also check out their fantasies of what is going on in the agency; it is remarkable how easily messages can become distorted. If counselors would like to confirm this, they should try passing a verbal message through 10 or more people (at a party, for instance). Usually even a simple message will show some dramatic change. Another way to confirm that multiple modes of communication work better is to write the message down and pass it both in written and verbal form. There should be a significant reduction in the distortion of the message. A similar issue occurs in counselors' anticipation of what is going to happen when they fantasize about what is occurring in an agency: these fantasies are usually partially, or entirely, wrong.

- If counselors are not physically located in the same facility, they should remember that they may have difficulty managing communication with their colleagues. Here you may have to create some method of maintaining contact with your coworkers. Some possible solutions might include (1) having coffee once a day in the central agency or (2) having lunch with fellow counselors once a week or more if counselors are located in the field rather than in a central office. The practical side of regular contact is that it allows counselors to deal with ongoing problems in the agency. Of more central importance is the fact that physical and psychological distance is reduced between counselors and their peers through regular contact. If people see and talk to one another on a daily basis, there is less likelihood that mistrust will become a problem. It should again be noted that colleagues provide a powerful support system for new counselors. Without the moral support of colleagues, many new counselors would not make an active effort to resolve their job-related difficulties and could withdraw into mindless conformity.

- Remember, there is a need to provide internal support for communication. Counselors should be aware that they have the most control over their own behavior. They should make every attempt to deal openly and honestly with their peers. Also, they should remember that overcoming mistrust can take time and, in an agency where there are problems, they may not receive much reinforcement for their attempts to deal with issues in a clear and straightforward manner. That will be particularly true when issues of peer insensitivity and defensiveness coexist in an agency; this is not an uncommon occurrence where mistrust is an issue.

A common failure in dealing with communication process issues is to assume that a one-time intervention that results in better communication is all that needs to be done. However, the same breakdowns in communication are likely to be recurring themes in an agency. Counselors should be aware that ongoing sessions devoted to specific breakdowns in communication may be necessary. They should not conclude, simply because there is decay in the communication process over a period of time following an intervention, that what they tried was ineffective or that repairing the communication pattern is hopeless. Rather, the problem should be viewed as a maintenance issue—one in which previously successful interventions can be utilized again.

Communicating with Supervisors

No matter what his position is as a newcomer to an agency, a counselor will need to manage effective communication with people superior, and subordinate, to him in rank or status. One factor that may directly affect counselors' survival is how they deal with people in authority over them, i.e., their supervisors. It is interesting that counselors can sometimes deal so effectively with clients and yet be very ineffective in using identical principles when they interact with their supervisors.

One thing that is very helpful is for counselors to become aware of their own personal feelings and reactions to authority. Frequently, counselors react to supervisors on the basis of long-held emotional reactions to authority figures. When they have a disagreement with a superior, the first question they should ask themselves is how much of this is their own emotional response to an authority figure. A good rule of thumb is that counselors should never confront a superior when angry and out of control (even if they are right!), because they may not present their ideas as clearly and precisely as they would like. If counselors are angry but are under control and can verbally express their anger (and their reason for it), their ideas are more likely to be well received. One thing that might be helpful to counselors when communicating something they feel strongly about is to ask themselves how they might feel if someone attacked them personally when complaining about some of their actions. One should not forget that people in positions of power are also human beings and that they have feelings, too. Counselors might also ask themselves if their motive is simply to let off steam, or if they really want to communicate with the person.

A common error in communication is for counselors to avoid interaction with their supervisor. It is almost as if counselors feel that the best way to manage their situation is to blend into the woodwork. If counselors get to know their supervisor as a person, the tendency and need to maintain distance are usually lessened and communication is improved.

Supervisors As a Factor in New Counselor Survival

Supervisors are critical to the initial development and continuing survival of chemical dependency counselors. Some specific ways that supervisors can aid in the development of competence in novice caregivers are outlined below. These include the following:

- Supervisors can provide technical suggestions and advice that can increase the counselors' effectiveness.
- Supervisors provide feedback to the new counselors; positive feedback can help alleviate anxiety, while negative feedback delivered constructively can help the counselor correct weaknesses.
- When the supervisor is readily available to the new counselor for consultation, the counselor feels less alone and isolated, and the fear of harming a client through ineptitude is decreased.
- Supervisors provide a reference point for the new counselor (e.g., if the new counselor sees the case in the same way as the supervisor, then the counselor is reassured that his own competence in understanding a case is adequate).

In general, for the new professional, a supportive, but discreet, supervisor has been found to be associated with positive career development, i.e., positive survival (Cherniss, 1980).

Interacting with Support Personnel

Regardless of their status in the agency, counselors will probably find someone with lower status than themselves with whom they must interact. For example, how will they, as entering counselors, deal with clerical personnel? Obviously, they will want to be sensitive to secretarial needs and will want to promote as much productivity as possible. One rule of thumb is to adopt a style of interaction with subordinates with which they can be comfortable. If counselors are easygoing individuals, it is likely that a brusque, business-like style with secretaries will be difficult to maintain. If counselors try to assume roles that are not consistent with their usual style of interaction, then typically they will under- or overplay them. Remember, a wide variety of approaches work in communicating with people. This can be confirmed by observing the different styles that fellow counselors use in interacting with people.

Cutting Through the Bureaucracy

One area that frequently seems to be overlooked is the general insensitivity of bureaucracies toward people. One result is that the professional role the counselor has been trained for may be difficult to carry out in the face of bureaucratic demands. For example, bureaucrats may see what is needed and demanded from a different point of view than the counselors do; this is particularly true in the area of professional autonomy. The irrational and sometimes destructive rules and policies of chemical dependency agencies may be a major source of frustration and stress for novice counselors. The new counselors find that one of their tasks is to mediate between bureaucratic demands and client demands. Frequently, alcohol counselors personalize some of the bureaucratic indifference that can occur in human care agencies. This can lead counselors to assume that what is occurring is a personal vendetta directed toward them. In point of fact, what is occurring may be totally unknown to the person (or persons) who could correct it, and it will remain that way unless counselors initiate action to open communication and resolve the problem. Frequently counselors find that the person responsible is just as eager to have the problem corrected as they are. In other words, counselors should check out perceived injustices to see if they are simply oversights.

The solution to another problem in communicating with the bureaucracy is also in the hands of the counselor. As noted above, many counselors find that keeping charts up to date, writing treatment plans, etc., is unexciting and boring. Counselors may do these tasks but gripe incessantly about doing them; or resist doing them at all. It may well be that this lack of response to the bureaucracy by counselors can lead to poorer care for their clients and more work for their colleagues. What can be overlooked is that these bureaucratic tasks, as onerous as they are, do help maintain communication within an agency and can ensure better care for the client.

In fairness, it should be noted that general griping about the bureaucracy is characteristic of human care agencies. In fact, if not taken to extremes, this griping can allow anger and frustration to be expressed toward a nonreactive source. However, when the griping includes passive resistance or active sabotage of the system, then a vital communication link is threatened.

The importance of establishing open, positive communication with colleagues cannot be overemphasized for new counselors. The role of a novice counselor is psychologically stressful and can be emotionally demanding even when the new counselors have open access to their more experienced peers and can depend on their advice and support. Without this support, the adjustment is infinitely more difficult.

If counselors could always rely on working out problems with colleagues, the world of work would be a happier place. However, the reality of life is that despite their strong efforts to communicate with peers, there will be some colleagues with whom counselors simply cannot communicate. At this point, they have to attempt to find ways to go around these colleagues and to do their job in spite of them. That is, they may have to live with these "problem colleagues" if they choose to stay in the agency. One question the counselor may have to answer is "Can I work out a way to live with this person or must I leave the agency for my own peace of mind?" Another way of phrasing the question would be "Do I like what I'm doing well enough to put up with working with this person?" In other cases, they will encounter colleagues who are already "burned out" and who have very negative attitudes toward the job. For the new counselors, these negative attitudes can be extremely contagious, and they can quickly lose their enthusiasm and drive for the job. Therefore, avoiding contact with these colleagues is essential for the new counselors, particularly during the first months on the job.

MAINTAINING COMMUNICATION WITH OUTSIDE AGENCIES

The practical importance of maintaining open and effective liaisons with other agencies, in terms of meeting the needs of clients, has already been demonstrated. The lack of adequate communication with other agencies also affects the overall morale and functioning of the entire agency and its personnel. Many of the same factors that apply to intra-agency communication also apply here. For example, openness, sensitivity to colleagues, candor, and trust are as necessary for inter-agency communication as they are for intra-agency communication. When the communication network is characterized by negative factors such as mistrust and insensitivity, poor communication will exist between the agencies in a community.

The establishment of positive inter-agency communication requires effort at several levels. For example, Rivers, Sarata, and Book (1974) have pointed out the potential role that chemical dependency agency secretaries can play in maintaining inter-agency communication. It is important for counselors to understand that adequate communication involves many levels. (They may sometimes assume that communicating with outside agencies is the responsibility of their superiors.) The actions of counselors can add or detract, in significant ways, to how well agencies may communicate. Another issue is that since interactions between some agencies may be very infrequent, the perception that one agency has of another may be based on the quality of interaction the agency had with a specific counselor.

As in intra-agency communication, it is critical that what is to be communicated is specified as clearly as possible. To reduce inter-agency ambiguity, it is necessary that the agency's intra-agency communication be firmly established and operating properly; this is a necessary but not sufficient condition for effectively communicating with outside agencies.

Some of the same factors that make intra-agency communication difficult are also problematic in inter-agency communication. The only difference is that inter-agency problems may occur more often and require more effort to deal with than the communication problems within a single agency. There is one built-in problem in inter-agency communication: that is distance, both physical and psychological. If the physical locations of agencies are in close proximity to each other, some natural communication might occur through various staff members bumping into each other in the parking lot, etc. However, these casual interactions are not as likely when agencies and their staffs are physically located in various parts of town. This physical distance can retard the development of close personal relationships between the various staffs. When these close personal relationships are not present, then it is possible for rumor and fantasy to increase drastically and for many imagined slights to occur. These negative fantasies can interfere with inter-agency functioning.

Distance As a Factor in Inter-Agency Communication

When groups of people are separated from each other, they attempt to maintain order in their perception of the outside group by filling in any missing blanks. Frequently, when they don't know the people in the outside group, they fill in these missing blanks in knowledge in a negative fashion (i.e., they imagine the worst thing that these people could do to them, and their agency, and proceed to make it fact). An illustration of how rapidly the establishing of distance can provoke suspicion, paranoia, and negative fantasy in fellow professionals is given in an exercise that was conducted with a group of professionals who were midway through a year-long training program. The group was initially broken into two subgroups. The exercise required one subgroup to learn an anagram task and then to teach it to the second subgroup. The subgroup that was to teach the task remained on the first floor and, like many community agencies, became totally focused on mastering the task. The members of the second subgroup were sent out of the room, with no explanation of their role or what was to be expected of them, except that the first group would teach them a task and that they were to remain in an upstairs room for about two hours. Shortly after reaching the second floor, the subgroup to be trained began to wonder what was going to happen to them. Then they began to wonder if, perhaps, the first subgroup would not try to present the material in such a way as to confuse them and to make them appear silly. As time passed (and the first subgroup was continuing to be totally involved in learning the anagram task), the second subgroup's fantasies became more real and members were convinced that this was the case. To deal with the anticipated humiliation, they established a password that, when called out, would signal the entire group to leave the building and abandon the training exercise. After two hours, the second group was brought back to the first floor for training by the first subgroup. The waiting group's initial reaction was so defensive that someone in the first group eventually thought to ask what was going on. Once the fantasies of the second subgroup were shared with the first group, an attempt was made to deal with their fears. Considerable time and energy were needed to dissipate the suspiciousness and anxiety of the second subgroup by members of the other group.

What is amazing about this situation is that the people in the two subgroups were well acquainted with one another and had formed close working relationships over the previous six months of training. They also had regular group meetings, where problems between them could be worked out. Despite the apparent closeness, separation for a short time—in a situation where one group had been given ambiguous information about the intentions of the other group—produced immediate paranoid fantasies. Following the completion of the exercise, it was pointed out that the first subgroup could have kept the second group in the room while the first group learned the task, and that this not only would have reduced the destructive fantasies of the second group but also would have facilitated the teaching and learning of the task.

Two things are apparent from this exercise. First, if well-acquainted colleagues can become suspicious of one another's motives in a two-hour period, separated by only a single floor in the same building, imagine the possible difficulties that can arise between agencies separated by several miles and without close working relationships. Second, if the first group had involved the second group in the task from the beginning, all of the problems could have been avoided. When one agency is planning policies that may affect another agency, bringing the second agency into the planning process from the beginning may significantly reduce the fantasies held by personnel in the second agency.

Dealing with Inter-Agency Fantasy and Rumor

Another problem created by distance and inadequate communication patterns is rumor. While the need to check out intra-agency rumors is important, the need to deal constructively with rumors concerning outside agencies is imperative. This is particularly so when these rumors consist of possible negative actions by the outside agency. (Unfortunately, these types of rumors *are* most frequently negative in nature.) As is the case with intra-agency communication, there is a strong need to confront these inter-agency fantasies and rumors and to build channels of communication that assure they can be dealt with quickly. Some principles that are potentially helpful in dealing with these problems are outlined below.

Maintaining an Avenue of Communication

In every community it is necessary to maintain some vehicle of communication between agencies. A coordinating committee (with representatives from all local chemical dependency agencies) that meets regularly is essential. Not only do the meetings allow for dealing with ongoing practical issues, but they also offer the opportunity to establish a network of people who can check out rumors and fantasies between meetings. A related issue is the need to deal with fantasies and rumor quickly and definitively. Delaying dealing with these problems only allows them wider circulation and therefore makes them more "real." Not being as definitive as possible when debunking these erroneous communications gives credence to such rumors and fantasies.

Unambiguous Communication

An agency has the same responsibility to communicate clearly and with minimum ambiguity with other agencies as do individuals. Whenever agencies are dealing with issues and announcements that could draw strong reactions from another agency (e.g., because it is potentially threatening to that agency), it is wise to use multilevel channels of communication. Do not send a memo! One possible approach might be to first go and talk with an agency representative, discussing the proposed issue at some length and asking for feedback. Whenever possible, an agency should incorporate any suggestions made and perhaps ask the agency or agencies affected if they would like a representative to come and discuss the issue at a staff meeting. While this may not be necessary with minor issues, the time spent may be less than that needed to resolve poorly communicated messages later. Also, it leaves a given agency with better, not worse, communication links with other agencies.

LONG-RANGE COUNSELOR JOB ADJUSTMENT: DEALING WITH ETHICAL ISSUES

While new counselors may be overwhelmed with the adjustments necessary to manage their new job, in a seemingly brief period of time they may be making adjustments to long-term problems of the profession. For example, the new counselor may enter the agency with considerable eagerness to change its policies and procedures and effect rapid and drastic change. The "young counselor" may see his enemy as the entrenched bureaucracy. One of the adjustments that young counselors must make over time is the transition from neophyte to member of the establishment. While this transition may not seem important to new counselors initially, most counselors will eventually face adjustment to the increased job demands and responsibilities of the experienced counselor (i.e., they will be faced with the responsibility for setting and maintaining the policies of the agency). In brief, the counselor will eventually become part of the establishment.

In the process of surviving working in the agency to reach the point of being a part of the establishment, counselors must learn to pace themselves, learn to cope with the ethical dilemmas confronted in the job place, and avoid job burnout. A consideration of some of the ethical issues that counselors may face will be presented first. Finally, a discussion of job burnout will be presented and steps that may reduce burnout will be outlined.

Dealing with Unethical Behavior in an Agency

As an alcohol counselor, you will be entering a caregiving area where problems with appropriate ethical behavior abound. It is *not* true that alcohol counselors are more, or less, ethical than other caregivers; however, they will face as many ethical issues as counselors in the mental health field and the guidelines provided for them are frequently less well defined than those of mental health professionals.

In order for new counselors to manage their own ethical behavior, it is frequently necessary for them to consult one or more counselors more experienced than themselves. Neophyte counselors should never hesitate to ask about an ethical issue, and most professional counselors will continue to seek advice about ethical dilemmas throughout their careers. While concern for following proper ethics should be a central value for counselors, it also has practical survival implications. Every year one of the major reasons for dismissal from alcohol and drug agencies, for a significant number of counselors, is that they are judged to have behaved unethically.

It would be impossible to specify all the possible ethical dilemmas that counselors could encounter in their work. To do so would require a listing lengthy enough to fill the entire New York City phone book. This section will cover only some of the more obvious potential ethical problems.

Propriety in the Client-Counselor Relationship

A key factor for counselors to consider, when dealing with clients, is that in the treatment situation the counselor has considerable power over a person who may be very vulnerable emotionally. Whenever counselors are in a power relationship in a professional setting they should provide safeguards for themselves and their clients so that this power is not deliberately, or inadvertently, misused. One of the best safeguards is to be alert to the power relationship. Counselors should ask themselves if their actions are likely to be interpreted as taking advantage of the client. Of course, counselors are frequently attempting to get their clients to try new behaviors and to do something that the clients do not choose to do, i.e., to change. Counselors often use the relationship they have with clients to get things accomplished. Most of these interventions are both appropriate and necessary. However, there will be times when counselors' actions toward clients could be seen as questionable. A brief discussion of some of the ethical issues that are most problematic for chemical dependency counselors follows.

Dating a Current or Ex-Client. While this situation is one most chemical dependency counselors would be acutely aware of, it is surprising how many do violate this taboo. Most fail to remember that the relationship begins in an unequal power relationship and that this differential power can place the client at a strong disadvantage. Dating an ex-client seems more clouded as an ethical issue until it is remembered that the relationship began with this same power differential, while the client was in a vulnerable and impressionable position. Therefore, post-treatment dating has some of the same problems that exist in dating a client in active treatment.

Sexual Intercourse with Current or Former Clients. This represents the epitome of taking advantage of the unequal power relationship and the client's vulnerability. This type of relationship is by far most frequent with a male counselor and a female client. Many alcohol counselors see this action as grounds for dismissal from the agency.

Failing to Maintain the Confidentiality of a Client. This is a very shady area and one that is sometimes more difficult for chemical dependency counselors than it is for some other caregivers. In many settings considerable treatment is done by volunteer counselors, and personal data is shared in a casual and open manner. While this atmosphere may be helpful in treatment, it opens up the possibility that information shared by a counselor about a client may be revealed unthinkingly by one of these volunteer counselors. Also, there are frequent visitors to chemical dependency settings, and counselors must be careful about who is within hearing distance when discussing a client. A related problem occurs when information about the client has to be shared with outside agencies. Frequently, law enforcement authorities or the client's employer may request a report on the client's progress and possible prognosis; making the judgment of just what should be included in these reports must be done very carefully. Here, the seeking of advice from more experienced counselors and finding out how the reports will be used are important steps.

Sharing Information with Family and Friends. While the client may frequently give blanket permission to share information, the counselor still may have to make judgments as to how much information is shared and how it is presented.

There are several other less dramatic examples of unethical behavior: not assuming professional responsibility for clients and not maintaining adequate supervision for oneself is one example; another is misrepresenting one's credentials to an agency in order to gain employment.

The preceding ethical dilemmas are based on the individual actions of a counselor. Frequently, however, the agency in which a counselor is employed may have a supervisor who is engaging in actions that are unethical or not in the best interests of clients or staff. For example, supervisors in an agency may attempt to use their positions to seek sexual favors from subordinates. Or, an agency may not systematically obtain its clients' permission before releasing information. In many states, the latter action would be a violation of state law (in addition to violating federal regulations).

Of course, there will be other situations that are not so clear-cut. In many cases the counselor will have to make more subtle decisions. When agency policy or actions do not agree with one's perception of correct procedure, it would seem wise to think of these problems as lying on a continuum. For example, counselors might want to see problems of agency procedure improved but allow their supervisors to deal with such problems. A second point on the continuum might be "I hold the agency responsible, and I intend to document what is happening." A final point on the continuum might be "These are actions I can't be a party to, and if I cannot get them changed, I must resign. These actions violate my professional (or personal) ethics and values." In other words, some actions by an agency involve minor borderline violations; others are more serious and may need to be monitored carefully by counselors; still others are so clearly beyond the pale that counselors can only opt for leaving the agency if things are not changed.

Resolving Ethical Problems

In terms of proceeding to deal with these issues, counselors might discuss their concerns at the first level with colleagues, soliciting their opinion, and perhaps even talk to their supervisors about the changes they perceive as needed. This approach might lead to the elimination of agency policies that the counselors find annoying; of course, it is possible that the counselors will simply have to live with the issue. In the second level, the problems are more acute, and the documenting of the issues should occur after the counselors have approached their supervisors and pointed out the problem. If no solution is provided, the counselors verbally (or, as in many cases, in writing) should inform superiors that they will be documenting events because they view the issue as an ethical problem for the agency and as one that causes the counselors considerable concern. In the final level, it is assumed that the counselor has gone through the steps described above and, in addition, has met with trusted colleagues inside and outside the agency prior to deciding to leave. Leaving an agency because of unethical practices is sometimes the only thing that can be done; however, the counselor should remember that leaving the agency usually means losing powerful leverage in getting unethical actions and policies changed.

LONG-RANGE COUNSELOR SURVIVAL: JOB ADJUSTMENT AND AVOIDING BURNOUT

Modifying Work Goals

Over the span of their careers, social service workers show several changes in the way they approach their job. A study of professional workers in several social service agencies found the following changes in new professionals:

- Professionals modified the work goals they had set out to accomplish. The modification was frequently in the direction of accepting more modest goals in terms of job accomplishment.
- There was a strong tendency for professionals to reduce their level of personal involvement in the job. Physical and emotional withdrawal from clients was a common occurrence. This reduced investment in clients was accomplished by a reduction of the role of work in their lives and an increase in seeking fulfillment in their lives outside the workplace.
- There was a tendency for new professionals to shift responsibility for failure from themselves to things outside themselves (e.g., they blamed the clients or the system for failures on the job).
- Over time, young professionals became less idealistic, less trusting, and more conservative in their attitudes toward clients and people in general.
- There was increasing concern about self-protection and enhancing their own lives (e.g., gratification of their own needs at work became more important). Also, there was increasing concern about salaries and maintaining freedom of action in the job place (Cherniss, 1980).

Reality Shock

These changes were described as occurring because of reality shock. Most of the professionals discussed had little experiential or internship training and thus entered their jobs with idealistic expectations that were not based on the realistic demands of their jobs. Most chemical dependency counselors do have considerable experiential training before taking their first job; however, while the proportion of the training occurring in real life settings is high, most chemical dependency counselors spend much less absolute time in training than did the professionals in the above study. In other words, while the experiential training certainly helps to insulate chemical dependency counselors against some of the stresses suffered by these professionals, it is probably still insufficient to prevent many of these same changes from occurring in the lives of substance abuse counselors. In fact, some degree of change in job perception and attitudes toward work in the direction of the changes noted above is probably normal and to be expected. These changes may be necessary for counselors to survive in the workplace. However, when pressures in the job place are extreme, there is the danger that chemical dependency counselors may experience job burnout.

Counselor Vulnerability to Burnout

Burnout has been described as a frequently occurring event in the lives of those counselors working with chemically dependent people. It has been noted, for example, that the role of the alcohol counselor is extremely vulnerable to burnout (Knauert & Davidson, 1979). One writer has suggested that human service workers are affected in the following ways:

- Human service work is psychologically fatiguing or stressful.
- Service providers experience and exhibit an identifiable pattern of "burnout" reactions.
- The behaviors associated with burnout reduce the individual's effectiveness with clients; indeed, burnout can cause the service provider to act in ways which are harmful to clients. (Sarata, 1982)

The effects of burnout are not only potentially harmful to clients but to the counselor's job performance, job satisfaction, and morale. Thus, burnout can play a crucial role in determining whether the counselor survives in the chemical dependency agency. It is important to first examine the characteristics of burnout that have been experienced and reported by alcohol counselors. Second, the ways these same counselors describe the recognition of burnout in their colleagues would seem to be important. As the following findings indicate, both perspectives are important, because one's perception of burnout changes drastically depending upon whether it is being experienced personally or viewed in another person.

Personal Responses to Burnout

Sarata presents a list of the personal responses to burnout given by participants in a burnout workshop for alcohol counselors (see Table 7-1). As Table 7-1 shows, the response reported by the largest percentage of counselors was that of being drained and exhausted and tired of listening and thinking so hard. The fact that burnout can affect self-esteem is reflected in the counselors' responses indicating feelings of helplessness, incompetence, and being overwhelmed.

A chemical dependency counselor would be wise to become well acquainted with the types of experiences reported by Sarata's alcohol counselors. These warning signs can be used to alert counselors that they either need to spend some time away from their jobs or increase their involvement in the maintenance strategies and behaviors that are outlined below. Sarata found that 65 percent of the counselors involved in his workshop were at a point where they should examine their lives for some possible change; 7 percent of the counselors were clearly experiencing burnout. These findings suggest that chemical dependency counselors need to spend more time monitoring their job reactions and taking corrective action where needed.

Burnout as Viewed By Others

Table 7-2 presents the ways in which burnout was reported as being observed in others. As Table 7-2 shows, counselors suffering burnout are perceived as reacting

Table 7–1 Phrases Used by Alcoholism Counselors To Describe Their Burnout Experiences

Respondents (N = 93)	Responses (N = 348)	Type of Phrase
71%	19%	Drained, exhausted (e.g., "tired of thinking so hard and listening so intently")
45%	12%	Helpless, incompetent, overwhelmed (e.g., "the faster I worked, the behinder I got")
34%	9%	Angry (e.g., "wanting to lash out")
30%	8%	Depressed
30%	8%	Anxious, fearful (e.g., "scared for self and clients")
26%	7%	Emotionally troubled, volatile (e.g., "losing control of self, uptight")
26%	7%	Irritable
17%	4%	Frustrated (e.g., "about what I failed to accomplish")
16%	4%	Alone (e.g., "dumped upon and unsupported")
16%	4%	Wanting to escape (e.g., "hoping clients don't show, dreaming about my vacation")
12%	3%	Resentful (e.g., "everyone is making demands")
10%	3%	Misunderstood and/or sorry for self
10%	3%	Uncaring
7%	2%	Caring too much (e.g., "taking cases home")
	6%	Other (e.g., "rigid, controlling, critical of others, having tunnel vision")

Source: Sarata, B.P.V. *Burnout workshops for alcoholism counselors.* Unpublished paper. Lincoln, Neb.: University of Nebraska, 1982.

in ways that are destructive to interagency communication; they behave in ways that can affect the morale of the people around them; and their style of dealing with their clients becomes drastically countertherapeutic. If these descriptions are accurate (they do agree with the author's observations), they stand as evidence that people who have been outstanding counselors and colleagues can show extreme deterioration as a result of not maintaining themselves on the job. Of course, one should remember that things occurring at home and in the counselor's personal life can be the cause of many of the behaviors linked to burnout; in other cases, the strain of the job is reflected in the person's home life. Not infrequently, there is an interaction between what is going on at work and the reaction of people at home. However, in some cases, the person will report feeling better and more relaxed away from work and then report headaches, anger, and frustration shortly after arriving at the workplace. Such dramatic changes may reflect burnout or extreme dissatisfaction with the job, or both.

Table 7–2 Phrases Used by Alcoholism Counselors To Describe Indicators of Burnout Among Coworkers

Respondents (N = 93)	Responses (N = 298)	Type of Indicator
45%	16%	Withdrawn, isolated, silent, shuts office door, won't discuss work with others.
35%	11%	Complaining, bitches about everything.
32%	10%	Spaced-out, can't follow conversation, only half listening, forgetful.
20%	7%	Avoids work, absent, clock watching, does personal errands, tardy.
19%	7%	Critical of others, blames coworkers, scolds clients, terminates problem cases.
16%	6%	Depressed, loss of confidence, perseverates about mistakes, turns every conversation to pessimistic side.
16%	5%	Procrastination, does only enough to get through each day.
13%	5%	Loss of objectivity, gets overinvolved with clients, misreads clients.
12%	4%	Emotionally flat, flat affect, lacks enthusiasm, loss of concern.
12%	4%	Emotionally volatile, paranoid, screams, throws things.
10%	4%	Physical problems.
10%	4%	Very busy, hassled, too busy for anything.
	15%	Other, e.g., inflexible, tunnel vision, poor hygiene, smokes too much.

Source: Sarata, B.P.V. *Burnout workshops for alcoholism counselors.* Unpublished paper. Lincoln, Neb.: University of Nebraska, 1982.

Maintaining Peak Counselor Efficiency: Avoiding Burnout

At this point, it is important to outline some ways in which chemical dependency counselors may maintain themselves at peak work performance and point out some of the traps that many chemical dependency counselors fall into in the workplace. These issues are discussed below.

Maintaining a Life Outside the Agency

Many counselors feel that a measure of devotion to their job is the fact that they are committed to it totally. Counselors should be acutely aware that they need to discriminate between values directed toward work and values directed toward other

things in their life. Both are important in maintaining long-range peak performance on the job. For example, maintaining relationships with family and friends
can give counselors a "time out" from the job place that allows the needed
emotional support and psychological repair following a bad day at the office.
Failure to maintain a life outside of the job place may not have drastic effects on
counselor performance in the short run, but grave risks are run if the counselor
remains totally involved over a long period of time (e.g., several years). For one
thing, the necessary network to emotionally support the counselor once he burns
out is simply not there when it is needed (i.e., family and friends will be more
distant and less readily available when the counselor needs their support). With
individuals who have not practiced personal maintenance, it may be necessary to
leave the alcohol or drug field for several years to recharge their batteries. This
practice is not unknown to chemical dependency counselors who simply do not, or
cannot, work without making their job their total life commitment.

Making a more qualified commitment to the alcohol field is particularly difficult
for those counselors who are themselves recovering alcoholics. For example, it is
frequently difficult for recovering counselors to discriminate between their job, the
work needed for AA maintenance, and maintaining close relationships with
friends (many of whom are recovering abusers themselves). In this situation, there
is generally considerable mutual support. However, there is also the tendency to
get into a pattern where one talks shop constantly, and the arena of one's life is
drastically narrowed. Thus, the very necessary distractions of doing other things
and not obsessively dwelling on job-related issues are lost.

Modeling a Balanced Life

While the above adjustments are important for preventing burnout, there are
some other issues that are just as crucial. Alcohol counselors, like all caregivers,
are models for appropriate behavior for their clients. In fact, modeling is emphasized by recovering counselors, and they will frequently point out similarities
between their history and personality and those of the client. In some cases,
counselors give specific advice about methods and procedures that clients can use
to deal with their problems with alcohol or drugs from the perspective of "This is
the way I managed it and so can you." However, when recovering counselors also
model a life that is filled with little but work, they are modeling behavior that the
large majority of people would see as inappropriate. In other words, maintaining a
balanced life allows the counselor to present a healthier model for the client to
emulate. This notion of a healthy, balanced life as a useful tool in caregiving has
frequently been underestimated by substance abuse counselors. Many recovering
counselors seem to turn their obsession with alcohol into an obsession with work;
they become workaholics.

Dealing with Excessive Agency Work Demands

Recovering counselors (and many nonrecovering counselors) are extremely dedicated and committed to the alcohol field and to the clients they serve. Frequently, chemical dependency agencies take advantage of these dedicated counselors. They are the ones who are persuaded to spend extra hours at the facility and who can be counted on to volunteer for the many extra services needed by the agency. Often the supervisor will involve the dedicated counselor in additional tasks simply because the supervisor is not alert to the possible consequences of his actions. Some supervisors are unscrupulous in their use of people or are eager to find a quick and simple solution. Whatever the reason, the counselor should be alert to the possibility of being used since it increases the risk of early job burnout.

Maintaining a Reasonable Caseload

The heavier the workload, the greater the tendency for counselors to suffer burnout. It has been pointed out that it is not simply the long hours that create burnout; rather, it seems to be the greater direct contact with clients (Cherniss, 1980). Since intense involvement with clients is characteristic of the substance abuse field, counselors should be particularly wary here. A heavier client workload is manageable if there are frequent timeouts from client contact; another way of saying this is that quality of workload as well as amount of time spent with clients affects the burnout rate.

Another "quality of workload" factor is the scope of client contact, i.e., the range of problems addressed by a professional working with a client and the extent to which the counselor sees the client in different kinds of situations. For example, counselors may never have the opportunity to follow up their successful cases, and thus they only see those clients who are readmitted for treatment. Therefore, counselors only receive negative feedback from populations with high relapse rates (e.g., a detox unit) and receive almost no feedback about the people they have helped, because all their time is spent meeting the needs of their "failures." For this reason, establishing some sort of follow-up system for successful cases may be a useful strategy, not just to better evaluate effectiveness but also to help prevent burnout. In brief, counselors will deal more effectively with job stress when they are exposed to the full range of clients' lives, from detoxification to long-range recovery.

Ambiguous Agency Goals and Objectives

A factor that seems to affect new professionals' burnout rate (and one that is present in some substance abuse agencies) is a lack of clarity about agency goals and expectations (Cherniss, 1980). When the guidelines that counselors are expected to follow are changed from week to week, counselors who are still uncertain about their competence face an additional stress in the job place. When counselors survive the initial stress created by a lack of structure, they may, with more experience and confidence, exploit this ambiguity. For example, in an unstructured situation, it may be possible to secure more advantageous working conditions for counselors and better services for their clients. However, in the initial stages, the ambiguity or conflict in goals only increases the new counselors' sense of helplessness.

Maintaining a Reasonable Job Perspective

Frequently counselors fail to maintain a perspective on their own job and on the agency in which they work. The ability to maintain an awareness of one's own limitations, the limitations of the agency where one works, and the limitations of the substance abuse field in general is crucial to chemical dependency counselors. In order to obtain a realistic perspective on these factors, the chemical dependency counselor may need to do several things. For example, counselors should attend outside conferences and communicate with other agencies in and out of the substance abuse field as often as possible. If counselors do not maintain contact with other agencies, they begin to see the way their agency does things as the only way to approach the treatment of substance abuse. This egocentric approach to treatment is a particular problem in the substance abuse field.

Maintaining Contact with Other Professionals

The author has been at several conventions where different groups described approximately the same type program as new and innovative. None of the groups were aware that the other groups had similar programs (and similar problems), so an opportunity to compare how specific problems could be dealt with was lost. This tendency to become self-centered and self-satisfied can lead to a selective gathering of information and a failure to appreciate other ways of doing the job counselors are doing.

Being open to new information and seeking it out have an important role in preventing burnout. One of the things that seems to work to prevent burnout is to be involved in new and different ways of thinking about the job. Maintaining inservice training programs and attending outside workshops and various other outside training experiences is one way of insulating against burnout and the consequent drop in the quality of care for clients. A penny-wise-and-pound-foolish stance by an agency is to fail to subsidize attendance at these training experiences and to insist that all of the counselor's time be spent with clients. The result of this lack of professional stimulation is that counselors become less motivated and show many of the signs of burnout noted above. An indirect benefit of having counselors involved in outside training experiences is that they become more open to other points of view (and to other agencies), thus improving communication possibilities with other community agencies. They also keep up with new ideas and innovations in the field much better.

Staff Support Groups

There are some additional strategies that may help to prevent burnout in the counselor. These methods of dealing with job burnout are somewhat more dependent upon the existing structure, policies, and attitudes of an agency than those noted above. One strategy would be for newer counselors to develop a staff support group. These groups provide opportunities to regularly discuss and analyze burnout experiences with others working in similar situations. These types of groups can reduce burnout and its effects. In support groups counselors from the same agency or from different agencies come together, usually on a regular basis, to talk about their work experiences. There is usually no formal leader and as little structure as possible. Typically, counselors share job-related satisfactions, frustrations, and uncertainties. Those with specific problems can present them to the group and receive concrete suggestions. There is an atmosphere of acceptance and concern by group members. The danger here is that these groups can turn into "bitch" sessions. A genuine effort must be made to go beyond simply sharing emotions and to suggest new attitudes and strategies for dealing with problems. A real danger is that the group can become dominated by members who have already burned out. Since the attitudes associated with burnout are highly contagious where a high degree of burnout already exists in an agency, the forming of a support group from existing staff may be counterproductive for the less experienced counselors.

Rotating Workloads

Another strategy designed to provide variety for counselors in the workplace is to rotate counselors' workloads. For example, taking a turn at performing the intake sessions in an agency offers an opportunity for relief from ongoing routine. One alcohol intake-and-referral agency asks each counselor to spend one day each month visiting clients who have been referred for inpatient treatment (and their agencies). These visits improve communication with outside agencies and provide some variety for the alcohol counselors. Another possible adjustment is to make sure that counselors see a variety of clients. In some alcohol agencies, new counselors may be assigned more revolving-door alcoholics initially because these clients are seen as less rewarding by the rest of the staff. While many of these alcoholics recover, the success rate is usually low, further placing stress on new counselors who may already be struggling with feelings of self-doubt about their competence.

Performance Feedback

Still another procedure to help reduce the burnout rate is to increase performance feedback for new counselors. Many agencies are casual about feedback, and the new counselor must be assertive enough to ask for feedback. (This is sometimes difficult for counselors to do when they are already unsure of their ability.) Feedback is particularly important during the first six months of the job and should be given frequently during these initial months.

One way that an inexperienced counselor can obtain feedback is to work with a more experienced counselor in seeing one or more clients. For example, the new counselor might work with an experienced counselor on a family case or a marital problem or colead a group with another counselor. These experiences are both a learning experience and a chance to gain some estimate of one's performance relative to that of a more experienced counselor in the agency. This procedure also helps to reduce the new counselor's social isolation in the agency.

Finally, factors that are not under the counselors' control may reduce or speed up burnout. For example, burnout is less likely for those counselors working in agencies with clear and consistent goals. Defining clear and consistent goals is, unfortunately, a task that is difficult for many substance abuse agencies. New counselors should be aware of this job stress and realize that it may have a severe impact on them. They should also be aware that changing this may be beyond their control; learning to live with the ambiguity or leaving the agency may be the only choices they have. An associated issue is that the agency should have realistic goals. Many agencies have grandiose notions about their missions. Administrators in these agencies may demand that counselors carry 40 clients per week in individual counseling, maintain liaison with local agencies, and keep all records and charts up to date. Unfortunately, these high work demands cannot be met, and it is precisely those dedicated and committed counselors who hate cutting corners and doing shoddy work who suffer the most (i.e., they are the staff most likely to burn out, in their attempt to keep up with the unrealistic work demands).

As this discussion shows, burnout is indeed a very serious problem for substance abuse agencies. However, the points outlined above should allow the chemical dependency counselor to avoid many of the problems associated with burnout. In the final analysis, it may be necessary for some people to work at other jobs periodically in order to regain the motivation and drive to work effectively in the alcohol or drug field.

JOB SELECTION: A CRITICAL CHOICE IN COUNSELOR SURVIVAL

Taking a job is a difficult experience under the best of circumstances, especially for a new counselor. Whether the job applicant is a newly trained counselor or very experienced, he or she will be making choices about whether to take a job with incomplete knowledge of how a given agency functions. Knowledge about the agency may be so lacking that the counselor may not even know what questions to ask. In some cases, counselors may feel they shouldn't ask too many questions since that might make them appear too "pushy" to the potential employer.

In the author's experience, most agencies are impressed by an applicant who is able to ask informed and appropriate questions about a position. Most interpret such questions as reflecting interest in their agency and as coming from an applicant who will be a thoughtful, knowledgeable, and invested employee. Of course, the major issue here is *how* questions are asked about the job. Applicants who are insensitive to the needs of the interviewer, or are too blunt in posing questions, may do themselves considerable harm. On the other hand, most agency employers will respond positively to well-thought-out questions that reflect some knowledge of the agency and a genuine interest in learning more about the job.

Finding Out About Your Potential Employer

Getting to be an informed job applicant does require some effort, but it will usually pay off in better job selection. Some of the procedures for getting prepared to ask sensible questions about the job are discussed below.

Read As Much About the Agency As Possible

Frequently, agencies will put out pamphlets to describe their mission, types of clients served, etc. While these pamphlets are frequently idealized descriptions of the agency and therefore should be accepted with caution, they do give the counselor an idea of how, ideally, the agency sees itself functioning. They can also allow the counselor, in conjunction with information gathered through other sources, to find out how well the agency has met its idealized goals. If there is minimal overlap between how the agency sees itself and how it seems to function, it would be important to ask, in the interview, what the agency does, how it functions, and what its mission is (to see if these inconsistencies can be resolved). An agency that has gross inconsistencies between its mission statement and what it actually does may be an agency in considerable turmoil—and it may be a tough place to work.

Find Out As Much As You Can About the Agency from Other Community Agencies

Again, this information must be used with caution. The intense politicization of the alcohol field can produce some distortion in one agency's views of another agency (because of vested interests), and this factor must be weighed when very negative impressions of a given agency are being expressed. Coordinating groups made up of local alcohol and drug counselors who deal with several chemical dependency agencies in the community may provide some important feedback. In any case, it would be wise to ask several agencies, in an informal way, how they see the prospective employing agency. As noted below, an agency that maintains clear and open communication with other agencies is likely to be more efficient and create less frustration for its employees. Less conflict with outside agencies means counselors will have more resources available to do their job and will be less likely to suffer burnout.

How the Agency Fits into the Overall Community System

Another factor that job applicants are likely to overlook is how the agency fits into the overall service delivery system in a community. For example, what need is the agency meeting in the community, and is it likely that the need will continue to be a high priority for the community? The reality of all job situations is that they are more likely to continue *if* they are perceived as needed by the people who provide the funding. Therefore, establishing whether the agency plays an important role in the continuum of care (in the opinion of coordinating agencies and other agencies in the community) may give the counselor a sense of job security potential in the agency. In this same vein, it might be important to ask outside sources (and try to glean from the written information on the agency) what the future role of the agency is likely to be. Not infrequently, agencies can make drastic changes in role and function, and counselors who thought they were taking a job in an agency with one mission suddenly find they are in an agency with another mission altogether. Also, even if the counselors have worked in agencies with the same explicit role and function, they cannot take for granted that they know what the new agency does. It is wise to treat each new job situation as one in which the counselor goes through considerable data collection prior to the interview, regardless of how much the counselor thinks he knows about the agency. Both the counselor and his future employer will benefit from this approach.*

Agency Overseeing Authority

A question that may initially escape the counselor (but which may prove to be important once employment is undertaken) is this: to whom does the agency answer in terms of ultimate responsibility? Is it the city council, county commissioners, a state agency, a board of directors, or some other group? If possible, you should also try to find out how actively the overseeing body is involved in agency decisions and day-to-day administration. Generally speaking, overseeing au-

---

*The author is indebted to Phillip Tegler, Director of Directions, an employee assistance program, for suggestions about things for counselors to inquire about prior to taking a job at an agency. Mr. Tegler is a former staff member of the survival skills program, Southeast Community College, Lincoln, Nebraska.

thorities are responsible for setting policy, while supervising personnel in the agency are responsible for day-to-day decisions on how the work is done (i.e., how the policies are to be implemented). A rule of thumb is that overseeing authorities should not be involved in program administration because they are not as aware of how the agency functions as are the on-site administrators. Where the overseeing agency is heavily involved, it frequently means that the agency has serious internal problems. For example, it may mean that the board has lost confidence in the administrative head of the agency. It could also mean that the governing board is composed of people who will not allow the agency to function without their steady input. Or, it could mean there have been serious blow-ups within the agency or between the agency and the community at large. None of these things bode well for a counselor and will most surely increase the job stress under which the counselor must work.

Basic Personality Types in Caregiving Agencies

In addition to what you find out about the agency, it is important to have an awareness of who you are and what you want from a job before you proceed with the interview. While there are several ways to answer this type of question, one way may be to look closely at what your primary needs are. Cherniss (1980) has outlined four basic types of people that he found working in human service agencies. While any general description of caregivers is bound to be an over-simplification, these career orientations may be helpful to counselors in outlining their own primary needs.

Social Activists

These individuals want to do more in their daily work than provide help to a given client. Personal security and status seem to mean very little to these people: their primary objective is to bring about some type of social and institutional change that would better the lives of the people they seek to help. In brief, these individuals seem to be concerned with social values and wish to work with people who share their ideology and commitment to social change. In the chemical dependency field there are many people seeking to change the way the system delivers services or meets the needs of chemical dependency clients. Many of them are frustrated because they have entered agencies where it is difficult to be involved with or bring about these system changes. The types of agencies in the chemical dependency field that are most apt to accomplish these goals are not likely to be direct service agencies; instead, they are likely to be state agencies, coordinating and advocacy groups such as the local alcohol and drug councils, or alcohol and drug foundation groups.

Careerists

Cherniss sees the individuals in this group as seeking success as it is conventionally defined. Prestige, respectability, and financial security are what is important to careerists. These individuals want to make a good impression on colleagues, supervisors, and anyone else who might control career advancement. While the chemical dependency field frequently disparages people who seek career advancement, these individuals usually are sympathetic, caring, and helpful to the clients they serve, and they provide a high level of service—it is just that their *primary* goal is to secure recognition and advancement. If career and job advancement are important to counselors, then they should find what opportunities exist in the agency for advancement and whether a job there can be a solid preparation for seeking a better job in another agency. The use of a job to advance one's career may initially seem distasteful to some counselors, but careful career planning may mean that they get to where they want to go in a more efficient and better prepared manner.

Artisans

To these individuals, the issues of career advancement and financial success are less important than the intrinsic quality of their work. Professional service and growth are also important to these service givers. They wish to perform well, according to their own internal standards. Cherniss sees the individuals in this group as the most individualistic. They tend to value autonomy and independence more highly than do social activists or careerists. They tend to be less competitive than individuals in these other groups, and they like working with people who know more than they do, because they can learn from them. Cherniss found that artisans will tend to leave a job (even when seen as successful by the agency that employs them) simply because the job is no longer stimulating and challenging. Those who feel that this description fits them should be concerned about things like the ability to work independently, with minimal constraints from supervisors. Individuals such as these would probably prefer an agency that stresses the individual professional responsibility and authority of the counselor; they would also like to be in an agency with stimulating personnel from whom they can learn. Frequently, these attributes are found in agencies that are trying a new approach to treatment or are trying to deal with chemical dependency issues in a new way. These individuals would be very unhappy in an agency where there were severe bureaucratic barriers and demands and where there was a rigid authoritarian chain of command in terms of supervision.

Self-investors

Self-investors are more involved in their life outside work than in their careers. These individuals are not motivated by work-related concerns. In general, they seek interesting work that is moderately challenging but which does not demand too much of them. They also desire pleasant, friendly coworkers and supervisors. If your job is not going to be the central part of your life, you may want an agency that is less demanding in terms of workload. You might also seek a place where the people seem to get along well with one another and value their interaction with one another very highly. While some people might view this work role as inferior to some of the others mentioned, it may be realistic for many counselors. For example, if a man or woman has a major investment in maintaining the family, such a job may be the most appropriate choice. It should be noted that Cherniss found that people with this career orientation were committed to maintaining an adequate performance level and that they would work extremely hard to bring their work level up to an acceptable standard.

Cherniss has been careful to point out that most people are really a mixture of all four of these types. In fact, he has a fifth category called a "mixed type," which combines qualities of the other four types. At the very least, a consideration of these types of career orientations should allow counselors to come up with their own set of job requirements: requirements that will fit their specific needs. Such a procedure should help clarify exactly what the counselor may want from a job and lead to the asking of appropriate questions in the job interview.

The Job Interview

If you are well prepared and have an understanding of the things you want to ask, you can obtain a considerable amount of important information from a job interview. For example, you will want to get as precise a job description as possible from the person who is responsible for hiring you. You may want to know who will supervise you and to whom you will answer in the agency. It may be important to ask about where you will be housed, office availability, etc. It goes without saying that you should also ask about salary and the possibility of salary increments. All of these questions are relevant and important: however, there may be other issues that are even more important.

Orientation Period

Find out if the agency usually has an orientation period where the new counselor can become acquainted with the agency and the job. This will provide the means and the time for new employees to learn the administrative tasks, etc., that will allow them to do their job more easily and effectively. Cherniss found that if counselors were dropped into a new job without orientation or a chance to get their feet on the ground, they were less likely to have a positive attitude toward the job and more likely to suffer burnout.

Workload Demands

Try to establish the workload demands expected by the agency. Generally speaking, the greater the workload, the greater the probability for burnout. Even a heavy workload can be managed if there are frequent opportunities for timeouts from face-to-face contact with clients. It is also important to determine the range of client contact available. Being responsible for a variety of different clients and being able to follow the same client through the system can help prevent burnout.

Degree of Job Stimulation

It is important to determine the amount of intellectual stimulation, challenge, and variety in the job. These factors will determine whether a counselor suffers burnout: the more of these characteristics present in the job, the less likely the counselor will suffer burnout.

Degree of Job Freedom

Try to find out how much freedom you will have on the job, because rigid bureaucratic control of a counselor's actions in the job place can lead to more rapid burnout. (This may be an important thing to find out about an agency during the interview. For example, psychiatric hospitals usually have more rigid bureaucratic control than an out-patient alcohol treatment center.) If freedom to do the job your way and on your own schedule is important to you, it would be especially wise to ask current employees about the amount of autonomy they feel they have.

Clearly Defined Agency Goals and Expectations

Try to find out in the interview (or from counselors currently working in the agency) how clearly the goals and expectations of the agency are spelled out to counselors. If guidelines and policies are unclear or if they change from week to week, it increases the danger of job burnout.

Compatible Outlook and Beliefs

Try to establish if the agency and the people working in it have an outlook on life and beliefs that are compatible with your own. Differences in outlook and beliefs are major sources of dissension in human care agencies.

An awareness of these issues will give you a chance to ask questions about all of the above areas of concern. Finally, you should establish the job's time demands. You must also ask yourself whether these time demands are consistent with your life roles. If you are married, with heavy family responsibilities, 15-hour days may not be appropriate for you. In conjunction with this question, you should try to ascertain whether the agency has realistic expectations and goals. Sometimes chemical dependency agencies expect staff to work extremely lengthy days because the agency is unrealistic about the goals it is attempting to accomplish. One final comment: it is totally unrealistic for applicant counselors to believe that they can come into an agency and carry out dramatic change. That is why it is so important to know the agency as well as possible before becoming a part of it: to not be fully aware of the agency eventually leads to lowered morale, frustration and fatigue (i.e., burnout), and the counselor is unlikely to survive.

This chapter outlines some of the problems faced by chemical dependency counselors in working with clients and the agencies that employ the counselor. As we have seen, chemical dependency counselors are faced with heavy, sometimes unreasonable demands from the clients they have in treatment. These demands are exacerbated by the fact that the treatment of the substance abuser requires a strong commitment to caring by the counselor in order to be effective. This situation places the chemical dependency counselor at risk for burnout. Stress on the counselor is increased when emotional energy is demanded to deal with communication problems within and between agencies. These intra-agency staff struggles (e.g., between lay and professional counselors) rob counselors of emotional energy and have negative effects on the clients under their care. It has been pointed out here that there are things alcohol counselors can do to ensure survival as viable helping therapists throughout their stay in the chemical dependency field. Factors to consider when choosing a job (such as matching oneself with the appropriate agency depending upon one's own needs and the agency's expectations of counselors) have been noted. It has also been pointed out that chemical dependency counselors should be aware of some of the possible adjustments they may need to make over time in their role in an agency. Finally, an attempt has been made to show the counselors some of the issues they will face in the chemical dependency field and how they can often effectively prevent or reduce problems that could affect their emotional and vocational survival.

This chapter has focused on issues of survival for the chemical dependency counselor working in a substance abuse agency. Adjustments that a chemical dependency counselor might have to make in other agencies (e.g., a correctional facility, the general hospital, industry, and the many other settings where the counselor could be employed) have not been dealt with specifically. It is hoped chemical dependency counselors working in these settings will find many of the things discussed here useful to them. As chemical dependency caregivers become involved in new agencies there will doubtless be job place adjustments that differ somewhat across all settings.

At the present time the growth of personnel in the chemical dependency field has increased markedly. While some of this increase is no doubt tied to increased funding in the substance abuse area, it is also due partly to the discovery, by many people, that working with chemically dependent people is highly rewarding. While this chapter has focused on managing some of the difficulties of working as a chemical dependency counselor, it should be noted that most chemical dependency counselors find the work exciting and gratifying. There are few places in the human caregiving system where a remarkable turnaround in a person's life can be accomplished as dramatically and rapidly. It is hoped that the issues covered in this chapter will help counselors maintain the enthusiasm and excitement with which they initially entered the field. In our opinion, their excitement is justified.

REFERENCES

Cherniss, C. *Professional burnout in human service organizations*. New York: Praeger Publishers, 1980.

Jellinek, E.M. *The disease concept of alcoholism*. New Brunswick, N.J.: Hillhouse Press, 1960.

Kalb, M., & Propper, M.S. The future of alcohology: Craft or science? *American Journal of Psychiatry*, 1976, *133*, 641–645.

Knauert, A., & Davidson, S. Maintaining the sanity of alcoholism counselors. *Family and Community Health*, 1979, 65–70.

Rivers, P.C., Sarata, B.P.V., & Book, T. The effect of an alcoholism workshop on attitudes, job satisfaction, and job performance of secretaries. *Quarterly Journal of Studies on Alcohol*, 1974, *35*, 1382–1388.

Sarata, B.P.V. Beginning employment as a child care worker: An examination of work experiences. *Child Care Quarterly*, 1979, *8*, 295–302.

Sarata, B.P.V. *Burnout workshops for alcoholism counselors*. Unpublished paper. Lincoln, Nebr.: University of Nebraska, 1982. (A later edition of this paper, with the same title, is currently in press in *The Journal of Alcohol and Drug Education*.)

Wegscheider, S. *Hope and health for the alcoholic family*. Palo Alto, Calif.: Science and Behavior Books, 1981.

SOME QUESTIONS TO CONSIDER

1. What do I want from my job?
2. What type of people do I want to work with?
3. How can I go about achieving my goals for employment?

Chapter 8

Some Questions and Answers

Gary W. Lawson
P. Clayton Rivers
James S. Peterson

INTRODUCTION

In our experience, alcohol counselors frequently have certain questions about clients and the counseling field that they would like answered. We have gathered together several of these frequently asked questions in this chapter and have attempted to provide answers. These answers are based on the current clinical and research literature and our own experience; however, these questions can only be answered in terms of what is known by the authors at this time. The rapid explosion of information in the alcohol field means that new information may shortly make these answers incomplete or insufficient. However, with these questions as examples, we hope to illustrate to counselors that keeping up with new clinical and experimental research in the alcohol field can potentially be very helpful to them. We also hope to encourage counselors to continue to read the research literature and to attend meetings where new research information is disseminated. As these questions and their answers will illustrate, the new-found information in the alcohol field has great potential for program planning and for direct treatment of alcoholics and their families. However, until the new information is utilized by counselors, it will be not be employed to provide better care for the alcoholic—a goal all counselors share.

Are There Differences Between Male and Female Alcoholics, and How Should They Be Treated?

If one examines the literature, the answer is yes. For example, Bourne and Light (1979) outline several psychological and sociological differences between male and female alcoholics that they have gleaned from the research literature. These differences include the following:

- Women usually begin drinking (and problem drinking) at a later age than do their male counterparts.
- Women move more rapidly from the early stages to the later stages of drinking than men do.
- Women, more often than men, will cite a specific stress or traumatic event that precipitated their problem drinking. Frequently the events cited have to do with female physiological functioning.
- Women appear to do more solitary drinking, much of it in the privacy of their homes. This presumed isolation may be due to the female's greater sensitivity to social disapproval of public drinking and general guilt and shame about using alcohol. (Author's note: Bear in mind that alcohol abuse and alcoholism are frequently viewed as a graver social risk by the female alcohol abuser. Therefore, the female drinker may be more strongly motivated to disguise her problem than the male drinker, although both generally attempt to hide their abuse of alcohol.)
- A frequent finding is that female alcoholics are more likely to have affective (emotional) problems and that males are more likely to be sociopathic.
- The consequences of alcohol for men and women show different patterns. Men feel the consequences more frequently in the work situation, whereas women feel them more often in the family situation. Women alcoholics are more likely to be divorced than are male alcoholics.
- Women are more likely than men to have an alcohol model in their family. The frequency of alcohol problems among alcoholic women's husbands is markedly greater than in the general population or in the wives of alcoholic men.
- There appear to be different medical consequences for alcohol abuse, depending upon the sex of the individual. In general, women get sicker earlier and develop health problems associated with alcohol abuse more rapidly (and, thus, earlier in their drinking careers).
- Alcoholic women, as noted above, are more frequently characterized as feeling guilty, depressed, or anxiety ridden than are alcoholic men.
- Another factor, identified by Schuckit and Morrissey (1976), is the correlation between drinking practices and socioeconomic status among women. Lower socioeconomic status women have drinking histories similar to those reported for males; higher status women fit the stereotype of the woman alcoholic described above.

Considering these differences (and there may be others that will become known in the near future), the question can be properly asked: have these differences led to differentiated treatment strategies for men and women?

Much of what has been written about the treatment of the female alcoholic has appeared in the past decade. Even today, little is known about what procedures work best with women, and only recently have treatment programs modified their approaches to meet women's needs. Therefore, the reader is cautioned that what follows is the best reading, at the moment, of differential treatment of females and will surely change in the next few years. Another limitation is the current absence of broad-based empirical research. What is given here has, in the main, been gleaned from clinical reports and the observations of those working with alcohol-addicted women.

Subtypes of Alcoholic Women

One of those writers cognizant of both research and clinical data is Wilsnack (1982). She sees several issues that must be considered in meeting the treatment needs of women. First, it is important to distinguish among subtypes of alcoholic women. For example, if a woman is suffering from an affective disorder, it may be necessary to seek psychiatric consultation to determine the extent of the depression and the potential usefulness of antidepressant medication. If the depression has preceded the alcoholism and is longstanding, it may be important to consider using antidepressant medication.

Another issue where female subtypes may be useful is when considering those women who drink in response to stressful life events and those who drink in response to sex role-related conflicts and stresses. It is possible that each of these subgroups may account for 25 to 30 percent of female problem drinkers. For those alcoholic women who are reacting to stressful life events, resolving their feelings about precipitating life transition issues and helping them to find alternatives to alcohol and other drugs for coping with the crisis and its associated stress should be the main focus of treatment. Treatment of women in the second group should include attention to the woman's feelings about herself and her roles as a woman. Women's therapy and support groups may help such women identify social pressures to conform to traditional sex role expectations and may increase their acceptance of themselves as persons, independent of sex role stereotypes. This means that alcohol counselors must be acutely aware of their own expectations of male and female behavior so that they do not unwittingly reinforce rigid and contrasting sex role stereotypes.

Enhancing Self-Image

The negative self-image and low self-esteem of the female alcoholic is another area that Wilsnack sees as crucial in the treatment of alcoholic women. These negative feelings should be actively addressed during treatment. To help the woman feel better about herself, pleasant and attractive surroundings are helpful. Helping the woman restore her physical appearance and at the same time introducing her to other recovering alcoholic women who can serve as role models are also important goals. Expressive activities and activity therapies that can help restore confidence and self-esteem (e.g., dance, physical fitness, sports, and movement therapy) are also important adjuncts to traditional counseling. The alcoholic woman's vulnerable self-esteem may mean that a somewhat less confronting but more supportive counseling approach is needed.

Because unexpressed anger is believed to be a major source of low self-esteem in alcoholic women, counseling that explores the source of anger and provides direct training in assertive behavior can help women identify, accept, and express appropriately the anger they feel. In other cases, where the woman's low self-esteem is linked to destructive interpersonal or living situations, direct environmental intervention may be required to provide an environment supportive of the woman's self-image and the recovery process. What should be emphasized here is that enhancement of self-esteem early in treatment may increase the alcoholic woman's sense of personal worth and result in increased motivation to change her drinking behavior. Therefore, early self-esteem enhancement may prove more effective than simply waiting for self-esteem to improve as a result of changes in drinking behavior.

Since interpersonal crises and losses are more likely to precipitate alcohol abuse in women, it is possible that the involvement and support of significant others may play an even greater role in the treatment of women. (Certainly this is true in the second author's clinical experience.) Understanding, concern, and expressed affection from significant others all seem to be very powerful tools in the treatment process. In point of fact, however, some alcoholic women are surprised to learn how much those around them care about them: such relationships not previously shared may be first encountered around the alcoholic crisis. Because the alcoholic female so frequently reports problems associated with her marriage or her children, at least one writer (Tamerin, 1978) feels that the most appropriate therapeutic approach for all alcoholic women is marital or family therapy.

Counseling Needs of the Alcoholic Woman

Because sexual problems and concerns seem to be so prevalent in alcoholic women, sexual counseling should be made available to them and their partners. This means that counselors should be comfortable discussing sexual experiences and sexual problems and should know well-qualified professionals to whom they can refer clients with problems they do not feel competent to treat.

Another special area of concern is the use of psychoactive medication. In particular, women are more at risk for polydrug abuse. This is because physicians are more likely to prescribe a wide variety of psychotherapeutic drugs for women than men. However, the use of major tranquilizers and mood control agents may not only be appropriate but necessary for women with major psychiatric difficulties.

It is probably better to offer both mixed- and single-gender groups for the treatment of the alcoholic female. For example, alcoholic females frequently have major difficulties in relations with both males and females, and the mixed groups allow work on these issues. However, females also have major issues to resolve that are best done with women, who are more understanding and supportive, and provide better role models for dealing with issues of self-esteem and role definition.

What is also frequently overlooked is that a woman with alcoholic problems may lack some very basic survival skills. Retraining in vocational skills, financial management, life and career planning, and parenting skills may make life less overwhelming and give the woman a sense of mastery of problems.

One overlooked issue is that women need to have child care available in order to maintain treatment. Child care may reduce a woman's ambivalence about entering treatment and reduce guilt about how her drinking has affected her children. (Another possible benefit is that intervention with children with potential problems is possible. If the counselor works with the children while the mother is in treatment, potential readjustment problems for the children can be reduced or eliminated. Without this treatment, it is possible, particularly in adolescent children, that problems will occur after intense treatment for the mother has been completed.) Finally, there is the need to have specialized care (e.g., Women for Sobriety) available for the recovering alcoholic female following treatment.

Is Alcoholism a Disease?

Like most questions about alcoholism, this seemingly straightforward question is more complex than one would anticipate. By definition, disease is "an alteration of a living body that impairs its functioning" (Webster, 1977); thus, such severe alteration of body functioning occurs only in the drinker who is physically addicted to alcohol. The onset of physical addiction usually follows a long period (5 to 20 years) of abusive drinking. This type of physical addiction is usually only diagnosed when the alcoholic is deprived of alcohol. The major characteristics are intense withdrawal symptoms (shakes, nausea, agitation), changes in cell metabolism rates, and increased tolerance for alcohol. The addicted drinker has usually experienced "loss of control"—a physical urge to continue drinking against his conscious will.

While Jellinek (1960) thought the above type of addiction was symptomatic of the most common type of alcoholism in North America (Gamma Alcoholism), many other types of alcoholism also exist. Many of these "non-disease" types of alcoholism are equally difficult to rehabilitate, and some of these individuals may eventually become cell addicted and move into what Jellinek labels as the disease type of alcoholism.

The disease concept of alcoholism has been an important impetus in changing the public's perception of alcohol problems as being based on moral failings to a perception where the alcoholic is seen as medically ill. This shift in perception has led the general public to see alcoholism as a treatable disease. Following this change in perception has been the reduction of the stigma that has been so long associated with the disorder. It has also led to considerable support, from legislators and other policy makers, in the form of financial support for instruction and treatment of the alcoholic. In brief, the positing of alcoholism as a disease has had considerable positive benefit for the alcohol field in general and the alcoholic specifically.

However, declaring alcoholism to be a disease may be misleading to caregivers, according to writers such as Cahalan (1970) and Pattison, Sobell, and Sobell (1977). These researchers note that neither the recovery of the alcoholic nor the problem itself is necessarily aided by labeling the problem a disease. Even some physicians (e.g., Kissen, 1977) see the recovery of the alcoholic as being primarily concerned with psychological and social problems and having little to do with medical issues. Taken to the logical extreme, one could agree that using the disease concept to guide alcohol treatment might lead the counselor to provide unrealistic and inappropriate care. (The reader is also referred to Robinson (1972) for a further discussion of potential problems with the disease concept.)

However, until society becomes sophisticated enough to understand the gamut of social and psychological problems that the alcoholic must overcome, the disease concept will serve the alcohol field well. In addition, as Wallace (1978) has noted, being able to blame the disease for many of one's problems can be extremely therapeutic for the recovering alcoholic, particularly at the beginning of treatment.

Is Alcoholism Inherited?

This question has been raised because of the fact that alcoholism seems to run in families. For example, Goodwin (1979) has noted that children of alcoholics are four times as likely to become alcoholics as children of nonalcoholics. Therefore, the risk to the children of alcoholics is high; as Goodwin notes, alcoholism does run in families.

However, the fact that alcoholism runs in families is insufficient, by itself, to support a genetic cause of alcohol abuse; we need other supporting data before we can say that alcohol abuse is inherited or genetically linked. To obtain these types of data, researchers have followed several strategies. (See Goodwin (1979) for a complete discussion of all these strategies.) We shall focus here on the two sources that have produced, over the past decades, the most dramatic evidence in support of a genetically linked cause of alcoholism. These two strategies are twin studies and adoption studies.

Twin Studies

Twin studies assume that monozygotic twins (born from a single egg and fertilized by the same sperm) and dizygotic twins (born from two separate eggs fertilized by two different sperm) differ in the amount of genetically linked characteristics they share. For example, monozygotic, or identical, twins have almost exactly the same genetic makeup; fraternal twins share only about 50 percent. It is further assumed that the fraternal and identical twins' environments will not differ significantly. Given these assumptions, it is predicted that alcoholism will tend to co-occur more often in identical than in fraternal twins.

This strategy has been applied in at least two major studies. Kaij (1960), in a Swedish study, located 1,974 male twin pairs where at least one was registered at a temperance board because of conviction of drunkenness or some other indication of alcohol abuse. The concordance rate for alcohol abuse in the identical twin group was 54 percent; in the fraternal twins the concordance rate was 28 percent; (a statistically significant difference in concordance rates for the two types of twin pairs). Kaij also divided the alcohol abusers into subgroups, based on severity. When this was done, the 14 identical twin pairs classified as having the most severe alcohol problems showed a concordance rate of over 71 percent; there was no significant increase in concordance rates for the fraternal twins when one member of the pair was classified as having severe alcohol problems.

In a Finnish study, Partanen et al. (1966) found less definitive support of a genetic predisposition to alcoholism. Using male twins, these researchers found no differences between monozygotic and dizygotic twins in terms of the consequences alcohol had on their lives (the primary criterion used for diagnosing alcoholism). However, more or less normal patterns of drinking, i.e., frequency and amount, were more concordant in identical than fraternal twins.

These two studies reflect the mixed findings in twin studies. While they do not provide conclusive evidence that a predisposition to alcoholism is inherited, the results do suggest that heredity is a factor in alcoholism and should be considered when diagnosis and treatment are initiated. We shall return to this issue later.

Adoption Studies

The second strategy, the adoption strategy, has also shown somewhat mixed results. However, the recency of some of this research and the increased sophistication in viewing the issue has made these studies highly visible in the alcohol literature. Goodwin (1979), in a study of 55 Danish male adoptees with an alcoholic biological parent and 78 control adoptees without such a history, found that the adoptees with alcoholic biological parents were nearly four times more likely to be alcoholic themselves than were the control adoptees. Adopted away sons of alcoholics were then compared with their own brothers, who had been raised by the alcoholic biological parent. Alcoholism rates were similar in the two groups, suggesting that regardless of whether one was reared by or away from the biological parent, the alcohol risk would be the same. These findings argue strongly for a genetic predisposition to alcoholism and tend to call into question the importance of family environment.

Bohman and his colleagues (1978) reported on an adoption study of 2,323 illegitimate children born in Stockholm, between 1930 and 1949, who were placed in adoptive homes before three years of age. Male adoptees whose mothers or fathers had been registered as alcohol abusers were themselves more likely to be registered. Following this, Bohman and his colleagues selected 50 male adoptees whose fathers had been repeatedly registered for alcohol abuse (i.e., they were probably alcoholic) and very carefully matched them with adoptees whose parents had no history of alcohol abuse. Bohman found that 20 percent of the sons of frequently registered parents were also registered as alcohol abusers, while only 6 percent of the male children from nonalcohol-abusing parents were registered. Thus, this study also suggests a genetic contribution to alcoholism in men.

As these studies show, the significance of the genetic factor is clear in males, but the findings do not indicate a major genetic transmission factor in females. Cotton (1979) found, in a review of 39 English-language studies, that 27 percent of the fathers of alcoholics were themselves alcoholic but that less than 5 percent of the alcoholics had mothers who were alcoholic, suggesting that genetic predisposition may be sex linked. These findings, taken in concert with those of Goodwin, would certainly suggest such a conclusion. However, the possibility that drinking (and, particularly, abusive drinking) occurred at such low levels in females in Scandinavia (and elsewhere) over the time period studied may also account for the differential results in terms of sex.

Familial and Nonfamilial Alcoholism

So what conclusion can we draw from this type of research? Goodwin (1979) has suggested dividing alcoholism into two types: familial and nonfamilial. Familial alcoholism would be characterized by early age of onset, rapid development, and an explosive course requiring early treatment at an early age. On the other hand, intervention into nonfamilial alcoholism would require somewhat more diverse approaches and treatment programs.

Nonfamilial alcoholism would occur in a substantial number of alcoholics, according to Goodwin (1979). Another pair of writers (Murray & Stabenau, 1982) conclude:

> . . . the better of the studies of normal drinking have suggested a
> modest but significant genetic influence. . . . The family, twin, and
> adoptive studies concur in finding more evidence for male drinking
> being under genetic influence than female drinking. . . . One of the
> reasons why researchers have been slow to elucidate the exact nature of
> genetic predisposition is that they have been looking for simple answers.
> The present evidence is incompatible with simple Mendelian inheritance
> through a single dominant or recessive gene. . . . Any successful

etiological model must obviously take into account environmental factors such as price and availability of alcohol, plus the effect of occupation and family attitudes to alcohol. . . . (p. 142)

In brief, the status of the genetic predisposition research suggests that genetic factors can account for some part of alcohol problems but that even when this factor is most clearly isolated, environmental factors probably mediate its effects.

Are Recovering Alcoholics More Effective Alcoholism Counselors Than Nonalcoholics?

A large number of observers have debated the advantages and disadvantages of utilizing counselors who themselves are recovering alcoholics (e.g., Blume, 1977; Falkey, 1971; Pattison, 1973; Rosenberg, 1974; Strachen, 1973). In their favor, it has often been noted that recovering alcoholics, because of their personal experience with alcohol abuse, may have a greater understanding of the problem. This understanding gives them an ability to quickly form a close relationship with the alcoholic—an ability that nonalcoholic counselors supposedly do not have. Both through the use of the close relationship and their personal awareness of denial, recovering counselors can challenge denial more forthrightly and forcefully than the nonalcoholic counselor. Involved in this ability to confront and to treat the alcoholic in general is the recovering counselor's greater ability to select and use language that is appropriate and understandable to the alcoholic client.

Potential Problem Areas with Recovering Counselors

Some of the same writers who have noted the positive qualities of the recovering counselor have also noted negative characteristics. Specific problems include the defensiveness of the recovering counselor, overidentification with clients, overcommitment to one mode of treatment (usually AA oriented), and hostility toward the use of medication, toward the value of research, and toward mental health professionals in general.

Several writers have suggested that the alcoholic counselor's defensiveness is linked to his need to maintain his own sobriety. The argument is that if the recovering counselor does not maintain the view of alcoholism that is keeping him sober, then his self-esteem will be threatened. A common example is the individual whose own recovery rests on AA principles: this individual may be deeply and personally threatened by information that calls these AA principles into question. Conversely, the nonalcoholic counselor may see the challenge to traditional beliefs as an academic matter in need of discussion, debate, and further investigation.

Another area of potential threat to the recovering alcoholic is the frequent disparity in education between recovering and nonrecovering counselors. Because the pattern seems to be for the recovering counselor to be comparatively older and less well educated, the constant fear is that "these young guys" may know more than the recovering counselors. This sense of being one down also contributes to the alcoholic counselor's defensiveness. Resistance to new learning may also be based on economic reality. Personal experience with alcoholism and a personally successful recovery may constitute marketable certification to work in the field. When new treatment concepts are not (or cannot be) incorporated into the recovering counselor's own experience, then the alcoholic counselor may view them as potentially undermining his expertise and source of livelihood. Whatever the reason, all of the above stances tend to produce a counselor with a narrower view of caregiving, who may not be able or willing to use knowledge and skills that are potentially helpful to his clients.

Possibly as a result of this narrower view, recovering counselors exhibit a tendency to utilize one approach to treatment (usually AA oriented) for all clients, regardless of the individual problems they present. Kalb and Propper (1976) as well as Rossi and Filstead (1976) have suggested that recovering counselors tend to avoid serious consideration of alternative views on the nature of alcoholism and refuse to question their own premises in light of new research evidence. Therefore, despite new research findings that suggest new directions for treating alcohol abuse, these counselors cling to empirically invalidated approaches. Kalb and Propper maintain that clinical knowledge is governed by the craftsmanship of AA-oriented recovering counselors. Thus, established traditions have become sacred wisdoms, which survive because of the protection of loyal disciples. As Jellinek noted:

> In spite of the respect and admiration to which Alcoholics Anonymous have a claim on account of their great achievements, there is every reason why the student on alcoholism should emancipate himself from accepting the exclusiveness of the picture of alcoholism as propounded by Alcoholics Anonymous. (1960, p. 38)

As Wallace has pointed out (1978), many recovering alcoholics employ assimilative projection, i.e., the tendency to see everyone else as much like themselves. This identification with the client can be used to rapidly establish a client-counselor relationship and to reduce defensiveness in the alcoholic client. However, the individuality of the alcoholic client can be overlooked using this strategy and specific treatment needs may not be met. Thus, overidentification with the client can blind the alcoholic counselor to the real and special needs of a specific client and interfere with recovery.

The recovering counselor is frequently opposed to medication of any type. This means that in those alcoholics who need psychotropic medication for a psychotic disorder, the counselor's insistence on a drug-free approach could contribute to a psychotic break. In other clients suffering from depressive disorders, the elimination of lithium could lead to severe depression and suicide.

This attitude toward the use of psychoactive drugs is related to a general tendency of some recovering counselors to discount mental health issues and mental health professionals. In many cases it is because these counselors' own experience with mental health professionals has been very negative. However, discounting mental health problems and not using mental health personnel deprive those alcoholic clients who need these services of the best possible care. The best possible care for a client should be the professional goal of every caregiver; therefore, learning to wisely use other professionals in the mental health area would seem to be an important goal for all alcohol counselors.

Just as mental health resources should be used when needed, any new information or approaches that could be used in client treatment should be reviewed by counselors. The constant upgrading and learning of new skills and ideas would seem to be an appropriate goal for all counselors. Discounting all research as useless is a failure on the part of counselors to better prepare themselves to deal with problems. To the degree, then, that an alcohol counselor ignores new information that might be helpful, that counselor is being unprofessional and destructive of client welfare.

We have spent some time discussing these potential problem areas because the positive aspects of recovering alcoholics as therapists are frequently noted, but the potential dangers and blind spots of the recovering alcoholic are seldom discussed. However, these problematic areas are usually more than balanced by the empathy and commitment of the recovering counselor.

The final answer to the question of whether a recovering or nonrecovering counselor is the best therapist for alcoholics is not a simple one. Many people suggest a mix of about one-half recovering counselors and one-half nonrecovering counselors. The reason for this mix is that the alcoholic in treatment can then be the beneficiary of the commitment, empathy, and ready identification of the recovering alcoholic *and* the somewhat different viewpoint of the nonrecovering alcohol counselor. The nonrecovering counselor may look more closely at broader, non-alcohol-related adjustment issues than would the recovering counselor. To sum up, neither the recovering nor nonrecovering counselor is inherently the better caregiver for the alcoholic client. Instead, what is needed is a warm, empathic, and caring person who can work effectively with people.

How Does Alcohol Abuse Affect the Sexuality of Alcoholics?

The general impact of alcohol on human behavior has been described in a frequently quoted line from Shakespeare:

Lechery, sir it [alcohol] provokes and unprovokes; it provokes the desire, but it takes away the performance: therefore much drink may be said to be an equivocator with lechery . . . (from Macbeth, Act II, Scene III)

This view of how alcohol affects human sexual behavior is shared by both the public and professionals. More specifically, alcohol is a central nervous system depressant that progressively disrupts sensorimotor performance in a dose-related manner.

Sexual Difficulties of the Alcoholic Male

A general finding from animal research is that ingestion of alcohol leads to a delay in ejaculation and reduced duration of erection (Gantt, 1940, 1952). Some researchers believe that alcohol abuse in men can result in irreversible damage to the neurogenic reflex arc serving the process of erection (Masters & Johnson, 1970). Other, less severe psychophysiological responses may be suffered by the male. For example, several studies have suggested that penile tumescence is severely reduced by moderate to heavy ingestion of alcohol, with significant reduction of tumescence occurring after the ingestion of 75 milligrams or more of alcohol (e.g., Farkas & Rosen, 1976). In addition to these difficulties, reports of more severe consequences abound in the clinical literature. Atrophy of the gonads and enlargement of the breasts are frequently reported in men with chronic, long-term heavy-drinking histories.

In addition to these difficulties, male alcoholics suffer from the sexual difficulties that occur in the population at large. Clinical information would suggest, however, that these difficulties occur much more frequently in the abusive drinker than in the nonabuser. These difficulties include:

- *Erectile insufficiency.* The inability to achieve or maintain an erection sufficient for successful sexual intercourse. (This disorder was previously called impotence.) There are two types of erectile insufficiency: primary and secondary. We will focus on the latter since alcohol can most clearly contribute to this disorder. The male with this problem is unable to maintain the required level of penile rigidity. While prolonged difficulty with erections is rare in the population at large, it occurs more frequently in the heavy-drinking male because alcohol tends, at high dosages, to reduce sexual responsiveness. In addition, failure to achieve erection can set up an expectancy of sexual inadequacy that can become a self-fulfilling prophecy. As Masters and Johnson have noted, the greatest contributor to sexual inadequacy is fear of sexual inadequacy (1970).
- *Premature ejaculation.* This refers to an unsatisfactorily brief period between the commencement of sexual stimulation and the occurrence of ejaculation.

This results in the failure of the female partner to achieve satisfaction. In the drinking male, the needs of the female partner are lost in the general dulling of interpersonal sensitivity that occurs with heavy alcohol intake. Therefore, the male frequently focuses on satisfying his own needs and ignores those of his partner. Upon recovery, it may be necessary for the male to relearn the needs of his sexual partner (or learn them for the first time if sexual intercourse was usually conducted while the male was drinking). Sex counseling with both partners may be necessary to deal with this problem.

- *Retarded ejaculation or ejaculatory incompetence*. Here the problem is that the male cannot ejaculate while inside the female or cannot ejaculate at all. While the clinical literature would suggest that some alcoholics have sexual difficulties that lead them to use alcohol in order to perform the sexual act (and hence, alcoholics with the inability to ejaculate while inside the female are likely to be part of this problematic population), the more frequently occurring problem in abusive drinkers is the inability to ejaculate at all. This inability is frequently keyed to the alcoholic attempting intercourse while severely intoxicated and when the sexual response is so depressed that ejaculation is impossible. Or, the alcoholic attempts intercourse after drinking for several days and in a physiologically exhausted state. In both cases, several failures will lead to an expectation of ejaculatory incompetence that may result in a continuation of this difficulty when the alcoholic begins recovery. In these cases, intense sexual counseling may be needed to deal with the recovering male's psychological apprehensions.

These characteristics are certainly not exhaustive, and we are still learning how alcohol affects the male sexual response. Generally speaking, alcohol at low levels may be disinhibiting and even increase the pleasure of the sexual act. At moderate to high levels it clearly impairs sexual performance and can make the sexual act impossible. While in some cases, heavy drinking may permanently impair the male sexual response, a more likely outcome is that negative psychological expectations about sexual performance will be established; these expectations will have to be dealt with by the counselor during the recovery process.

Sexual Difficulties of the Alcoholic Female

Sexual difficulties also occur in females who abuse alcohol. While the initial literature regarding alcohol and the female described the alcoholic female as a "loose woman" and as very promiscuous, more recent research *does not* support this generalization.

Many females do report that alcohol has a disinhibiting effect on their sexual performances. Interviews by P. Clayton Rivers (one of the authors of this chapter) with women in treatment for alcoholism indicated that the vast majority of these women reported sexual intercourse while drinking was much more exciting and enjoyable. However, studies of actual physiological responses suggest that the sexual response is inhibited even when the females are reporting more arousal in response to erotic stimuli. For example, Wilson and Lawson (1976) measured vaginal pulse pressure of women at differential dose levels of alcohol. The more alcohol consumed, the lower vaginal pulse pressure was (i.e., lower physiological arousal), but as intoxication increased more of the women reported enhanced sexual arousal. So, while physiological arousal seemed to be reduced by alcohol in this study, the subjective experience of arousal increased.

Despite the heightened psychological expectation, studies of women with severe alcohol problems suggest that orgasm is severely curtailed by chronic alcohol intake (Levine, 1955) and that the sexual drive is inhibited (Glatt, 1961). Other factors that are closely associated with alcoholism in women are sexually related physiological difficulties. For example, one of the earliest descriptions of alcoholic women reported that problem drinking was associated with dysmenorrhea, abortion, childbirth, and sexually related physical disease. Menstrual periods have also been shown to be instrumental in precipitating excessive drinking in females (Lindbeck, 1972). Wilsnack (1982) has noted the prevalence of sexually related physical problems among alcoholic women and has suggested that alcohol may be used by many women to compensate for feelings of inadequacy. (This brief overview does not do justice to the complexity of alcohol use by the female: the reader is referred to Schuckit (1976) for more information.)

Although the following problems also occur in nonalcoholic women, they should give substance abuse counselors some awareness of potential sexual problems and will aid the counselor in diagnosing these problems in alcoholic females and in the spouses of male alcoholics.

- *Orgasmic dysfunction* can be *primary* or *secondary* in nature. The former refers to the failure by the female to ever achieve orgasm (by any means), whereas secondary orgasmic dysfunction occurs in women who have experienced orgasm but who have since lost that ability.
- *Vaginismus*. This is a psychophysiological difficulty (a spastic contraction of the muscles of the perineum and outer third of the vagina) that prevents the woman from completing intercourse. It is an involuntary response brought on by imagined, anticipated, or actual attempts at vaginal entry. Assessment of this problem should include a thorough history and a pelvic examination.
- *Female Dyspareunia*. Dyspareunia denotes pain that occurs during or following intercourse. Causes can range from physiological difficulties (e.g., infection, cysts, lack of lubrication) to psychological difficulties (including lack of interest in the sex act or fear of intercourse). In some instances, the spouse of

an alcoholic male has been subjected to sexual abuse and rape. These factors should be carefully explored and evaluated in the therapy situation. Lack of interest in sex can sometimes be a complex issue in the female and may reflect more widespread problems in a couple's relationship.

Outlining specific treatment approaches for these problems is beyond the scope of this chapter. The reader is referred to Miller and Mastria (1972, pp. 103–124) for an excellent overview of alcohol-related sexual problems and their treatment in the alcoholic.

The Counselor's Personal Comfort Level in Discussing Sexual Issues

A topic that Miller and Mastria also cover (and which is frequently overlooked or downplayed by the alcoholic counselor) is the counselor's personal acceptance of his own sexuality and the counselor's personal comfort and openness in discussing sexually related issues with clients. As Miller and Mastria indicate, discussing, clarifying, and thinking through one's own feelings about sex is a necessary first step for the counselor in preparing to help others with their sexual problems. In fact, this may be more important than knowing about all the technical and treatment information available on sex. While reading treatment manuals, research information, and other literature can be helpful, Miller and Mastria suggest that the use of formal discussion groups with other counselors, where opposing views are presented, is helpful to many counselors in desensitizing themselves to the topic and exposing them to views that are different from their own. They also suggest that blind spots in sexual counseling with couples can be compensated for by pairing male and female counselors. Such an arrangement allows both clients to feel they have an ally; it also provides the opportunity for the counselors to model how men and women can relate to each other in an adult and constructive manner.

Is There a Difference Between an Alcoholic and an Alcohol Abuser?

This question could be asked in another way: Is there a difference between a drug abuser and an alcoholic? However, both questions are only relevant with regard to the extent that they affect treatment procedures. That is to say, if the treatment for a drug addict is thought to be the same as the treatment for an alcoholic, then why bother to differentiate between the two states? Differences in problems should be represented by differences in treatment. It is our opinion that each person, although similar to others, in some ways is different from all others as well. It is the ability to recognize these similarities and differences and to use them in a treatment setting that separates quality treatment from nonquality treatment.

To be more specific about this particular question—yes, there is a difference between an alcoholic and an alcohol abuser. However, neither term is totally satisfactory when used to describe the condition of an individual. Abuse and misuse are unsatisfactory concepts within a scientific approach because they involve value judgments. Terms such as unsanctioned use, hazardous use, dysfunctional use, and harmful use are less value laden and go further toward describing the situation (just as uncontrolled drinking or uncontrolled behavior go further toward describing a situation than the term alcoholic drinking). As Jellinek (1960) has pointed out, there are many types of alcoholism, each type representing different behaviors and different levels of addiction to alcohol. (For those who are not familiar with it, Jellinek's classic *The Disease Concept of Alcoholism* is highly recommended.) Many people quote Jellinek and speak of alcoholism as a disease. But they hardly ever mention that Jellinek himself only saw two of the several types of alcoholism he described as a disease, that he presented his work as a "working hypothesis," not fact, and that he took no explicit stand on issues such as irreversibility of the syndrome. It is, then, the person's own behavior in relation to alcohol or drugs that we must examine. What does this behavior mean in the context of the individual's own life? One man's normal drinking could be another man's alcoholism. Or with regard to the original question: one man's alcohol abuse might be another man's alcoholism. The bottom line is how will you, as a counselor, treat clients differently according to their needs?

As a chemical dependency counselor you need to have the resources to be able to refer a wide continuum of drug and alcohol problems to an appropriate treatment source. You may be able to offer the Cadillac of treatment, but you must be able to recognize that some people don't want or need a Cadillac; they may only need a Volkswagen.

This leads in to the very controversial issue of total abstinence versus controlled drinking as treatment goals. If one assumes that addiction is addiction and that the alcoholic is just like the heroin addict (and that either you are an alcoholic or you are not), then things are simple: treat everyone as if they were the same, and maintain total abstinence as a goal for everyone. This narrow approach, however, has limited success. On the other hand, if one believes that each person is at a different point on a continuum of chemical dependency problems, then different treatment approaches are a necessity. This not so simple way of looking at the problem calls for some answers to difficult questions. For example, how do you differentiate candidates for controlled drinking from those for whom abstinence is necessary? It is no solution just to say that this is impossible and too risky, so let's not do it. The answers to problems of differential diagnosis are there, but to find them one must look, and this means work. The counselor must keep an open mind and continue to study the field. With regard to controlled drinking and total abstinence, Miller (1983) and Heather and Robertson (1981) would be excellent places to begin reading about the issues involved.

The more that counselors can differentiate problems for individuals and identify specific treatments for each problem, the more successful they will be. (For more information on this, see Chapter 3.)

How Should the Counselor Use Alcoholics Anonymous or Narcotics Anonymous in the Overall Treatment Plan?

First, the counselor should have a thorough understanding of the AA or NA program. For the nonalcoholic counselor this would involve reading the "Big Book" of AA and attending open meetings. For the recovering alcoholic or drug abuser who is a member of either group, this would include a recognition of the limits of AA or NA. It is not unusual to find the counselor who is sober by way of AA or NA who sees his method of achieving sobriety as the only means for others to achieve it. It is important for counselors, regardless of whether they are recovering alcoholics or not, to recognize both the assets and limitations of the self-help group.

Again, this realization leads us to an appropriate differential diagnosis that is translated into an appropriate treatment plan. There are some individuals who will respond very favorably to a referral to AA or NA. There are others for whom this type of referral would be inappropriate or at least insufficient as a total treatment plan.

For example, American Indians, who have been taught to keep their problems to themselves, often do not respond to the traditional AA meeting, where they are expected to share their drinking history with other members. This is especially true when all other members of the meeting are white. Chicanos with a macho self-image might have problems with the idea of admitting one's powerlessness over alcohol (the first of AA's 12 steps). The nonbeliever might have problems with the concept of a "higher power," even with the addendum "[God] as we understand him." As a patient once explained to this author, "They told me at AA that I needed to turn my life over to God. I said I didn't believe in God. Then they said that's OK, turn my life over to my "higher power" as I see him, even if my higher power was a door knob." He then looked up at me and in all seriousness said, "They wanted me to turn my life over to a door knob!"

Perhaps this understanding of AA was a bit distorted. But it is hard to convince an antireligious person that AA is not a religious program, when 6 of the 12 steps mention God or "your higher power" specifically. Some people are unable or do not want to differentiate between religious and spiritual. This does not mean these people are untreatable or a poor treatment risk. They may very well respond to an alternative to AA. Thus, use AA and NA where appropriate, but don't depend solely on them for the treatment of the chemically dependent person.

What Is the Most Effective Treatment Model for Chemically Dependent People?

This is a difficult question to answer. Evaluations of various treatment models are either not available or not generally agreed upon by various theoretical orientations. Outcome results are subject to question because programs are often self-selective with regard to clients. For example, private programs that require payment end up mostly treating people who have money or a job with an insurance policy that pays for treatment. The outcome with these people is likely to be better than with those who have no job and no money. Often the success rate reported by a program does not include the people who started the program but dropped out during treatment.

The most widely accepted approach to treatment is Alcoholics Anonymous. The 12 steps of AA are used in more treatment programs than any other approach. These steps have been revised for a variety of programs including overeating, gambling, and others. The success of AA is perhaps overrated when viewed in an overall perspective. The latest reported number of AA members is around 1 million. Given that there are over 10 million alcoholics, that would mean 1 in 10 alcoholics has found AA to be an acceptable program for their sobriety; one in ten is not enough.

What is needed in the field of chemical dependency is a variety of treatment approaches that meet the needs of a variety of individuals. This should include the family members, as suggested by Lawson et al. (1983). This family approach has the added appeal of preventing intergenerational alcoholism or chemical dependency and working as a prevention program for the children of alcoholics or chemical abusers. The most effective treatment program will look at all aspects of a person's life and will provide treatment for each of these areas as necessary. The questions of inpatient versus outpatient treatment, AA versus psychotherapy, family treatment versus individual treatment are all answered by looking objectively at the needs of the person being treated. If a man gives up drinking but commits suicide because he is so depressed, what good is the treatment that got him off alcohol? If a person attends AA regularly but neglects his family, treatment is not complete.

The most effective treatment model for the chemically dependent person is a treatment model that meets the individual treatment needs of the individual. This may seem like a simple answer to a complex question; however, it is as simple as it is true!

How Would You Approach and Confront a Close Friend, Colleague, or Coworker about His Alcohol Problems?

To answer this question we obtained the assistance of some special people who have a great deal of experience in the chemical dependency field. We have summarized their interviews and have attempted to capture, as accurately as possible, the flavor of their comments. The interviewees' answers to this question are given below:

Ellen McCrory, Director
St. Monica's Halfway House
Lincoln, Nebraska

I'd start out by shooting the breeze—make them comfortable, get their defenses down a bit. Then come right out and talk to them directly about their problems. I'd share my concerns and feelings about what I've seen and how they've changed. If I know them well, I'll point out what they used to be able to do. I'd also point out that their job is suffering. Most of the time when I confront it is from a feeling level— they know that I care about them. I feel that many times an alcoholic is waiting for someone to say something. I usually go into these sessions with the same plan—I let them know I'm willing [to help]. I've never had someone turn me down. I also place the responsibility [for doing something about their problem] on them, except at work, where it is an either/or proposition.

Women are, in a sense, easier to confront; [there is] almost a sense that they're supposed to do what is expected of them. If you know the individual, you know where they are vulnerable. For example, you can break through a woman's defenses through her children—if the woman is guilty about the children [or it can be assumed they will be better off without her while she's in treatment in terms of long-term effects] then the woman is more likely to be able to accept treatment.

If the family is involved, the better off you are; the more leverage you have, the better off you are. That's why late stage alcoholics are hard to intervene with, i.e., there's no leverage. Also, when a family member is alone they may be rather ineffectual in confronting the alcoholic; however, when the same family member is part of an intervention team confronting the alcoholic, they have considerably more impact. Generally speaking, when confronting the alcoholic it is better to have more than one person, and it is better to have more than one family member whenever possible.

Duke Engel, Director and Intervention Specialist
Independence Center
Lincoln, Nebraska

Originally our confrontation [at Independence Center] was based on a heavy confrontation model, i.e., lay out the facts very hard and without qualification. But with coworkers and friends this is not appropriate. We are now moving to a more invitational model. We think this model suggests:

1. Getting across your personal concern for the person being confronted.

2. If at all possible, talk about the facts of alcoholism and how these facts relate to the confrontee's problem.

3. Staying away from moral judgments. And stay away from opinions and use facts when discussing the drinker's drinking behavior. For example, don't say "you are drinking too much," but instead indicate the person had 10 beers, i.e., be specific.

4. Have an open invitation—put forth hope that the drinker can get better, that treatment can help. Leave the door open, but don't nag them. These types of interventions may go on over a period of several months. With a friend or coworker it may take months, years, and may involve several people talking to the abusive drinker before they agree to enter treatment.

We do more interventions of this type now, i.e., the open invitation kind. We expect that this type of intervention approach [involving gentle persuasion instead of harsh confrontation] will be the one we will use in the future. If you're successful using this approach, then the friend, coworker, or relative enters treatment with a better attitude. We may still use heavy confrontation if the alcohol problem has placed the person and those around them in crisis (i.e., something bad might happen if we don't take action). However, it is only in this type of situation that we would really put pressure on the drinking individual.

Dr. William Leipold, one of the originators and former director of the first Valley Hope Alcohol Treatment Center, Norton, Kansas. He is currently president of the Valley Hope Association, Norton, Kansas.

I try to create a crisis in their lives. I try to get the alcoholic to confront his or her drinking problem. Frequently, their denial system is so well established that they will not accept that they have a problem and will not enter treatment. In these cases, I try to persuade people close to the alcoholic to create a crisis in their life. For example, we recently suggested to the wife of an alcoholic that the next time he went driving while he was intoxicated that she should call the police and have him arrested for DWI. She wouldn't do it because she was afraid it would create difficulty for the family. It is interesting that similar circumstances finally created the crisis that brought the man to treatment. Whether it's a friend, colleague, etc., we have to work with anything that gets past denial—we try to get them to face up to their denial. In another case, the person soiled himself, vomited, and generally was a filthy person following his drunken bouts. We suggested to the wife that she put in a full-length mirror in the basement, where he normally drank himself into unconsciousness. While the alcoholic refused to accept that this dirty and di-sheveled person was really him, he did enter treatment for his problem. If the individual is an alcoholic, you try to get him to treatment any way you can. If they come to treatment angry and resistant, we'll deal with that issue in the treatment setting as a part of treatment. You must remember that frequently when we get calls about someone's drinking problem it is generally very late in the person's drinking history, and there is some type of emergency for the person who is drinking and/or for those around them.

In recent years we are getting more and more cases where we get someone who is still in the early stages of alcoholism. This is because our education of the public has made the detection of alcoholism possible earlier [in the person's drinking career]. Here we may make a more subtle approach, e.g., leaving brochures about alcoholism and alcoholism treatment in the living room.

We have also found that if we have family members come into treatment [before the alcoholic is willing to come], that not only does the family feel better and happier but we eventually get the alcoholic into treatment in 95 percent of the cases. In other words, anything that can be utilized should be utilized; what we find most effective for referrals are the employee assistance and industrial programs. We have also found that the education of judges and probation officers and prosecuting attorneys is also helpful in getting people into treatment. To sum up, it depends on the severity of the problem what confrontation methods you use. Helping the families and getting them involved in pressuring the alcoholic seem to be the best approach. In several cases we've had alcoholics come to treatment [following the treatment of their families] saying that all the happiness and relief in the family brought them to treatment. They just couldn't stand all that happiness around them!

Ralph Fox, Executive Director
Houses of Hope, Inc.
Lincoln, Nebraska

I feel pretty strongly about this. I would refer them to someone else who could be objective.

James S. Peterson, Ph.D.
Professor of Rehabilitation Counseling
Southern Illinois University
Carbondale, Illinois

This is a ticklish situation; not only due to its very personal nature, but also because one expects the response to be defensive and hostile. However, most professionals agree that ignoring the problem is not the answer.

Circumstances and individual differences do dictate [the response] to a certain extent, but there are a few things to keep in mind when approaching the problem drinker.

First, do your homework. It is important to cite specific examples; a general accusation can be easily denied and/or discounted.

Second, use a straightforward but supportive approach. Avoid uses of guilt, blaming, or angry confrontation. This will prevent the problem drinker from reacting to the *way* it's said, and focus more on the content of what's being said.

Third, have some resources at your finger tips which you can recommend. Be specific, cite a name and a phone number, and offer to help make some arrangements. If possible, do it right then and there—often the problem drinker will agree to seek help, but never follow through on his own.

Finally, be willing to come away with less than a completely successful encounter. Don't press on indefinitely once you have made your point—it is often enough to "plant the seed" and allow some time for reflection. Leave the door open for future contact.

Ann Lawson, M.A./M.F.A., Director
Children From Alcoholic Families Program
Child Guidance Center
Lincoln, Nebraska

Having lived in an alcoholic family as a child, I learned not to confront people about their drinking. This is a strong taboo for those who are close to the person with the drinking problem. It allows the person to drink more comfortably.

If I were concerned about a friend or family member I would use a family systems approach to define the drinking as it affects the family system and each of the members. I would work with all of these people together, including the children. With this approach it is necessary to help each person describe specific behaviors of the drinker and how the behaviors have affected them. Often it becomes more difficult for that person to continue drinking with the new knowledge of how this affects those closest to them.

It is advisable to look for adaptive consequences of the drinking in a family—what does the family gain when the person is drinking? This may be closeness, distance, sexual intimacy or distance, freedom, martyrdom, or a number of complicated relationship dynamics that may stem from the families of origin.

It is important to remember that one person cannot force someone else to change a drinking pattern, but the family can express themselves and reduce enabling behavior, thus making it more difficult for the drinking to continue. There is also help for those family members who hurt as a result of another's drinking. Children who live with alcoholic parents need counseling to reduce the risk of intergenerational alcoholism.

REFERENCES

Blume, S. Role of the recovered alcoholic in the treatment of alcoholism. In Kissen, B., & Begleiter, H. (Eds.), *The biology of alcoholism: Treatment and rehabilitation of the chronic alcoholic*. Vol. 5. New York: Plenum, 1977.

Bohman, M. Some genetic aspects of alcoholism and criminality. *Archives of General Psychiatry,* 1978, *35,* 269–276.

Bourne, P.G., & Light, E. *Alcohol problems in blacks and women.* In Mendelson, J.H., & Mello, N.K. (Eds.), *The diagnosis and treatment of alcoholism.* New York: McGraw-Hill, 1979, 84–123.

Cahalan, D. *Problem drinkers.* San Francisco: Jossey-Bass, 1970.

Cotton, N.S. The familial incidence of alcoholism. *Journal of Studies on Alcohol,* 1979, *40,* 89–115.

Falkey, D.B. Standards, recruitment, training, and use of indigenous personnel in alcohol and drug misuse programs. *Selected papers of 22nd Meeting of Alcohol and Drug Problems Association,* 1971, 38–41.

Farkas, G.M., & Rosen, R.C. The effect of alcohol on elicited male sexual response. *Journal of Studies on Alcohol,* 1976, *37,* 262–265.

Gantt, W.H. Effect of alcohol on sexual reflexes in dogs. *American Journal of Physiology,* 1940, 360.

Gantt, W.H. Effects of alcohol on sexual reflexes of normal and neurotic dogs. *Psychosomatic Medicine,* 1952, *14,* 174–181.

Glatt, M.M. The drinking habits of English middle class alcoholics. *Acta Psychiatria Scandinavia,* 1961, *37,* 88.

Goodwin, D. *Genetic determinants of alcoholism.* In Mendelson, J., & Mello, N. (Eds.), *The diagnosis and treatment of alcoholism.* New York: McGraw-Hill, 1979, 59–82.

Heather, N., & Robertson, I. *Controlled drinking.* London, New York: Methuen Press, 1981.

Jellinek, E.M. *The disease concept of alcoholism.* New Brunswick, New Jersey: Hillhouse Press, 1960.

Kaij, L. *Studies on the etiology and sequels of abuse of alcohol.* Department of Psychiatry, University of Lund, Sweden, 1960.

Kalb, M., & Propper, M.S. The future of alcohology: Craft or science? *American Journal of Psychiatry,* 1976, *113,* 641–645.

Kissen, B. *Theory and practice in the treatment of alcoholism.* In Kissen, B., & Begleiter, H. (Eds.), *The biology of alcoholism: Treatment and rehabilitation of the chronic alcoholic.* Vol. 5. New York: Plenum, 1977, 1–51.

Lawson, G., Peterson, J., & Lawson, A. *Alcoholism and the family: A guide to treatment and prevention.* Rockville, Md.: Aspen Systems, 1983.

Levine, T. The sexual adjustment of alcoholics: A clinical study of a selected sample. *Quarterly Journal of Studies on Alcohol,* 1955, *16,* 675–680.

Lindbeck, V.L. The woman alcoholic: A review of the literature. *The International Journal of the Addictions,* 1972, *7,* 567–580.

Masters, S.H., & Johnson, V. *Human sexual inadequacy.* Boston: Little, Brown & Co., 1970.

Miller, P.A., & Mastria, M.A. *Alternatives to alcohol abuse: A social learning model.* Champaign, Ill.: Research Press, 1977.

Miller, W.R. Controlled drinking: A history and a critical review. *Journal of Studies on Alcohol,* 1983, *44*(1), 68–83.

Murray, R., & Stabenau, J. Genetic factors in alcoholism predisposition. In Pattison, E.M., & Kaufman, E. (Eds.), *Encyclopedic handbook of alcoholism.* New York: Gardner Press, 1982, 135–144.

Partanen, J., Bruun, K., & Markkaners, T. *Inheritance of drinking behavior.* New Brunswick, N. J.: Rutgers University Center on Alcohol Studies, 1966.

Pattison, E.M., Sobell, M., & Sobell, L. *Emerging concepts of alcohol dependence.* New York: Springer, 1977.

Pattison, E.M. *A differential view of manpower resources.* In Staub, G., & Kent, U. (Eds.), *The paraprofessional in the treatment of alcoholism.* Springfield, Ill.: Charles C Thomas, 1973.

Robinson, D. The alcohologist's addiction—some implications of having lost control over the disease concept of alcoholism. *Quarterly Journal of Studies on Alcohol,* 1972, *33,* 1028–1042.

Rosenberg, C.M. The responsibility of direct treatment. *Alcohol Health and Research World,* 1974 (Spring), pp. 3–5.

Rossi, J., & Filstead, W.J. *"Treating" the treatment issues: Some general observations about the treatment of alcoholics.* In Filstead, W.J., Rossi, J., & Keller, M. (Eds), *Alcohol and alcohol problems: New thinking and new directions.* Cambridge, Mass.: Ballenger, 1976.

Schuckit, M.A., & Morrissey, E.R. *Alcoholism in women: Some clinical and social perspectives with an emphasis on some possible subtypes.* In Greenblatt, M., & Schuckit, M.A. (Eds.), *Alcoholism problems in women and children.* New York: Grune & Stratton, 1976, 5–35.

Strachen, G. *Non-alcoholics vs. recovered personnel.* In Staub, G., & Kent, U. (Eds.), *The paraprofessional in the treatment of alcoholism.* Springfield, Ill.: Charles C Thomas, 1973.

Tamerin, J.S. *The psychotherapy of alcoholic women.* In Zimberg, S., Wallace, J., & Blume, S.B. (Eds.), *Practical approaches to alcoholism psychotherapy.* New York: Plenum, 1978, 183–203.

Wallace, J. *Working with the preferred defense structure of the recovering alcoholic.* In Zimberg, S., Wallace, J., & Blume, S. (Eds.), *Practical approaches to alcoholism psychotherapy.* New York: Plenum, 1978, 19–29.

Wilsnack, S. *Alcohol abuse and alcoholism in women.* In Pattison, E.M., & Kaufman, E. (Eds.), *Encyclopedic handbook of alcoholism.* New York: Gardner Press, 1982, 718–735.

Wilson, G.T., & Lawson, D.T. Effects of alcohol on sexual arousal in women. *Journal of Abnormal Psychology,* 1976, *85,* 489–497.

Index

About the Authors

Gary W. Lawson is a Professor of Counseling Psychology at the University of Nebraska. His area of specialization is alcoholism counselor training. He has 13 years experience in the field of chemical dependency, including directing an inpatient alcoholism treatment center. Dr. Lawson has published articles and presented related materials both regionally and nationally. He has recently published a book entitled *Alcoholism and the Family: A Guide to Treatment and Prevention*. He is a consultant to the Alcoholism/Drug Counselor Training Institute of Nebraska as well as many other agencies. He also maintains a private practice in psychology where he does outpatient treatment of chemical dependency, marriage counseling, and family therapy.

Dan C. Ellis has worked in the field of chemical dependency, as both a trainer and a practitioner, since 1974. Dr. Ellis was the founding director of the Alcoholism Counselor Training Institute of Nebraska. Currently, Dr. Ellis conducts training workshops and does consulting nationally on chemical dependency treatment. Dr. Ellis has a private therapy practice with the Hudson Center in Omaha, Nebraska.

P. Clayton Rivers received a B.A. in psychology from Berea College, Berea, Kentucky, and an M.A. and Ph.D. in clinical psychology from Southern Illinois University, Carbondale, Illinois. He completed a post-doctoral study in Alcoholism Leadership Training at Harvard Medical School and Massachusetts General Hospital, where he studied with Dr. Morris Chafetz and Dr. Howard Blane. Since 1972, he has been an Associate Professor and Director of the Alcohol Training Program in the Psychology Department at the University of Nebraska at Lincoln. In 1979, Dr. Rivers was a visiting senior psychologist to the North Canterbury Hospital Board, Christchurch, New Zealand. While in New Zealand he helped with the development of their new alcohol assessment centers, was a consultant to the Alcohol Liquor Advisory Council, and was a presenter at several national seminars on alcohol use and abuse for psychologists, nurses, and other personnel.

He also was an invited lecturer at Canterbury University. He has published articles in the *Quarterly Journal of Studies on Alcohol* and the *Journal of Alcohol and Drug Education*. He has presented papers at the American Psychological Association, the Southeastern Psychological Association, and the Ortho-Psychiatry Association. His current research interests include procedures for implementing community resources in the treatment and prevention of alcoholism; the cross-cultural differences in the perception of deviance; training and job perception differences in caregiving personnel; and the interface of psychology and the law in terms of the alcohol abuser.